China in Contemporary Capitalism

Studies in Critical Social Sciences Book Series

Haymarket Books is proud to be working with Brill Academic Publishers (www.brill.nl) to republish the *Studies in Critical Social Sciences* book series in paperback editions. This peer-reviewed book series offers insights into our current reality by exploring the content and consequences of power relationships under capitalism, and by considering the spaces of opposition and resistance to these changes that have been defining our new age. Our full catalog of *SCSS* volumes can be viewed at https://www.haymarketbooks.org/series_collections/4-studies-in-critical-social-sciences.

Series Editor
David Fasenfest (York University, Canada)

Editorial Board
Eduardo Bonilla-Silva (Duke University)
Chris Chase-Dunn (University of California–Riverside)
William Carroll (University of Victoria)
Raewyn Connell (University of Sydney)
Kimberlé W. Crenshaw (University of California–LA and Columbia University)
Heidi Gottfried (Wayne State University)
Alfredo Saad-Filho (Queen's University, Belfast)
Chizuko Ueno (University of Tokyo)
Sylvia Walby (Lancaster University)
Raju Das (York University)

CHINA IN CONTEMPORARY CAPITALISM

Edited by
Esther Majerowicz
Edemilson Paraná

Haymarket Books
Chicago, IL

First published in 2024 by Brill Academic Publishers, The Netherlands
© 2024 Koninklijke Brill NV, Leiden, The Netherlands

Published in paperback in 2025 by
Haymarket Books
P.O. Box 180165
Chicago, IL 60618
773-583-7884
www.haymarketbooks.org

ISBN: 979-8-88890-548-7

Distributed to the trade in the US through Consortium Book Sales and Distribution (www.cbsd.com) and internationally through Ingram Publisher Services International (www.ingramcontent.com).

This book was published with the generous support of Lannan Foundation, Wallace Action Fund, and the Marguerite Casey Foundation.

Special discounts are available for bulk purchases by organizations and institutions. Please call 773-583-7884 or email info@haymarketbooks.org for more information.

Cover design by Jamie Kerry and Ragina Johnson.

Printed in the United States.

Library of Congress Cataloging-in-Publication data is available.

Contents

Foreword: toward a Southern Perspective on China's Capitalist Development   VII
  Ho-fung Hung
Acknowledgements   IX
List of Figures and Tables   X
Notes on Contributors   XI

Introduction   1
  Esther Majerowicz and Edemilson Paraná

PART 1
The Fundamentals of the Chinese Economic Transition: Politics, Economy and Society

1   Developmentalism with Chinese Characteristics   9
      Carlos Aguiar de Medeiros and Esther Majerowicz

2   The Trajectory of Chinese Developmentalist Action and Its Contemporary Challenges   46
      Edemilson Paraná and Valéria Lopes Ribeiro

3   The State and Domestic Capitalists in China's Economic Transition   77
      Isabela Nogueira and Hao Qi

PART 2
China's Global Expansion and the Technological Dispute

4   Recent Chinese Expansion: State, Capital and Accumulation on a Global Scale   105
      Valéria Lopes Ribeiro

5   The Sino-American Dispute in Information and Communication Technologies   143
      Esther Majerowicz

Conclusion 181
 Esther Majerowicz and Edemilson Paraná

Index 199

Foreword: toward a Southern Perspective on China's Capitalist Development

For quite some time, discussions surrounding China's ascent within the capitalist world economy in the West, particularly in the United States, have been rife with myths and biases. Throughout the 2000s and 2010s, especially in the wake of the 2008 global financial crisis, numerous economists and financial analysts endeavored to depict China as a captivating capitalist paradise for profit-making. They lauded the Chinese Communist Party for its purportedly superior management of the market economy compared to Western governments. Wall Street's fervent efforts to entice investors into pouring their portfolios into Chinese-related stocks contributed to the myth of a perfect capitalist machine in China. Phrases like "the China model" and "Beijing Consensus" proliferated. It became widely accepted that China could sustain double-digit or near-double-digit economic growth for decades to come.

However, the narrative took a turn when China's stock market crashed, and its currency tanked in the summer of 2015. This event marked the first time Western observers began to discern cracks in China's developmental model. Post-2015, the Chinese economy continued to decelerate, and the financial strains on heavily indebted local governments and major enterprises became increasingly difficult to conceal. The collapse of Evergrande, once hailed as a shining example of China's economic success, alongside other business failures and rising youth unemployment, exposed the contradictions and crises within China's developmental model. Western observers swiftly adopted a more pessimistic outlook on China's political economy, attributing the crisis to China's repressive party-state authoritarianism.

The Western portrayal of China has historically vacillated between extremes of fantasy and contempt, dating back centuries. This phenomenon traces back to the polarized views of the Catholic Church regarding China in the seventeenth century, where some viewed the Chinese as adherents to a monotheistic God, embodying superior morality, while others depicted them as idol-worshipping Satanists with values radically divergent from Christianity. The contemporary discourse surrounding China's capitalism mirrors earlier debates about Christianity, reflecting Western anxieties regarding China's status as a formidable empire or nation and its potential impact on Western norms and values.

While geopolitical and cultural tensions between Western developed countries and China hinder nuanced analysis, intellectual communities in the

Global South are uniquely positioned to offer more accurate and complex perspectives on China. Scholars and policymakers in developing and middle-income countries seek positive developmental lessons from China while remaining cognizant of the challenges it poses to their own industries and working classes. They view China's rise as a counterbalance to Western hegemony but remain wary of its geopolitical assertiveness.

The unique geopolitical and geo-economic position of the Global South in the escalating US-China rivalry provides scholars from these regions with exceptional insights into Chinese development and global expansion. This volume showcases numerous outstanding works that testify to such insights. Through my interactions with scholars and policymakers, many of whom are contributors to this book, from BRICS and other developing countries, I've come to appreciate the value of a non-dogmatic Southern perspective on China's capitalist development. This community of scholars offers a potent corrective to the prevalent fantasies and biases about China in the Western world. Hence, the publication of this volume is a cause for celebration. It should be widely disseminated not only in Brazil but also across the Global South and in the West.

Ho-fung Hung

Acknowledgements

This book is the result of multiple dialogues. The authors thank Professors Virgínia Fontes, Leda Paulani, Célio Hiratuka, Maria de Lourdes Mollo, Franklin Serrano, and Ambassador Celso Amorim for their comments. Special mention should be made of the fruitful discussions hosted by the Department of Economics at the Federal University of Rio Grande do Norte, the Graduate Program in Global Political Economy at the Federal University of ABC, the LabChina research group at the Institute of Economics of the Federal University of Rio de Janeiro, and the Latin American Council of Social Sciences (CLACSO). The authors also thank the Brazilian National Council for Scientific and Technological Development (CNPq) for their support.

Figures and Tables

Figures

2.1 China – Gross Domestic Product growth rate (2000–2019)   60
2.2 China – Average (nominal) wage of employed persons in urban unities (1995–2015) (yuans)   65
3.1 Distribution of net value added in the corporate sector, 1992–2020   82
3.2 Growth of real estate profits and net land transfer income, 2000–2015 (2000 = 1)   91
4.1 Chinese foreign direct investment (2000–2018), in billions of dollars   121
4.2 Chinese foreign direct investment in the technology sector (2005–2019), in millions of dollars   123
4.3 Chinese foreign direct investment (stock) – share of state and non-state enterprises in total (2006–2017)   124
4.4 Belt and Road – Sector distribution of total investment (2013–2019)   132
4.5 Belt and Road – Destination of investments by world region (2013–2019)   133
5.1 The stacking and coevolution of the key technologies in the ICT system   149

Tables

2.1 China – GDP components from the expenditure perspective – share in GDP and annual growth rate (2000–2019)   62
3.1 Factions of domestic private capitalist class   84
3.2 Relationship between the Chinese state and the domestic private capitalist class   97
4.1 Foreign direct investments by selected Chinese private companies (2005–2019)   125
4.2 Selected Chinese private companies – foreign direct investment by regions, % of total invested (2006–2019)   126
4.3 Selected Chinese private companies with projects via BRI (2013–2019)   135

Notes on Contributors

Esther Majerowicz
is Assistant Professor at the Department of Economics and at the Graduate Program in Economics at the Federal University of Rio Grande do Norte, Brazil. Her research deals with China's insertion into the global economy, the formation of the Chinese labor market, and the international political economy of information and communication technologies. Majerowicz has worked as a postdoctoral researcher at the Federal University of Rio Grande do Norte. She holds a Ph.D. in Economics from Université Paris 13 and the Federal University of Rio de Janeiro. She is the coordinator of the Research Group on Political Economy of Development at the Federal University of Rio Grande do Norte. Email: estherzinhamj@yahoo.com.br

Carlos Aguiar de Medeiros
is Emeritus Professor at the Institute of Economics at the Federal University of Rio de Janeiro, Brazil. His main areas of teaching and publishing are economic development, income distribution, economic growth, technology, and development institutions and patterns. Carlos has held a visiting professor position at the University of Cambridge, United Kingdom. He holds a Ph.D. in Economics from the University of Campinas, Brazil. In 2011, he was awarded the James Street Latin American Scholar award by the Association for Evolutionary Economics (AFEE). Email: carlosaguiarde@gmail.com

Isabela Nogueira
is Assistant Professor at the Institute of Economics and the Graduate Program in International Political Economy and Coordinator of LabChina (Laboratory of Studies in Political Economy of China) at the Federal University of Rio de Janeiro. She has held the positions of postdoctoral researcher and lecturer at the Institute of Socioeconomics at the University of Geneva, visiting professor at Aalto University, Finland, and visiting researcher at Tsinghua University, China. She holds a Ph.D. in economics from the Federal University of Rio de Janeiro. Email: isabela.nogueira@ie.ufrj.br

Edemilson Paraná
is Associate Professor in the Department of Social Sciences at LUT University, Finland. He has taught at the University of Brasília and the Federal University of Ceará, Brazil, and held research fellowships at the Institute of Applied Economic Research (IPEA, Brazil), and the Brazilian National Council for Scientific

and Technological Development (CNPq). He holds a Ph.D. in Sociology from the University of Brasília, Brazil. Paraná has lectured and published in the areas of Political Economy, Economic Sociology, and Social Theory. Email: edemilson.parana@lut.fi

Hao Qi
is Associate Professor at the School of Economics at Renmin University, China. He holds a Ph.D. in economics from the University of Massachusetts, Amherst, and a master's and undergraduate degree in economics from Renmin University. His research areas include Marxian political economy, labor economics, distribution, inequalities, and Chinese economics. He has articles published in *Review of Radical Political Economy, Critical Asian Studies, International Review of Applied Economics, Science & Society*, among many other international and Chinese journals. Email: hq@ruc.edu.cn

Valéria Lopes Ribeiro
is Assistant Professor at the Center for Engineering, Modelling and Applied Social Sciences at the Federal University of ABC, São Paulo, Brazil. She is also Assistant Professor at the Graduate Program in World Political Economy and at the Program in International Relations, both at the Federal University of ABC. A researcher in the fields of International Political Economy, Economic Development, Political Economy, and Foreign Policy, with an emphasis on China's economic growth and development and China's global impact on peripheral countries (Africa and Latin America), she holds a doctorate in economics from the Federal University of Rio de Janeiro. Email: valeria.ribeiro@ufabc.edu.br

Introduction

Esther Majerowicz and Edemilson Paraná

China's impressive economic, technological, and military trajectory in recent decades has not only been associated with fundamental transformations in the country's socioeconomic structure but has also been decisive for key processes in the global economy and the international system. From the world factory of cheap manufactures, China has become a manufacturing and technological great power, with a mix of private-owned, state-owned, and partially state-owned global companies in which capitalists and bureaucrats operate.

For advanced countries, especially the US and its military allies, the Chinese rise is perceived as a central challenge for their cutting-edge technologies and the industrial system, and ultimately a potentially military threat. In the case of Latin America, this rise has a double meaning. On the one hand, it presents itself as a reinforcement of their productive specialization based on the export of commodities and imports of industrial goods. On the other hand, for developing countries in general, China's successful economic development appears as an experience from which to derive eventual lessons.

In this context, a strong anti-China movement emerges led by the United States, in alliance with several advanced countries, with projection onto the global periphery; while the perception grows among certain governments and leftist sectors in developing countries[1] that China would constitute an alternative, be it as a model to be followed, or as a promoter of a beneficial international order. In this scenario, derogatory or celebratory rhetorical outbursts find fertile ground and have been echoed more and more in debates about China. In some cases, they substitute the analysis of concrete reality, theoretical rigor, and critical thinking, which should guide a frank and sovereign reflection, factoring in the peculiarities – historical-cultural, socioeconomic and political – of each country.

It is in this complex terrain that the present book is inserted. A collective effort to critically apprehend China in contemporary capitalism entails, on the one hand, inquiring ourselves about China's development itself and, on the other, considering what such development represents for the global economy.

---

1 In Brazil, the Chinese economic success and greater international projection have been provoking a predisposition to dazzle in part of the Brazilian intelligentsia. Such enthusiasm, it should be noted, is not a monopoly of this sector, since it is also verified, for example, among the ranks of Brazilian agribusiness and large mining companies.

The work brings a range of authors dedicated to political economy, whether mobilizing Marxian approaches or heterodox theories of development.

The authors, Esther Majerowicz (Federal University of Rio Grande do Norte), Carlos Aguiar de Medeiros (Federal University of Rio de Janeiro), Isabela Nogueira (Federal University of Rio de Janeiro), Edemilson Paraná (LUT University), Hao Qi (Renmin University) and Valéria Lopes Ribeiro (Federal University of ABC), carry out this expedient in two moments, reflecting the two analytical axes that, intrinsically related, structure the book in different parts.

Part 1 is dedicated to the fundamentals of the Chinese economic transition in its political, economic, and societal dimensions. From different perspectives, Medeiros and Majerowicz and Paraná and Ribeiro characterize that the Chinese economic transition established a capitalist economy led by a developmental state, with economic nationalism as its cornerstone. As the economic transition entailed the creation of a domestic capitalist class, Nogueira and Qi analyze the role of the party-state in its formation, the impact of this new class on the state, and the evolution of the state-bourgeoisie relationship within the dynamics of class conflicts, contradictions, and regimes of capital accumulation.

In Chapter 1, debating with multiple currents regarding the nature of the Chinese economic system, such as those arguing it is "market socialism", "socialism with Chinese characteristics" and "state capitalism", Medeiros and Majerowicz denominate the Chinese experience as "developmentalism with Chinese characteristics". The authors discuss the complex but necessary combinations between market and non-market relations both in the genesis and in the reproduction of capitalism, showing that the State has always been present in capitalism and highlighting that capitalist development entails that non-capitalist institutions fulfill their role, in a way that, in concrete reality, every capitalist economy presents itself as a hybrid economy.

If every actually existing capitalist economy is a hybrid economy, would the matter of determining whether it is "market socialist", "state capitalist" or capitalist *tout court* depend on specifying whether more than half of this economy is privately-owned or state-owned? The rigorous analysis by Medeiros and Majerowicz helps us to deal with and transcend this issue as it moves within the scope of Political Economy.

Thus, articulating Political Economy and comparative experiences of development, Medeiros and Majerowicz argue that, in the last forty years, "developmentalism with Chinese characteristics" creatively combined the main dimensions that in the post-war period boosted the industrialization process in the economies, especially those of East Asia, in which the national state, through planning and control mechanisms, governed markets and led economic growth and the process of structural change. The main characteristic that distinguishes the Chinese experience is the structure of its political power formed by the party-state, which has great political autonomy and strong penetration in economic power. This power structure helped China to persevere its state-led national development strategy at a time when most national economies adhered to global neoliberalism, giving up this coordination in favor of an accumulation regime led by private corporations.

Characterizing Chinese development in contemporary capitalism also requires an appreciation of its articulation with the global capitalist economy. In Chapter 2, Paraná and Ribeiro argue that the economic rise of China was functional to the transformation of capitalism in the last four decades, having fulfilled a necessary role in the context of production restructuring, transnationalization, and financialization of capital. There would be, for the authors, a "symbiosis" between the Chinese economic miracle and globalization led by the United States, at least until the 2008 crisis.

In this context of relatively favorable conditions for the reorganization of the world economy, Chinese developmentalist action was competent in strategically mobilizing these conditions in favor of an accelerated economic development of the country – institutionally boosting, moreover, its potentialities, resources, and internal characteristics. It was this combination that guided the exceptional result of such unparalleled developmentalist action in the history of capitalism. Bearing in mind that, "in the rough dialectic of history, past success does not guarantee future success", Paraná and Ribeiro wonder to what extent the Chinese developmental State will continue to be able to maintain this delicate balance in favor of its development; considering the paradoxes of recent Chinese development and the new limits and challenges posed to its developmentalist action.

In Chapter 3, Nogueira and Qi analyze the formation of the Chinese bourgeoisie in its relationship with the party-state. In contrast to part of the academic literature that considers the developmental State as supraclassist, capable of instrumentalizing capitalists at will for autonomously determined purposes, the authors maintain that the relationship between the party-State and the new capitalist class is the product of a bidirectional movement from top to bottom and bottom to top forces. If, on the one hand, the State was fundamental to the formation and transformation of the Chinese capitalist class, then on the other hand, it itself was transformed throughout this process.

For the authors, the patterns of relationship between the State and the Chinese capitalist class have changed over time, being permeated by capital-labor conflicts, by changes in the pattern of accumulation in the country's economy and by external determinants. Nogueira and Qi therefore consider the State as a social relation with historical dynamics, which is expressed in different arrangements, compositions, and tensions with a domestic bourgeoisie that differentiates itself into different fractions as it develops in post-reform China. Based on the identification of three factions of the Chinese capitalist class – the low-road, the innovation, and the finance factions – the authors propose that the relationship between the domestic bourgeoisie and the Chinese State would have moved from what they called a "great compromise" to the current period defined by a "strained alliance", a context which characterizes, among other developments, Xi Jinping's anti-corruption campaign and the technological, military, and commercial disputes with the US.

Therefore, gestated and governed by the party-state, capitalist accumulation in China proved such a resounding success that not only gave renewed impetus to the capital valorization on a world scale through global manufacturing value chains, but also gave substance to the emergence of large domestic capitals. Since particularly the 2010s, the spheres of valorization of domestic capitals, both private and state, have been overflowing the national sphere. This last movement naturally tends to cause friction with the United States, as both nations dispute spheres of capital valorization. More than that, this dispute over spheres not only reflects an expansion movement in a quantitative dimension, but also a qualitative one, as Chinese economic development has been able to sustain impressive results in terms of technological development and the incorporation of technical progress into its productive apparatus. This is the problem that Ribeiro and Majerowicz deal with, in Part 2 of this book, dedicated to China's global expansion and the technological dispute.

In Chapter 4, when addressing the recent Chinese expansion considering the State, capital, and accumulation on a global scale, Ribeiro highlights a problem that has become increasingly relevant for the periphery of global capitalism. Does Chinese global expansion actually correspond to that represented by the official discourse of the CCP – which portrays the external projection and actions of "socialism with Chinese characteristics" as constituting an opportunity granted to other countries to enhance their development and maintain their sovereignty, while China seeks to "solve the problems of mankind"?

Examining how China's expansion has effectively unfolded, Ribeiro seeks to understand how the country's external projection is affected both by the relationship between the State and capital and by the characteristics of the current stage of capital accumulation in China. Thus, the Chinese external projection is conceived in light not only of its strategic interests, but also of the interests of the capitalist class, interests that are constituted in a dialectical relationship. After undertaking an analysis of the specific characteristics of its recent economic growth cycle, the author investigates two vectors of the current Chinese external expansion: Chinese investments abroad and the Belt and Road strategy. Regarding investments, Ribeiro seeks to scrutinize how they reflect the current stage of capital accumulation in the country and to what extent they derive from private capital, while she seeks to analyze the presence of private interests in the Belt and Road strategy, even if to a lesser extent, beyond state interests.

In Chapter 5, Majerowicz addresses the current technological disputes between China and the United States in information and communication technologies (ICT). Is a new Cold War under way – as several authors propose and in some instances the US rhetoric suggests – that will lead the world to a "digital divide", with the formation of two compartmentalized ICT systems, led by each of these great powers?

Even though Majerowicz considers that the Sino-American dispute takes place within the framework of capitalism – which would be more than enough to significantly differentiate it from the Cold War, having as a reference the perspective of the working class – the author investigates the entangled hypotheses of the new Cold War and the "digital divide" based on the productive and technological dynamics of ICTs. Majerowicz considers ICT as a technological system embedded in a global machinery system composed of three key technologies, namely, semiconductors, mobile telecommunications infrastructure, especially 5G, and "artificial intelligence". From such an integrated perspective of analysis, the author scrutinizes and frames the structural conditions of possibility of the Sino-American dispute in this field, as well as some of its potential consequences.

Overall, the collection offers, in addition to a detailed analysis of its domestic economic transformations, a careful assessment of the rise and current role of China in the world economy – an investigation without which, given its core importance, a correct understanding of contemporary capitalism cannot be derived. This is an additional reason why the theme should invite reflection, not only from researchers and specialists in the subject, but also from all those attentive to the new directions of international affairs, society, politics, and the world economy. It is a work inspired by the scientific spirit and by the necessary distance from the denunciatory or celebratory euphoria around which the debate has become, in some environments, polarized, to the detriment of analyzes focused on complexity. This is what is asked for by the political moment in which geopolitical tensions and inter-capitalist competition intensify: the ability to analyze the complex reality of Chinese dynamics with theoretical rigor and critical thinking.

The book also crowns a pioneering line of research in the political economy of Chinese development in Brazil led by Professor Carlos Aguiar de Medeiros, whose direct and indirect contribution is essential for this volume. To cite just one of many reasons, in addition to the opening chapter of this book, which has the professor as the first author, in every text of this collection at least one of the authors was formally supervised, at some point in her previous research trajectory, by Medeiros – whom we honor for his broad and solid contribution to this field.

May the invitation to read and debate with these and other examples of this line of research make it possible to broaden horizons and new critical-reflexive engagements around such a fundamental theme for a better understanding and transformation of the world in which we live.

PART 1

The Fundamentals of the Chinese Economic Transition: Politics, Economy and Society

CHAPTER 1

Developmentalism with Chinese Characteristics

Carlos Aguiar de Medeiros and Esther Majerowicz

1 Introduction[1]

Since Deng Xiaoping's "reform and opening", initiated in 1978, China maintained for four decades a high rate of per capita product growth, creating an industrial and exporting base that has recently elevated China to the top position in international trade and second highest GDP in current dollars. Hundreds of millions of people were lifted out of poverty, a vast middle class with increasing consumption power was formed, and, in many areas, China reached the technological frontier. Today, China's investment in R&D is only surpassed by the U.S.

This extraordinary evolution occurred in a context of profound changes in the economic and social institutions inherited from the 1949 Revolution, based on state property of all means of production, compulsory central planning, and social egalitarianism. Under the coordination of Five-Year Plans, economic development took place under a corporate structure formed by large state-owned enterprises (SOEs) and public banks, which assumed a central role in driving capital accumulation, and a large – national and international – private sector. At present, the country has the third largest Stock Exchange, and although it has a relatively lower financial integration than its international trade integration, China is also the second country in the world both as a destination and a source of foreign direct investment (FDI).

This economic performance has led to profound demographic and social changes. Most of the population is now urban. Despite the high upward social mobility and the recent development of a welfare system, the basically egalitarian society of the Mao years has disappeared, giving way to high income and wealth concentration. Contemporary, China has, after the U.S., the largest number of billionaires. Throughout this period marked by such profound structural and institutional transformations, China maintained the political

---

1 This chapter is a modified version of a homonymous paper published by the authors at the *International Journal of Political Economy* 51 (3). We thank the journal for authorizing a revised publication. We thank Franklin Serrano for the constructive comments to a version of this text.

system inherited from the socialist revolution based on the monopoly of the party-state, which demonstrated a great capacity for coordinating the processes of change.

Controversies over China's social regime and pattern of economic development have gained ground in contemporary literature on economic development. After all, no successful post-war catch-up experience claimed to possess a specific social regime, the "socialist market economy" – as established in the resolutions of the Chinese Communist Party (CCP) –, and a national pathway, "socialism with Chinese characteristics". "Is China socialist?" – asked Naughton (2017). Is it a variant of hybrid capitalism, as The Economist (2020a) describes? A "political capitalism", as Milanovic (2019) argues? A mixed economy, as Rodrik (2020) observes? A state capitalism, as Naughton and Tsai (2015) claim? Or a version of neoliberalism, as in Harvey (2005)?

Several recent formulations (Losurdo, 2017; Gabriele, 2020; Fan, Morck, and Yeung, 2012; Jabbour and Gabriele, 2021) argue that "socialism with Chinese characteristics" would constitute a variant distinct from both the "central planning economy" – which characterized real socialism in the 20th century – and capitalism. This interpretation is based on the central (or dominant) role played by SOEs and comprehensive economic planning. Recently, this perspective gained greater prominence under Xi Jinping's leadership (initiated in 2012) due to his political and ideological campaign against corruption and the boosting, in the description of The Economist, of a "top-heavy state-dominated growth model", arising from the affirmation of the CCP's power over private companies and the expansion of state participation in investment, in a movement in which the "the state sector advances, while the private sector retreats" (Lo, 2020). In 2021, the Chinese government launched a series of crackdowns on big technology companies and several other activities – further strengthening such interpretation.

The formulations that classify contemporary China as capitalist or socialist generally assume a dichotomous position. Those who argue that China is not capitalist (hence, socialist) assume neoliberal capitalism by capitalism; those who argue that China is not socialist (hence, capitalist) assume by socialism a centrally planned economy. This is the case of several neo-Marxist formulations (Harvey, 2005; Li and Qi, 2014) describing China's reality resulting from the dissolution of rural communes and the privatization of SOEs in the 1990s as the formation of a capitalism characterized by low wages, intense working hours, and integration into global markets. For these authors, the prevailing regime today, referred to as "neoliberalism with Chinese characteristics" (Harvey, 2005), would be a wild yet dynamic variant of capitalism.

However, outside of these opposing positions, the issue becomes more complex to the extent that a given economy can combine capitalist and non-capitalist elements and institutions (statists or socialists) at different levels. Thus, the strategic question is to identify which dimension prevails. In a way, this has been the approach adopted by institutionalist economists and social scientists. Among the liberal institutionalist economists of neoclassical formation (Lardy, 2018), China's success was due to the development of markets and the integration into the global economy – capitalism – while the main problems would arise from the closed political regime – statism or socialism – distorting the allocation of resources. Other authors who follow this methodological perspective with greater pragmatism do not consider, however, that "political capitalism" (Milanovic, 2019) or state capitalism (Bremmer, 2010; The Economist, 2020a) is a negative factor for economic development, limiting their criticism to political aspects, including the high degree of corruption. In the non-neoclassical perspective of development economics, several authors (Knight, 2012; Haggard, 2018; Naughton, 2017; Naughton and Tsai, 2015; McNally, 2019; Xu, 2011) consider the Chinese experience as a (more or less) close variant of developmentalism as affirmed in East Asia – particularly in the experiences of Japan, South Korea, and Taiwan, examined by Johnson (1982), Amsden (1989) and Wade (1990) – in which cohesive authoritarian states (Kohli, 2004) led and coordinated comprehensive industrialization and capital accumulation process.

This chapter aims to examine such interpretations and some central aspects that formed and distinguish the Chinese way of industrialization. As we will argue, the transition from a centrally planned socialist economy to the current social structure of accumulation (Wolftson and Kotz, 2010), which here will be referred to as "developmentalism with Chinese characteristics", was the way in which the transition from a relatively underdeveloped socialist economy to an industrialized economy integrated into the world economy was affirmed in China. In this transition, China gained, lately, some essential features of the system that Galbraith (1967), in his analysis of post-war American capitalism, termed the "Industrial State", converging, in China's own way, "to the model of the Golden Age" traversed by advanced capitalist economies in 1950–73 (Lo, 2020) and, particularly, the variant of developmental states that was affirmed in Japan, South Korea, and Taiwan. The uniqueness of the Chinese route can be attributed to its initial conditions – a command economy –, its geopolitical position – which will be referred here only indirectly – and the way in which the relations between political power (exercised by the CCP) and economic power were structured and, in a way, merged.

We develop this interpretation in the following sections. Section 2 discusses how the basic characteristics of the capitalist system incorporate distinct national varieties and how historically different social structures of accumulation have been affirmed. Subsequently, section 3 delves into some general traits and national variants of the "actually existing socialism" of the 20th century and the issue of economic development as a central priority. In section 4, we describe the process of institutional change in China since the reforms initiated by Deng and, in section 5, we analyze the economic and political formation of contemporary China with emphasis on the relations between economic and political power. In the final section, we derive some conclusions.

2   Capitalism and Its Varieties

Marx understood capitalism as an economic system historically formed by the transformation of the means of production into capital and its concentration "in the hands of a minority of individuals" (Marx, 2017: 941). In this system, the commodity produced as a product of capital "constitutes the dominant and determining characteristic of its product", and there is "the production of surplus value as the direct aim and determining motive of production" (Marx, 2017: 941–942). Competition between multiple individual capitals in the pursuit of profit both shapes the behavior of capitalists (representatives of capital) and governs the dynamics of this system. What characterizes capitalism is not the mere existence of markets, but the imperative of the market and profit. It is this imperative that makes capitalism, and its more abstract form, money-capital, a dominant social relationship.

In the Marxist tradition and the Schumpeterian and institutionalist neoclassical perspectives (North, 1990; Acemoglu and Robinson, 2012), several interpretations of capitalism deduce from its production relationships an endogenous dynamic that leads to the development of productive forces and the introduction of technical progress, unless it is hindered by institutional and political impediments. However, the accumulation of capital can only be affirmed when moving a fundamental contradiction – if we stick to the terms put by Marx and Luxembourg (2003) – which exists between the unlimited character of production and the limited purchasing power; or, from another perspective, capitalism – as Keynes and Kalecki considered – is a "demand constrained" economic system.[2] In addition, the dynamics of capital accumulation

---

[2]   Kalecki (1966) and Kornai (1980) described socialism as a "supply constrained" economic system.

needs to systematically resolve the contradictions that arise from the combination between, on the one hand, the hierarchy of power between capitalists and workers entirely based on the ownership and control of the means of production at the vertical plane, and, on the other hand, the anarchy in the relations between capitalists on the horizontal plane (Marx, 2017).

In the Marxist interpretation (Jessop, 2002), the state in capitalist economies, developed with its fundamental institutions (such as liberal democracy, the multi-party system, the separation of powers), although formally separated from the economy, not only represents the economic interests of the capitalist class over economic policy, but also has an internal mechanics based on the power of money that favors the general interests of this class in the defense and expansion of private property and capitalist relations over other interests and relations. This state was a nationally differentiated historical construction, and the processes of formation of this functional relationship were not synchronous and generated distinct institutionalities (Jessop, 2002).

"Actually existing capitalisms" arose in the midst of non-capitalist production relations and only incompletely subverted these relationships. In the transition processes – such as in the expansion of capitalist production relations in Europe –, economic and political power were historically dissociated for a long period. Once a functional state was constituted in the bourgeoisie's interests, the historical evolution of capitalism occurred by the systematic (albeit contradictory) introduction of extra-market mechanisms for regulating the "fictitious goods", labor, land, money (and knowledge, as Jessop, 2002 correctly added) (Polanyi, 2001). Neither capitalism nor the capital-labor relationship can be produced purely through the market, both require additional institutions and regulatory mechanisms (Jessop, 2002), in such a way that "actually existing capitalism" is always a hybrid system.

Markets are social constructs. Capitalism has historically established itself because it created both market institutions and counterbalancing forces to the process of commodification of social relations of production and the anarchy of intercapitalist relations. These forces – created essentially at times marked by wars and revolutions – did not eliminate the general tendencies of capitalism described by Marx, tendencies that lead to the domination of the commodity form and the power of money-capital over economic decisions, but systematically created forms of protection and coordination that, cyclically, enabled capitalism's socioeconomic reproduction. The way advanced capitalist economies combine market with non-market relations and face the problems of effective demand, investment coordination, and social cohesion shape distinct varieties of capitalism (Hall and Soskice, 2001).[3] These varieties stem from the wide national and historical differentiation over how markets are regulated.

In relation to capital accumulation, the social structures and institutions in late industrializations in the 19th century, as discussed by Gerschenkron (1962), were very diverse according to the nationally differentiated challenges and the degree of economic backwardness for the "industrial startup". In the industrialization of several economies, not only a systematic intervention was affirmed over global demand, tariffs, prices, resource allocation, financing, technical progress, and income distribution, but also a significant presence of state capital in oligopolistic activities in public utilities and heavy industry.[4] Hence, state action and its institutions and ideology in the late industrializations (as in Russia, discussed by Gerschenkron) were quite distinct from the English and Western European experiences. These national strategies aimed at "prosperity, civilization, and power", a formulation of economic nationalism advocated by List (1904). In peripheral economies and especially in economies under colonization (as China with the 19th-century Opium Wars), national states were subjugated, and local bourgeoisie rarely supported economic nationalism and industrialization. This only changed substantially after the Second World War in a limited set of countries.

In the post-war period, the interactions between capital accumulation and class struggle originated, in advanced capitalisms, a social structure of accumulation that Wolfson and Kotz (2010) called "regulated", in contrast to unregulated, as in 19th century liberal capitalism or in neoliberalism, starting in the 1980s. In regulated capitalism, the Keynesian Welfare State – built over war experiences and the socialist challenge arising from the USSR – implemented economic policies aimed at full employment, investment coordination through indicative planning, progressive taxation, and state provision of public and social goods and services. Non-capitalist institutions were developed operating with non-capitalist rationality. Full employment corresponded

---

[3] The authors focus on the different forms of labor regulation and Welfare systems. The analysis of varieties of capitalism discussed here also includes other coordination mechanisms involving investment allocation.

[4] As Sperber (2019) highlights, in contemporary literature on comparative experiences, the combination between statism (interventions) and state capital (SOEs) is associated to a particular variety of capitalism, state capitalism, or to national developmentalism. The greater or lesser presence of SOEs neither defines the accumulation regime nor the type of capitalism: it is a particular way in which the state action in the economy is exercised, distinguishing the industrialization of each country according to its degree of economic backwardness and institutions.

to what Kalecki and Kowalik (1971) called "crucial reform", which, as they predicted, predominated in advanced capitalism while there was high "social conformity".

During the Golden Age, the planning of the government and large corporations occupied a central place. In his analysis of the capitalism of large corporations in the U.S., Veblen (2001) argued that the fundamental issue for overcoming the problems of the U.S. economic system was shifting the power of financiers over corporations to "production engineers". For Galbraith (1967), this transition had occurred in the post-war U.S. in what he called the "new industrial state". Large companies were not run by proprietary shareholders and did not submit to consumer sovereignty. The important decisions were made by the "technostructure", that is, by Veblen's "production engineers", and both shareholders and consumers were passive actors. In this system, a combination of (private) planning of investment in large companies by the technostructure and Keynesian economic policy predominated.

In his formulation, the planning of large firms was an imposition of technology and required the stabilization and predictability of markets. Galbraith (1970) considered that the U.S. and the USSR converged in their business system to the extent that the firm's planning and the macroeconomic regulation of the market were intrinsically associated and eventually imposed in both economies. According to him, this reality would also be imposed in China when it industrialized. The enemy of the market, he warned, is not ideology, but the engineer. Galbraith (1967) considered that the industrial system was intrinsically associated with the state, "corporations were an arm of the state", and the state, an "instrument of the industrial system". This mutual determination has never been clearer, he argued, than in the post-war U.S. Department of Defense's public procurement, whose action engendered the "most developed planning of the industrial system" (Galbraith, 1967: 317).

Some of these characteristics examined by Galbraith were fully affirmed in the late industrializations of the 20th century, although state planning had greater prominence not only in the strategic areas of defense, energy, and innovations, but also in manufacturing in general. This was verified in France, with the General Planning Commission; in post-war Japan, with "Japan Inc." organized around conglomerates (*keiretsus*), under the leadership of the Ministry of International Trade and Industry; and, despite the initial differences, also reproduced in South Korea, with its corporate structure organized in *chaebols* under the leadership of the Economic Planning Board, and Taiwan, with the Council for Economic Planning and Development.

In Japan, South Korea, Singapore, and Taiwan, capitalism and the planning of their conglomerates and large companies developed under the command of a Developmental State (Johnson, 1982; Amsden, 1989; Wade, 1990), which held (until the 1980s) remarkable control and coordination capacity over the "commanding heights" of the economy, combining private appropriation of the social surplus with long-term development in a hierarchical and disciplined society. Through planning aimed at structural change and coordinated by pilot agencies, the Developmental State, with greater or lesser presence of state capital in key industries, established the "focal points" for industrialization and financed and promoted the construction of comprehensive national innovation systems. The co-optation and discipline of big business to the decisions of bureaucracies – control and reciprocity examined by Amsden (1989) and Evans (1995) – was remarkable. The success of this venture depended largely on the combination of these domestic efforts with the U.S. support and even induction, motivated by geopolitical reasons (Medeiros and Serrano, 1999).

If Keynesianism and planning occurred along with a social democratic commitment, leading to growth, the reduction of inequalities, and the virtual elimination of poverty; industrialization in developing countries was accompanied by workers' low bargaining power and harsh discipline in factories. In East Asian countries, the agrarian reform that preceded industrial startup was an essential socioeconomic basis for social cohesion and the elimination of poverty. The democratization and modernization of the countryside occurred along with the authoritarian control of urban workers, whose wages almost always grew below productivity.

Thus, throughout the history of the 20th century, capitalism in both central/industrialized and peripheral/lesser industrialized economies showed essential differences in the way in which it regulated the "fictitious goods" and coordinated investment and the development process. These national varieties and diversities did not cancel, as observed, the central characteristics of capitalism as a mode of production that moves through the expansion of markets, the continuous pressure for the commodification of social relations, and the imposition of its rationality based on the subordination of production to capital's valorization.

With the end of Bretton Woods, the widespread financial deregulation, and the dissolution of the USSR in 1991, these characteristics of post-war capitalism were progressively (in some cases abruptly) dismantled. The "variety of capitalisms" began to be reduced with global neoliberalism, affirmed from the 1980s and projected into the 21st century (Baccaro and Pontuson, 2016), and capitalism became increasingly convergent with the Anglo-Saxon model (King, 2014). In fact, privatization processes, the commodification of public goods, the flexibilization of labor markets, and tax cuts to the richest individuals have substantially reduced the power of workers and dismantled planning mechanisms in capitalism. The structure Veblen advocated for U.S. capitalism, affirmed in the reality described by Galbraith in *The New Industrial State*, was partially undone by the triumph of shareholders over managers and the greater influence of large corporations on the state and public policies, imposing their logic and rationality on non-capitalist institutions.[5]

This process of institutional convergence to global neoliberalism has meant, in many countries, the decline of developmental states.[6] This general but not homogeneous process did not occur in China. As will be argued, China's transition from a centrally planned economy took place gradually, combining capitalist production relations under the leadership and coordination of a developmental state. By electing economic and technological development as the central priority of the government and the nation, China reproduced, with its national and political peculiarities, the central traits of economies led by a developmental state when these institutions had been replaced in most economies by neoliberal capitalist institutions.

3   Varieties of Socialism and the Development of the Productive Forces

Since Marx, the main formulators of socialism have conceptualized it both in relation to its means – the state ownership of the means of production – and ends – the elimination of social deprivations and the construction of a

---

5 An economic system is dominant not only because its constitutive mechanisms predominate in a given economy (which in the real world is always hybrid), but because they tend to impose themselves: they invade and progressively subordinate the other mechanisms, logics and rationalities. The question of capitalist expansion in the neoliberal period is not limited, as in 19th century classical imperialism, to the conquest and subordination of national territories to the capitalist space, but essentially includes the subordination of other institutions, whether communitarian or state, to the commodity form, private interests, and the principles of rationality aimed at profit. This domination is imposed both by formal and informal privatization, in which public companies and organizations abandon objectives and rationalities different from those that dominate in private corporations. Privatization not only occurs when the State sells its proprietary control to the private sector, but when SOEs, even under the state, submit to private corporate logics in the management of their activities and objectives.
6 Developmentalism occurred with a decrease in the wage share, a strong segmentation of labor markets in favor of skilled workers, and authoritarianism in labor relations, but, at the same time, a great upward social mobility due to industrialization was affirmed. Within this perspective, China, despite its distinct starting point and political and institutional characteristics, is trailing a similar trajectory of state-led industrialization.

society based on cooperation and distributive justice. The socialist experiences asserted in the 20th century, the "actually existing socialisms", also had different varieties. In the USSR, "war communism", the New Economic Policy (NEP) announced in 1921 by Lenin, and the command economy affirmed under Stalin's leadership presented very different characteristics regarding the means used, how the state controlled the economy and prioritized the development of productive forces, and how distributive relations were structured. Similarly, in China under Mao, relations between political power and the economy were very different before the period of the 1956 Great Leap Forward and the period of the Cultural Revolution. National differences were also very significant.

Despite the different varieties in these experiments, common elements were present. There was a total "expropriation of political power" of the economically dominant classes (Losurdo, 2017). Capital accumulation was subordinated to a central planning system based on use value and operated by SOEs, although the form and degree in which private property expropriation occurred has been quite uneven historically. With the forces of accumulation predominantly in the hands of the State, the economic system became entirely "supply-constrained" (Kornai, 1980; Kalecki, 1966), in which investment and production do not respond to market demand, but to general planning (Serrano and Mazat, 2013). The elimination of traditional classes, the provision of universal public services, and full employment have led to an extraordinary social leveling, the expansion of public consumption, and poverty reduction.

Underlying the CCP's formulation of "socialism with Chinese characteristics", officially proposed in the 12th National Congress of the CCP in 1982, and the "socialist market economy" (which is how Deng called the regime that would have been asserted in contemporary China) is the implicit proposition that previous socialist experiences, such as the USSR and China itself, were historical experiences, and not an archetype or model that necessarily defines socialism abstractly as a specific social formation. Indeed, the particular way in which socialism developed in the USSR and other Eastern European countries, with the total abolition of private enterprise and the adoption of central planning, was the result of a set of economic and geopolitical factors experienced by the USSR in the late 1920s (Gerschenkron, 1963) and later by the war economy and the Cold War with the U.S. (Serrano and Mazat, 2013; Medeiros, 2008).

The existence of markets is not what defines capitalism and, as Deng has repeatedly formulated, the presence of markets in socialism – state capitalism as Lenin had referred when launching the NEP[7] – is not a contradiction with

---

7   Lenin argued that the NEP consisted of using capitalism to develop socialism (Boer and Zhixiong, 2015).

the objectives of socialism, unless the power of money dissolves other social relations and a new bourgeoisie takes political power.[8] Arguably, for Deng, the central priority in his defense of reforms and openness was the development of productive forces, a project abandoned during the Cultural Revolution.

The international attraction exerted by socialism in the 20th century was based on its ability to overcome economic backwardness and eliminate mass poverty. This was affirmed, as examined by Robinson (1966) and Brus and Kowalik (1983), as an alternative way of promoting national industrialization and not a successor to capitalism. For this, a bourgeois national revolution was necessary, but due to the passive and subordinate social position of the "comprador bourgeoisie", this revolutionary process could only be led by workers under the direction of communists and socialists. For Sun Yat-sen, the first president of the Republic of China and founder of the Kuomintang party, industrialization was the essential basis for eliminating the "miserable condition among the Chinese proletariat" and to end the growing "economic domination" initiated with the Opium War (*apud* Helleiner, 2020). This formulation applies precisely to both the trajectory followed by Post-1949 Taiwan under Chiang-Kai-shek and the People's Republic of China. The Chinese revolution led by Mao was essentially a national and anticolonial revolution, and the focus on the development of productive forces remained until the Cultural Revolution when developmentalism was replaced by ideological struggle. Under the leadership of Deng, economic development gained absolute priority, subordinating the ideological struggle to economic performance and initiating a gradual dismantling of the command economy for what he called "socialist market economy", the form acquired by the economic nationalism advocated by Sun Yat-Sen and fully implemented in Taiwan.

Neither the transition to socialism nor its transition to capitalism can be interpreted as an economic necessity or historical inevitability. Both the development of productive forces and social relations should be seen in a specific historical context. Indeed, the passage of the USSR from the 1920s NEP to central planning was an imposition of geopolitical and economic circumstances; the reverse movement, from central planning to NEP, which roughly was affirmed in China from the 1970s onwards, was also imposed by economic and geopolitical circumstances. China's essential political challenge was to protect the country from a military attack (in that decade mainly associated with the USSR) and the separatism and fragmentation of the central power represented

---

8   As Sweezy (1970) observed, as there is no "law of movement" in socialism, its evolution depends entirely on class struggle. The system could evolve either to its larger project, communism, or to a restoration of capitalism.

by Taiwan's independent existence and U.S. relations with Taiwan. Considering these challenges, the development of productive forces and the technological modernization of the overall economy and the armed forces have become central national strategies, to which the rapprochement with the U.S. was instrumental (Medeiros, 2008). Under Deng's leadership, the government developed the perception that the acceleration and support of China's accumulation trajectory required expanding export production and consequently having access to the technology and foreign markets of large capitalist economies.

When, in the 1990s, liberalizing reforms were deepened and capitalist discipline was widespread in export factories, there was no longer an international socialist system; and China, under the leadership of its party-state, would forge a path of development combining various developmental experiences underwent by the post-war East Asian countries. As Xu (2011) observed, from the 11th CCP Congress in 1978, which officially launched the "Four Modernizations" (agriculture, industry, technology, and armed forces), a consensus was affirmed in the CCP: economic development must be interpreted as the essence of socialism, in fact for the basis of "prosperity, civilization, and power" in List's formula on economic nationalism. Before addressing this issue, we should summarize the developments that occurred in China.

4 Markets, Planning, and Political Power in the Chinese Transition

The structural reforms and transformations initiated in 1979 occurred gradually and under the control of the CCP (Medeiros, 2013). The periodization of this evolution proposed by Orlik (2020) identifies four major cycles.

The first started in 1979 with Deng's "Four Modernizations" and ended in 1989 with conflicts in Tiananmen Square. In this cycle, the central economic priority was obtaining foreign currency to import food and technology and increase agricultural productivity. The dissolution of rural communes, the establishment of the household responsibility system, the expansion of township and village enterprises (TVEs), and the creation of Special Economic Zones (SEZs) have initiated major changes. However, throughout this decade, they have not altered the fundamental characteristics of the pre-existing socialist economy, such as the control of the means of production by the state, with newly created private companies occupying a marginal position in the economy and society. From the 5th Five-Year Plan (1978–83), the central planning system progressively reduced its scope, forming a hybrid planning system that combined mandatory allocations, indicative planning, and market allocation ("out of plan") according to the pricing system. From the economic standpoint, the reforms started from the realization that there was a huge technological gap relative to industrialized economies and aimed to "learn with the West" while protecting the economy from the disruptive impacts generated by the opening. Indeed, these reforms (contrary to what occurred in the former USSR) did not include any reduction in the state control of foreign exchange (maintaining a dual system) and foreign trade, preserving a protectionist tariff structure.

This "defensive nationalism" (Zheng and Pan, 2012) took place in an international context characterized by new opportunities created by changes in the international and regional division of labor induced by the U.S. exchange rate policy and the reaction of Japanese capitals aiming at a spatial relocation of investments (Medeiros, 2008, 2013). Exports from SEZs have contributed to raising the growth and investment rates and gradually begun a comprehensive controlled process of change. In fact, in the SEZs established in Guangdong and Fujian, near Hong Kong and Taiwan, capitalist production relations were introduced (in a spatially delimited environment) through the institutionalization of a labor market and capitalist discipline in factories, and the regulation of a legal system with tax and exchange incentives for foreign investment and the formation of joint ventures with foreign companies. SEZs have also expanded in number and modalities: between 1984 and 1988, 14 economic and technological development zones and the first high-tech industrial development zone were created, while in 1990 the first free trade zone was established in Shanghai (Zeng, 2012). These modifications, like the others that followed later, were initiated by subnational governments exercised by executives appointed by the central government and, to the extent that they were successful, were progressively extended to other regions (Xu, 2011).

A second cycle began with Deng's Southern Tour (1992). The liberalizing reforms that will characterize this cycle and alter the social relations of production still in force were preceded and driven by three major events of great impact on the CCP: the 1989 Tiananmen Square protests, the dissolution of the USSR in 1991, and the first Persian Gulf War, in which the U.S. revealed a great military superiority (Medeiros, 2008) and provoked a sense of urge in CCP for pursuing military modernization. These events led to the maintenance of Deng's strategy of openness (contrary to CCP's orthodox currents), reaffirming three central points: the monopolistic power of the CCP over the State and the People's Liberation Army, in response to the protesters' claims for political liberalization and in order to avoid the collapse experienced by the USSR; economic development opened to FDI and foreign technology; and the elimination of personalism in decision-making processes in favor of the CCP's collective decisions (Xu, 2011). A consensus was affirmed – having as foundation the support of the Army, for whose modernization greater resources were promised by Deng and the administrators of coastal cities – based on the continuation of openness and reforms at the economic level, maintaining political power centralized under the direction of the party-state (Medeiros, 2013).

The main content of the reforms was the expansion of new production relations that were built in the SEZs to dozens of other special areas in major cities in inland China. Over the decade, the "special" regime of economic areas began to become widespread. The defensive economic nationalism of the previous period was progressively being modified with the tariff reduction and the quite comprehensive trade policy change preparatory to entry into the World Trade Organization (WTO), occurred in 2001 (Zheng and Pan, 2012), and gradually incorporated new strategies aimed at promoting exports, expanding domestic companies, transferring technology, and attracting FDI, whose inflow increased substantially in this decade. Market access conditional on technology transfer – which could also be leveraged for military modernization – began to be asserted as one of the main instruments of economic nationalism.

Already in the late 1980s, but especially in this second cycle, private capital and TVEs formed a hybrid structure – many of these companies ceded their proprietary rights to managers – and built with state bureaucracies, the CCP, and SOEs informal networks (known as *Guanxi*) to compensate for their institutional weakness and expand access to credits and investments (McNally, 2019). Many entrepreneurs registered their firms as collective companies, forming what was called "red hat collectives" (Dickson, 2008). Progressively, this structure was overcome with the formal recognition of private property.

In 1992, at the 14th CCP Congress, China was no longer described as a "planned commodity economy" but as a "socialist market economy" including various forms of ownership (private, individual, and foreign invested enterprises) (Dickson, 2008). Essential here was the decision that the CCP should facilitate and promote the development of private enterprises. With the decision, starting in 1992, to restructure state capital, which by the late 1990s would take shape in the rhetorical formula "grasp the big, release the small" for the privatization of small and medium-sized enterprises, the Chinese private sector gained a new economic and political dimension (McNally, 2019). The number of private companies grew 35% per year over the decade (Dickson, 2008). In 1990–91, stock exchanges were created in Shanghai and Shenzhen, and in 1993, the Company Law was approved enabling the transformation of SOEs into stock companies.

With the expansion of migration flows and the increasing mobility of the workforce generated by the great contraction of wage employment in privatized SOEs, a broad labor market was affirmed in coastal areas, as well as a dynamic process of capital accumulation, export growth, introduction of new technologies, and expansion of the financial sector. In relation to labor regulation, the Trade Union Law was introduced in 1992 and, in 1994, the Labor Law, providing for the maximum of eight working hours daily and 44 hours weekly.

Privatization and investment in SEZs and urban areas largely accrued to sub-national initiatives. With tax centralization promoted by the tax-sharing reform of 1994, local governments and administrative regions found in privatization, leasing of urban lands, and inflows of FDI forms of compensation and financing. In this cycle, using Polanyi's (2001) metaphor regarding the oscillation between social regulation and regulation by the market, the pendulum strongly moved towards the market. The socialist welfare system based on full employment and social provision by enterprises in the urban sector was eroded through the privatization of SOEs, the pursuit of flexibility in labor relations, and the privatization of health services and pensions.

Under the leadership of Zhu Rongji, with China's entry into the WTO, a third cycle began, expanding the economic transformations initiated previously, with the strong expansion of foreign investments, private companies, and market relations. There was an important emphasis on the internationalization of large enterprises, especially state oil companies (the "going out" or "going global"), and a dynamic growth regime was affirmed driven by public and private investments led by urbanization and exports. In reaction to the 1997 Asian financial crisis, the government kept its currency regime as a crawling peg to the dollar – initially, the renminbi was pegged at around 8.28 per USD until 2005, when the government started tolerating a progressive appreciation of the real exchange rate –, meanwhile keeping financial flows under strict control. There were strong FDI inflows in SEZs, the pronounced expansion of outward FDI, a great boom in exports, the formation of gigantic reserves, and the repositioning of China as a central link in the Asian production chain (Medeiros, 2008, 2013).

SEZs, in their different modalities, kept expanding – for instance, there were 54 national industrial parks by 2008 (Zeng, 2012) –, guided by the government's new priorities, focusing on endogenous technological development. The pursuit of technological catch-up was elevated to the central priority in 2006, and China, since then, substantially increased its technological effort (Medeiros and Trebat, 2017; Majerowicz and Medeiros, 2018) forming a comprehensive National Innovation System. The regulation of foreign capital inflows and the defense of national capital received more emphasis with the 2008 Antimonopoly Law. In this cycle, entrepreneurs gained a new political status and, since 2001, were admitted in the CCP. In 2003, the State-owned Assets Supervision and Administration Commission of the State Council (SASAC) was established as the main owner and controller of a block of large SOEs in the economy's central activities. In 2007, private property protection was included in the country's Constitution. In the 11th Five-Year Plan (2006–10), there were no more quantitative targets, consolidating the increasingly indicative nature of planning. Under Hu Jintao, the focus for economic growth was placed on the domestic market, and several measures were implemented to build a new system of social provision (the construction of a "harmonious society"). In face of the great urban unemployment generated by privatizations and the constant conflicts and violations in labor relations, a Labor Contract Law was enacted in 2008, aiming to institutionalize collective bargaining and regulate working conditions. New priorities were established such as equity, balanced development, energy diversification, and environmental concerns. The pendulum began to shift towards the social regulation of the market.

Still under Hu Jintao, a fourth cycle began with the 2008 Great Crisis, and, under the leadership of Xi Jinping, continues to this day. With the global financial crisis, the Chinese government launched a major anti-cyclical program (4 trillion yuan, one of the world's largest) with an emphasis on infrastructure investments and SOEs' protagonism. Under Xi, not only public investment and household consumption took a leading role, but also a greater priority was conferred to national technology with the Made in China 2025 plan, the augmentation of R&D spending, the expansion of incentives for the development and acquisition of technologies, and investments in technology parks. Economic nationalism in both its technological (the promotion of indigenous technology) and monetary (control over financial flows) dimensions has come under increasing U.S.-led international pressure. Simultaneously, there was an expansion of welfare policies aimed at building a "moderately prosperous" society, as established in the 13th Five-Year Plan (2016–2020).

On the political level, Xi began his government with a major political and ideological campaign against corruption (resulting in hundreds of thousands of prosecutions of CCP members, officials, and executives, many of which were arrested). Alongside this campaign aimed at expanding the state political power, the government faced, in 2015, the first crisis of its stock market, resulting in capital flight. Both movements led simultaneously to the deepening of reforms – with the progressive liberalization of the participation of foreigners in its financial market and Chinese residents in foreign financial markets – and the greater control of the CCP over enterprises (Orlik, 2020).

Regarding macroeconomics, the growth rate was much lower than in previous cycles, public investments in infrastructure modernization and household consumption became the main magnets for growth. A new phase of SOEs' restructuring occurred, regulating its shareholding structure, aimed at diversifying state capital. In addition, policies were introduced to regulate competition. One of the central aspects of this cycle documented by Bai *et al.* (2020) and Chen and Rithmire (2020) was the expansion of Chinese SOEs investments in joint ventures with the private sector, largely induced by the program of technological modernization and promotion.

Moreover, the reforms aimed at building a welfare state were institutionalized with the approval of the 2010 Social Insurance Law and the 2013 amendment to the Labor Contract Law aimed at extending the protection of legislation for outsourced activities. Externally, in the face of the growing protectionism practiced by the Trump administration against Chinese exports and foreign investment, the government strengthened its comprehensive program to build a regional infrastructure with the Belt and Road Initiative.

As a result of this evolution, the Chinese society arrived in this last cycle with the majority of the population living in the urban world, a vast segmented working-class (workers with and without local residence permit), a large middle class, a massive domestic market – which for various goods such as automobiles, mobile phones, and luxury goods is the world's largest (McKinsey, 2019) –, hundreds of large SOEs with global projection, a diversified national innovation system, a few giant private technology companies, and a numerous class of wealthy entrepreneurs with large individual fortunes, with a few hundred of these billionaires (a number comparable to the US) among the 500 largest fortunes on the Forbes list. In this context, in 2021, a series of regulations were introduced in distinct areas, from antitrust to cybersecurity and online gaming, particularly hitting China's private Big Tech, in a movement that has been justified, at least rhetorically, in terms of "common prosperity". However, as this is an ongoing process, it remains out of the scope of our analysis.

5   Developmentalism with Chinese Characteristics

The description of the four cycles of structural reforms and transformations is instrumental to delineate that what we postulate as developmentalism with Chinese characteristics. The first cycle, in the 1980s, is still marked by transition from socialism to capitalism, and the socialist regulation mode is still present. Developmentalism with Chinese characteristics, hence, is a growth regime or pattern initiated by Deng with the affirmation of capitalism in the second cycle, starting in 1992. Initially, this growth regime underpinned by economic nationalism included reforms that aimed at accelerating capital accumulation. However, due to the political and class conflicts that occurred in the 1990s and the beginning of the 2000s, the idea of a harmonious development and the technological policy gained more traction by mid-2000. These two characteristics are further consolidated under Xi Jinping in the fourth cycle.

Under Xi, "socialism with Chinese characteristics" is, in practice, the implementation of a party-state-led project based on economic nationalism (understood primarily as the pursuit of technological catch-up with advanced economies), the modernization of the armed forces (objective strongly entrenched in the former), and the achievement of satisfactory social cohesion (the maintenance of satisfactory levels of employment and social provision of public services). That is, what is described here as "developmentalism with Chinese characteristics", an intellectual-heir project of those formulated in other historical contexts by List and in the Chinese political history mainly by Sun Yat-sen,[9] and followed in the post-war period by Japan, Taiwan, and South Korea, albeit with different national characteristics. The main characteristic that distinguishes the Chinese experience is the structure of its political power formed by a party-state that has great political autonomy and strong penetration in economic power.

Despite this intellectual heritage and all the fundamental transformations China underwent over the last four decades, the CCP still sustains that China is a socialist economy, even if a socialist market economy. For that reason, it is important, first, to elucidate the main points that sustain our thesis vis-à-vis the official rhetoric and academic versions supporting it, before we proceed with further analyses of the other characteristics of Chinese developmentalism in its current phase.

5.1   *The CCP's Official Rhetoric*

The expression "socialist market economy", enshrined at the 14th CCP Congress in 1992 (Pearson, 2015),[10] has an important political-ideological connotation considering the persistent conflict of perspectives between the CCP's liberalizing reformist wings and the orthodox socialist currents. The reformist leadership seeks to keep alive the proposition that, with the expansion of markets and changes in the structure of coordination and planning – replacing the former State Planning Commission, which exercised a compulsory allocation

---

9   Sun Yat-sen advocated a program based on economic nationalism – understood as the basis for freeing China from foreign economic domination –, the democratic rights of the people, and the provision of welfare. For a discussion on the influence of Sun Yat-sen's thinking on Xi Jinping, see Helleiner (2020).

10   This resolution clearly established that the reforms' objective is to develop the market system, including the financial market, the Stock Exchange, and the real estate market, forming a unified internal market (Pearson, 2015).

of resources, by the National Development and Reform Commission, which has largely an indicative character –, China follows a direction in which socialist objectives, such as equality and social justice, will be achieved at a later stage when it obtains levels comparable to moderately developed countries. According to this narrative, the reforms of the 1990s – although they resulted in the large relative expansion of profit-oriented production and the commodification of labor power – did not essentially alter the socialist project initiated with the 1949 revolution, but only adjusted its course, adapting it to economic and political transformations. While achieving high growth rates provides broad acceptance to this narrative, it suppresses the existence of political conflicts and debates among currents within the party that have been important to the recent emphasis placed on building a "harmonious society" through welfare policies.[11]

Abstractly, there is not a commonly accepted formulation regarding market socialism. Fraser (Fraser and Jaeggi, 2018), without specifically referring to China, conceptualized it as a system in which markets are used for the distribution of consumer goods while non-market mechanisms (such as planning) are used for the allocation of credit, capital goods, raw materials, and the social surplus. If we include the regulation of foreign trade and control over capital flows in the planning system, we get a reality of an economy strongly regulated by the state as in contemporary China. However, since this formulation is limited to a discussion about the means of the economic system, excluding the objectives, it does not allow us for qualitatively distinguishing this regime from those that were historically asserted among developmental states, particularly in East Asia. In these, the power of private companies was subordinated to multiple planning and control mechanisms (Amsden, 1989), including, in some cases (as in South Korea and Taiwan), a strong presence of SOEs, although not comparable in extension with contemporary China.

---

11 The most well-known political polarization since the fall of Chongqing Party Secretary Bo Xilai, in 2012, is the one that has taken place between the "common prosperity", "the Chongqing model", and the reformist liberalizing line, the "Guangdong model". As Zhao (2012) argues, Bo Xilai cited in his internal political discussions a speech in which Deng warned against the risks of reforms to take an "evil path" of capitalism, creating a great social polarization, and considered that it was not possible to expect that only in the future could polarization be addressed, because the interests constituted would obstruct the process of change. He advocated within the CCP a strategy he called "common prosperity" based on the pursuit of social harmony. Objectively, what has been referred as the Chongqing's model is a development program based on public investments in socially necessary activities, social protection, and popular involvement.

Thus, bearing in mind the differences arising from China's starting point where the state controlled all means of production, the developmental planning system that came to prevail in China is comparable to the system that was affirmed in East Asia in which the state – as Wade (1990) said regarding Taiwan – ruled the markets.[12] In Taiwan, the relative presence of state capital in the 1960s was comparable to mainland China today.[13] Although the existence of this system refutes the thesis that China has a neoliberal accumulation regime, it does not allow us to conclude and characterize as socialist a developmental economy led or governed by the state.

5.2   SOEs in China Proprietary Structure: Defining a Form, but Not Necessarily a Content

The combination of SOEs, planning, and private accumulation would describe, according to Gabriele (2020), a socialist market economy in which the core of SOEs (affirmed after the 1990s) acts strategically and other state-controlled companies, although guided by a market logic, would not be capitalist. In this economic structure, the role of private companies would occupy a subordinate position because, although they predominate in number, they command a smaller fraction of the capital stock. Under Xi, this interpretation would gain more solidity with the realization that the movement, initiated in 21st century, in which the "the state sector advances, while the private sector retreats" would have been strengthened (Lo, 2020). Indeed, the privatization that occurred in the 1990s was quite selective, resulting in a structure of capital accumulation in contemporary China in which large SOEs constitute its fundamental core. In 2021, under the control of the SASAC,[14] there were 96 large companies, which

---

12   Taiwan's industrialization was coordinated by the Council for Economic Planning and Development, whose "responsibilities cover the formulation of the one-, four-, and ten-year macroeconomic development plans; analysis of the current situation of the economy; and evaluation of large-scale public enterprise projects" (Wade, 1990: 209).

13   "Throughout the 1950s they [SOEs] accounted for over half of industrial production. As new industries started the proportion fell, reaching 45 percent by 1963" (Wade, 1990: 90).

14   "In the name of the Chinese central government, SASAC holds ownership rights over a broad range of (nonfinancial) state firms, which means it has nominal control over enormous wealth. Forty-five corporations on the Global Fortune 500 list for 2012 are owned by SASAC, with combined assets worth U.S. $4.5 trillion". (Naughton, 2015: 46). It should be noted that also in Taiwan SOEs were under centralized coordination and subordinated to the Council for Economic Planning and Development: "The management board for each public enterprise is appointed by the ministry to which the enterprise is affiliated; in the major public enterprises, the senior positions are appointed directly by the president or premier.... Board members tend to be ex-ministers, ex-senior officials, or ex-military officers rather than private industrialists or academics" (Wade, 1990: 209).

controlled over thousands of companies. These companies – mainly in oil, petrochemicals, electricity, telecommunications, and the military industry – form the commanding heights of the economy and are key agents of long-term investment strategies established in the five-year plans. They form the apex of power of the Chinese productive structure. Beside these, there are many companies in which the state is the main shareholder; they are stablished in sectors such as machinery, equipment, automotive, chemistry, and pharmaceuticals. In these companies, the state's participation is much lower and is mainly exercised through industrial policy. At the base of the economic pyramid, formed mainly by the light consumption industry, the presence of SOEs is less prominent and private capital predominates.

Thus, the economic power exercised by the Chinese state – formed by the industrial and service enterprises administered by the SASAC, other state-controlled enterprises (even if they have a greater participation of the private sector) spread in manufacturing, and state banks that exercise absolute control of the financial sector – is arguably very high. According to Gabriele (2020), 60% of industrial assets, half of industrial product and one third of industrial employment are carried out by SOEs.[15] As Lo (2020) highlights, China had 106 companies listed in Fortune's top 500, of which 90 were SOEs.

The direct participation of SOEs in the product does not exhaust all their importance in the economy. The influence of Chinese state capital in the formation of private capital through joint ventures has grown widely in the last decade (Bai *et al.*, 2020). Private companies with "connected investors" – defined as SOEs or private owners with capital participation in state-controlled enterprises – rose from 20,000 in 2000 to more than 100,000 in 2019. This evolution in China's corporate structure, in which companies with state investments[16] substantially increased their participation in Chinese capital formation, was made possible by the changes in the legal framework created in 2003 and was affirmed in a macroeconomic context of strong countercyclical action led by SOEs' investments.[17] Considered together, SOEs' influence on the Chinese capital structure is an essential trait for understanding China's high

---

15   Statistics on asset ownership depend on how mixed-owned firms are considered. Qi and Kotz (2019) estimate that, in 2015, about 40% of industrial assets and 22% of the industrial product were attributed to SOEs only.

16   Alongside investments, private companies benefit from greater freedom of action conferred by connections with SOEs (Bai *et al.*, 2020).

17   "The primary means of implementing the policy has been the creation of 'government industrial guidance funds' … in strategic sectors … In 2014, the State Council called for the creation of multiple professionally managed private equity funds to make equity investments on behalf of the state" (Chen and Rithmire, 2020: 6).

rate of capital accumulation (especially post 2008) in a context where several countries sought to reduce this participation with neoliberal reforms. This evolution, in a way, reproduces with peculiarities the business strategies asserted in Japan with the *Keireitsus* and in Korea with the *Chaebols* at the height of their industrializations. The Chinese peculiarity is that at the top of this business structure there is a large SOE (Naughton and Tsai, 2015).

Instead of a socialist market economy, Naughton and Tsai (2015) prefer to call this reality a specific form of state capitalism. According to the authors, this structure combines state control of strategic sectors with advanced forms of financial capitalism, production networks integrated into global trade, capitalist incentive systems, and U.S. corporate techniques predominantly forming a market economy.[18] Among the essential traits of the Chinese economic system highlighted by the authors, three dimensions are particularly relevant for the purposes of this chapter: (1) the state control of strategic sectors through SOEs; (2) the control of executives by the party; (3) the market as the basis for a broad segment of the economy (in which the influence of the central government is indirect through local governments whose leaders are appointed by it).

As previously argued, state ownership defines a form, but not necessarily a content (or defines a function) in enterprises' investment decisions. There are two distinct but intertwined issues here. The first concerns the relationship between the state as the main actor who formulates the strategic objectives not reducible to the criteria of efficiency and profit rate maximization and the company as an agent of these strategies. The second, which tends to increase in importance when these companies acquire greater autonomy and have significant participation of minority shareholders, is whether these enterprises' decisions move according to the criteria established by their executives aiming at greater long-term growth – as in Galbraith's New Industrial State – or mainly

---

18 Convergently, McNally (2020) describes Sino-capitalism as a combination of different forces: "China adapted neo-liberal policies in various areas, such as allowing substantial access by foreign capital to its manufacturing and retail sectors; fostering the relatively rapid development of equity markets and intensive use of Hong Kong's internationalized capital markets; and, despite China's socialist legacy, the creation of some of the most flexible and brutal labor markets on earth in a 'market-liberal form of state capitalism'… Despite these elements, neo-liberalism was balanced with neo-statist interventions. China followed its East Asian predecessors in late development with the active use of industrial policy programs to subsidize investments in 'strategic industries' and provide other policy supports. The Chinese Communist Party (CCP) also employed 'financial suppression' that created high savings and investment rates to foster high-speed industrialization" (McCNally, 2020: 287).

aimed to increase their profitability, share value, and shareholder remuneration, as is the case in contemporary capitalist enterprises.

Gabriele (2020) considers that SOEs under SASAC have predominantly a strategic action focused on the long term, subordinated to the five-year plans, configuring the core of a socialist market economy. However, in parallel, through the reforms, more autonomy was granted to SOEs relative to the government, the activities and sectors of private capital were expanded, greater participation of investors and minority shareholders[19] was allowed, and corporate efficiency criteria and goals were incorporated,[20] such as IPOs launch by investment banks – these shares were traded not only in Shenzhen, Shanghai, and Hong Kong Stock Exchanges, but also (such as several Chinese SOEs) in New York and Nasdaq. These reforms aimed not only at centralizing the regulatory and control mechanisms of strategic companies, but also at increasing productivity through the incorporation of profitability-focused business practices – which we will call corporatization – using financial instruments and indicators, the deployment of shareholder value in investment decisions over assets, etc. (Chen and Rithmire, 2020), making the action of these enterprises closer to a capitalist rationality.[21]

---

19   "By transforming SOEs into different kinds of limited liability companies or shareholding companies, the state's responsibility for SOEs would then be limited up to the actual capital it invests, and SOEs would have to be responsible for their own profits and losses up to the point of bankruptcy. Regarding control, the state would reserve the power over the selection of the top management of SOEs and over their strategic decision-making. SOEs would receive investment from the state and other legal entities, and the state would enjoy proportional returns from enterprise profits" (Lo, 2020: 9).

20   "We will improve the distribution and structure of the state-owned sector of the economy and accelerate the development of mixed-ownership economic entities. We will establish a sound modern corporate structure and corporate governance. We will improve the system for managing state-owned assets, clearly define the functions of different SOEs, and carry out trials of investing state capital in corporate operations. We will … raise the percentage of earnings from state capital turned over to public finance by central government-owned enterprises. We will formulate measures for non-state capital to participate in investment projects of central government enterprises, and allow non-state capital to participate in a number of projects in areas such as banking, oil, electricity, railway, telecommunications, resources development and public utilities" (Li Keqiang Second Session of the 12th National People's Congress on March 5, 2014).

21   "SASAC firm profits quadrupled from 2002 to just shy of one trillion RMB in 2007, increasing from 2% of GDP in 2002 to 3.8% of GDP … With substantial sums of money at their disposal, SASAC firms have financial clout that reinforces their economic importance. SASAC trumpeted the record-breaking 2007 profit figures but since then has become much more circumspect, for two reasons. First, the arrival of the global financial crisis in 2008 dealt a major short-run blow to SASAC firm profitability. Second, SASAC's huge profits began to attract negative comment from people who pointed out that SASAC firms had been given

Contemporary, China's SOEs act both with strategies that govern or "replace" the market and follow or "conform" to the market, and the latter has grown in no less exceptional way with the intense growth of the private sector. A first and important block of capital accumulation is carried out by companies mainly in SEZs, where the most technology-intensive exports accrue primarily to foreign companies – attracted by a broad set of fiscal and regulatory stimuli –, and the less technologically sophisticated exports are carried out by private capital in joint ventures with SOEs and increasingly with foreign capital. While the penetration of multinational companies' subsidiaries in China producing both for exports and the domestic market – which, since the beginning of the century, has been the main source of expansion – is small relative to the total capital stock, it is higher in China than in the US (McKinsey, 2019). Indeed, 80% of the 500 largest non-Chinese companies listed on Fortune had subsidiaries in China.[22]

In parallel, the formation of Chinese private enterprises also evolved from another departure point quite distinct from other national developmental experiences. On the one hand, as local governments were (and still are) owners of a substantial portion of local and state enterprises, privatization constituted a strategy for subnational governments to finance their investments with the 1994 tax centralization. On the other hand (similarly to the other transitions from socialism to capitalism), a substantial part of the privatized companies that today forms the main block of national private capital in China was acquired by its managers, technical staff linked to the CCP (Fan, Morck, and Yeung, 2012).

Considering the employment composition that resulted from the asset structure evolution of China's economy, the National Bureau of Statistics (NBS, 2021) reported that urban employment in China constituted 60% of employment in 2019, of which: 19.3 percentage points corresponded to employment in private enterprises; 15.5, to self-employment; 7.3, to state units; 15.5, to other employers (collective units, foreign invested units, cooperatives, and others); and 2.6, to unspecified employment. In the urban world, despite the existence

---

monopoly or quasi-monopoly privileges in many markets by the government, but SASAC firms kept the monopoly profits and turned little or nothing back to" (Naughton and Tsai, 2015: 51).

22 In 2013, China began to have a "negative list" for FDI reduced to some activities considered strategic: "The number of specified restrictions fell from 139 in 2014 to 48 in the 2018 revision" (McKinsey, 2019: 35). In view of U.S. restrictive policies, these investments tend to be reduced, without, however, altering this fundamental feature of capital accumulation in China.

of cooperatives and hybrid forms of ownership, proletarianization or the commodification of labor power in the private and state sectors is predominant, which makes the Chinese economy, regarding capital-labor relations, a predominantly capitalist economy.

5.3   Capital-Labor Relations and the Welfare System

On the factory floor, China's reality is also very heterogeneous. On the one hand, low wages, high intensity, and long working hours faced by workers (largely migrants) in construction sites and assembly lines (such as Foxconn) mainly, but not exclusively, located in SEZs. On the other hand, workers hired by SOEs with urban citizenship have higher salaries and better working conditions. On average, wages have grown over the last decade – above productivity growth, from 2011 to 2015, and *in tandem* with productivity since then (Medeiros and Majerowicz, 2024) –, albeit with large dispersions between regions and occupational positions. This heterogeneity is reproduced due to loopholes in the 2008 Labor Contract Law, the resistance of employers, and the attitude of official unions (affiliated to the All-China Federation of Trade Unions), which tend to follow the guidelines of management.

With the dissolution of rural communes and privatization, the socialist system of universal provision of health, education, and income was dismantled throughout the 1990s. From there, a new welfare system was built with the 2010 Social Insurance Law. Although access to public and social goods and services is not universal and depends essentially on individuals' income, occupational position, and urban citizenship (segmenting migrant workers), it has been expanded in the last two decades, particularly in the provision of quality public education. Similarly, in a decentralized way, cities are establishing a basic subsistence income. For the most vulnerable in society, the poorest, – which are a potential source of social instability –, the Targeted Poverty Alleviation strategy was put in place. Launched in 2013, the strategy addressed the remaining 100 million people in extreme poverty out of 770 million existing in 1978, a mass campaign that eventually succeeded in eradicating extreme poverty by 2020 (Bertrand, 2022).

This evolution of social regulation of the market occurred in response to the increase in income and wealth inequality, as well as inequality between large cities and the interior, the growing striker movements of basic wage earners and peasants who lost their land use right (for many, the safest source of subsistence) – transformed into urban land –, and conflicts within the CCP on the issue of social justice. It is now an important dimension of class struggle in contemporary China. Indeed, it can be argued that China has been building, especially under Xi, a version of the welfare state (one of the central dimensions of post-war advanced capitalism), even though the Chinese version is closer to the liberal version, focusing more on efficiency than the social democratic concepts of justice and universality (Ringen and Ngok, 2013).

Recently, challenges for satisfactory social cohesion emerged from the further slowdown of economic growth[23] and the high level of unemployment among young adults that reached 20% in July 2022 (Cai, 2022). These developments were in a large extent a byproduct of the CCP's zero-Covid policy. Such policy, despite avoiding a tremendous number of fatalities and the overrun of the healthcare system – which could compromise social stability – had adverse effects on economic growth and global production networks.

5.4   Technological Catch-Up and Military Modernization

The CCP diagnosed that "digitalization, networkization, and intelligentization" amounted to a technological revolution, which represented a unique historical opportunity for China to leapfrog the advanced countries and climb the hierarchy of the international system, changing the structure of relative powers (Naughton, 2021).

This technological revolution was driving an industrial revolution, said Made in China 2025 (MIC, 2025), whose main goal is to transform China in the leading manufacturing power by 2049. MIC 2025 acknowledged that, since the beginning of the industrial society, the centrality of manufacturing was proven by the rise and fall of great powers (State Council, 2015a). The technological revolution would also imply a "new stage" in the revolution in military affairs (RMA). According to China's 2015 military strategy, in the new stage of the RMA, cyber-space and outer space were affirmed as the "new commanding heights in strategic competition", with the rapid evolution of the war form "to informatization", which were accompanied by the military restructuring pursued by world powers (State Council, 2015b)

In this context, in 2015, the concept of military-civil fusion was elevated to a national strategy. It expressed a two-way technological flow that had evolved historically from defense conversion in the 1980s to a dual-use economy and the employment of spin-on strategies in the late 1990s, in which civilian technologies were used to modernize the military sector (Cheung, 2009). In 2017, China published the Military-Civil Fusion Strategy, which asserted the objective of becoming a 'world class military' by 2049 (Jash, 2020).

---

23 For a discussion on the drivers of China's recent economic growth slowdown, see Medeiros and Majerowicz (2024).

Under Xi, hence, the perception held by the CCP that the country's economy and military were technologically lagging the West – a major driver for Reform and Open – has evolved into an innovation-driven development strategy as a world power strategy, which intends to seize the opportunity of a particular technological revolution that opens a breach for the manufacturing and military reconfiguration of great powers. Economic development, technological catch-up, and military modernization are intrinsically intertwined in this strategy.

These aspirations and plans, however, have been provoking a reaction from the U.S., putting in motion a trade and tech dispute that started under Trump and continues under Biden. The US growingly punitive measures and international pressures on its allies against Chinese tech enterprises are a central dimension of this response. Many of these measures count with the fact that China has not yet surmounted its dependency on foreign technology in the crucial high-tech components of information and communication technologies (ICT), that is, chips, and in semiconductor manufacturing equipment (see Chapter 5). Hence, China has a major vulnerability at the core of its world power strategy, as the country must count with the supplies and technology from the US and its military allies, namely, Europe, Japan, South Korea, and Taiwan. However, the possibility of growing approximation and/or absorption of Taiwan by China could potentially address a severe industrial bottleneck in chip manufacturing, while sophisticating its productive capacity, which would enhance its technological development and competitiveness in ICT as well as in its military through military-civil fusion. Behind the escalation of tensions in the Taiwan Strait, in 2022, lies this possible development as a major source of U.S. concern.

5.5 The CCP's Monopoly of Political Power and Current Tensions with the Markets

The characteristic that really distinguishes the Chinese experience from other transition economies is the fact that, in China, the expansion of private wealth did not lead – as in Russia and Eastern European countries – to the dismantling of the state's political power, which has the same form inherited from 1949.[24] This power structure and its permanence stem not only from internal aspects inherited from the 1949 revolution, but also from political and strategic

---

24 "Just as a Party position corresponds directly to each key position in government, a Party hierarchy parallels corporate governance in banks, SOEs, listed non-SOEs, hybrid enterprises, joint ventures, and sufficiently large private businesses. Party cells throughout business enterprises constitute parallel internal accountability systems to those established by enterprises themselves, keeping an enterprise's Party Secretary and Party Committee up-to-date and able to provide timely advice to its CEO and board. Imported corporate

aspects originated in the Cold War in which China affirmed itself as a nuclear military power. Contrary to what happened in the USSR, the transition did not break the strategic alliance between the military and the party and their unity (Medeiros, 2008). This alliance was personified in an exemplary way by Deng, whose official position was precisely that of chairman of the CCP Central Military Commission, and, contemporary, by Xi, who accumulates this function with the presidency of the country. It is under this centralized state that the transition process took place in China.

In a way, the change in production relations and the expansion of private enterprises were largely a politically induced evolution as a national development strategy under the CCP's political power. Considering this power dimension, the expansion of the private sector resulted in the progressive engagement of entrepreneurs in the party and the party in enterprises. In the 2000s, with the policy of the "Three Represents" under Jiang Zemin's administration, the CCP became representative of the "advanced productive forces", "advanced culture", and "the overwhelming majority of the people of China", terms attributed respectively to entrepreneurs, intellectuals, and workers and peasants. Since then, private entrepreneurs began to participate increasingly in the party and, hence, political power (Orlik, 2020). With this formulation, the CCP ceased to be a class party and assumed a physiognomy of a national party (Gilbert, 2017).

In China, a particular relationship was affirmed between the political power exercised by the CCP and the economic power of large SOEs and the domestic private sector. The tension between economic power and political power has not resulted so far in an essential change in the control that the CCP exerts over the means of coercion and administration of the state, as well as the media and the consensus in Chinese society. As Pearson (2015) observed, with the adoption of market practices, the control exercised by the state is done not only through cash incentives and performance requirements (classic control mechanisms of developmental states), but also, to a large extent, by the CCP control over executives – through SASAC's appointments of CEOs and the influence or supervisory action of the party in companies.

This power relationship, however, is neither a given nor does it follow a linear trajectory, but a process in permanent movement. The great campaign against corruption initiated under Xi was precisely to contain a process which, in his view, could destroy the party and the state (Orlik, 2020; Allison, 2017). As

---

governance regulations, mandating independent directors and the like essentially ignore Party involvement in enterprise governance" (Fan, Morck, and Yeung, 2012: 24).

Allison (2017) noted, Xi's nightmare was the transition process occurred under Gorbatchov. According to Xi, Gorbatchov's big mistakes were relaxing the political control of society before reforming the economy, allowing the Communist Party to become corrupt and subordinating the Soviet military to the nation instead of the Party and its leader (Allison, 2017). The fight against corruption and enrichment of party cadres – since 2012, more than 900,000 CCP members were prosecuted (Allison, 2017) –, the ideological political renewal, and the greater control over social media proposed by Xi aim precisely to prevent China from following the path that led to disaster in the Soviet transition.

Indeed, the tension between the markets and the CCP's political power has recently escalated, opposing, on the one hand, the interests of private big business and large fortunes in favor of greater financial opening and market deregulation, on the other hand, those of the Chinese state in defense of the strategic objectives of national development.[25] This tension is informed by three main movements: the expansion of the internationalization of Chinese companies (state and private) in the last decade, the U.S. political pressures, and the evolution of financial markets. The internationalization of national private companies constitutes an important fracture between the interests of globalized capitals and national states. According to the Ministry of Commerce (McKinsey, 2019), the number of Chinese companies operating abroad made an extraordinary leap – an effect of the 2008 global crisis – from just over 10,000 registered in 2010 to more than 37,000 companies, 110 of which were among Fortune's 500. Although it is led mostly by SOEs, China's private Big Tech, Baidu, Alibaba, Tencent, etc. have grown rapidly through mergers, acquisitions, and joint ventures. The tensions and conflicts of interest between globalized capital (which generally advocate financial deregulation and adopt U.S. legal norms and business practices) and the domestic economy have grown, particularly when these companies list their stocks in the U.S. financial market. In 2020 and 2021, the party-state launched a series of regulations and restrictive and punitive measures over private companies, particularly hitting the tech sector. Antitrust measures and cybersecurity reviews by the Cyberspace Administration of China were put in motion, especially to curb the development of fintech outside the regulatory framework of banking activities and to prevent Chinese tech companies from listing in foreign Stock Exchanges, especially in the U.S., without government clearance.

---

25   "Many of the businessmen who once fancied themselves as a Chinese Warren Buffett are in prison or worse" (The Economist, 2020).

Although this internationalization has been extraordinary, the income generated by Chinese companies abroad is still very low relative to the obtained in the domestic market (McKinsey, 2019). In addition, the main globalized Chinese enterprises are SOEs (albeit increasingly corporatized) and therefore more susceptible to government control. Moreover, with U.S. restrictive policies, North America's participation in the internationalization of Chinese companies has dropped substantially in recent years, contributing to its slowdown.[26] Thus, except for the giant private enterprises, in relation to the impact of enterprises' internationalization on national strategies, this fracture is smaller in China than other economies, even though it has grown extraordinarily over the last two years.

Concerning the financial system, tensions are higher. Despite the gigantic state banking system and the large size of its financial market, financial inflows are much more restricted in China than FDI inflows. Foreign participation in domestic financial markets has only recently begun to be asserted.[27] This reality stems in part from the government's control over financial flows – a centerpiece of its macroeconomic policy – and the nominal exchange rate of the yuan, which remains an inconvertible currency. However, SOEs' corporatization and the appreciation of large companies' stocks and bonds (especially in e-commerce and real estate), in a period of lower growth rates, fostered a boom in the financial market with speculative purchases of shares financed largely by loans granted by shadow banking on the margins of state banks. In 2015, there was a big fall on the Shanghai Stock Exchange, where the main shares traded are from state-owned and state-controlled enterprises, and capital flight.[28] There was a consequent drop in foreign reserves, without, however, affecting the sound position of its balance of payments.

This crisis has resulted in two actions signaling the two ongoing mechanisms in China since Deng. In response to external (IMF, World Bank) and internal pressures (especially large private companies) liberalizing (albeit controlled) reforms have been implemented. These include the opening for foreign

---

26   Inaugurated by Trump, this policy may undergo some inflection with the new Biden administration, but without essentially altering its main motivation to inhibit the expansion of Chinese companies in international markets.
27   "China's banking system is now the biggest in the world at $40 trillion, and its stock and bond markets are the world's second- and third-largest, respectively. However, the financial system remains far from globalized. Foreign ownership accounted for only about 2 percent of the Chinese banking system, 2 percent of the bond market, and about 6 percent of the stock market in 2018" (McKinsey, 2019: 30).
28   The Chinese Central Bank announced a small increase in the yuan's exchange rate against the dollar and, in that speculative context, there was a strong capital outflow.

participation in banks and the Stock Exchange and access (also regulated) of residents to foreign financial markets, such as the London-Shanghai Stock Connect agreement in 2019, enabling the trade of financial assets between residents and non-residents. Meanwhile, U.S. government pressures against Chinese companies in the U.S. market have strengthened the domestic capital market with the launch of shares of major e-commerce platforms. Recently, a stock market only for high-tech enterprises, STAR, was created seeking to rival Nasdaq. In contrast to this liberalizing movement, even if administered by the government, there was an increase in the control and power mechanisms of the CCP over enterprises.[29]

5.6 The Crucial Reform

It is suggestive to compare the transformation that took place in China with the "crucial reform" that Kalecki and Kowalik (1971) observed in post-war capitalism. In that context, Keynesian and social democratic politics constituted a crucial reform imposed on the ruling classes to stabilize the economic system without altering production relations. In economically underdeveloped nations, the crucial reform was state-led developmentalism. In industrialized economies, the crucial reform depended (the authors considered a democratic political context) on the acquiescence of the working classes, and, in economically backward nations, one could add, the subordination of the working class and acquiescence of the owning classes. In China, the crucial reform was the introduction of capitalist production relations without altering the political power centralized in the CCP. At present, the functioning of China's "crucial reform" depends on the acquiescence of capitalists (and the middle class) to the guidelines established in the Five-Year Plans and the monopoly of political power exercised by the party-state. Economic growth and nationalism constitute the essential basis of contemporary China's social cohesion, which has been further amplified and legitimized by the rhetoric of "common prosperity", even if the term remains so far vague.

---

29 The brokers and companies that participated in the speculative movement and capital outflow were mostly SOEs. This fact illustrates in a very didactic way how, under the current conditions, it is illusory to mechanically associate the state-ownership of an asset with a strategic action aimed at long-term growth.

6   Conclusions

This chapter discussed the transition made in China since the reforms initiated in 1978 by Deng Xiaoping, highlighting the profound changes in its social structure of accumulation and the persistence of its institutions of political power. China has gradually – but indeed – moved away from a centrally-planned and socially-egalitarian socialist economy to a sharply unequal mixed economy that we called "developmentalism with Chinese characteristics". The Chinese transition to developmental state capitalism took place in cycles of reforms in which the opening of space for private accumulation, contrary to the experiences of Eastern Europe and the perspectives of neoclassical economists (and liberal political scientists), was not towards the affirmation of neoliberal capitalism. National development constituted in China, in Deng's expression, an "ironclad truth", and was obtained through institutions in which the state, through planning and its enterprises and banks, maintained control over the economy's commanding heights. China has integrated deeply into the international economy through trade and FDI and created a vast internal market for Chinese SOEs, multinational companies, and extraordinary opportunities for the formation and development of a rich class of Chinese entrepreneurs.

This evolution occurred largely in reaction and response to internal conflicts and changes in the international context generated by the extinction of the USSR. Despite specific historical and political characteristics, China has combined in its trajectory several aspects historically followed during the "Golden Age" by advanced capitalist economies in the building of a modern Industrial State, especially in the version affirmed among the dynamic economies of East Asia, and in the construction (especially in the last decade) of a (liberal) Welfare State.

The peculiarity that essentially defines the Chinese path is political power and its relationship with enterprises and the market, affirming a unique relationship between political and economic power. On the one hand, this relationship is expressed by the way the party-state absorbs the transformations occurring in society (bottom-up), with the expansion of private companies and the labor market, as well as by the way it imposes itself on enterprises and workers. On the other hand, it is mainly effectuated by the greater role played by state capital, SOEs, in economic planning. This dual power relationship – of the party over economic agents and the government over investment allocation – has not evolved linearly as in other transition economies in which the state gives way to market forces, but has been affirmed cyclically, engendering different phases marked by internal struggles and contradictions and reactions to the external environment, even though maintained within a stable political context guaranteed by the party-state political system. In radical contrast to the chaotic experience that occurred in the Soviet transition, this evolution, despite having generated rapid primitive accumulation of capital and great private enrichment, did not lead to institutional rupture to the detriment of the economy as a whole. This tension gained greater latitude under Xi Jinping, with the campaign against corruption and the predominance of SOEs' function focused on growth and the plan, counterbalancing the autonomy of decisions conferred by the reforms to enterprises, at a time when global capitalism and corporate practices are subordinate to the logic of financiers.

References

Acemoglu, D.; Robinson, J. (2012). *Why Nations Fail: The Origins of Power, Prosperity, and Poverty*. New York: Crown Group.

Allison, G. (2017). *Destined for War*. New Yok: Houghton Mifflin Harcourt.

Amsden, A. H. (1989). *Asia's Next Giant: South Korea and Late Industrialization*. New York: Oxford University Press.

Baccaro, L.; Pontusson, J. (2016). Rethinking Comparative Political Economy: The Growth Model Perspective. *Politics & Society* 44 (2): 175–207. doi: 10.1177/0032329216638053.

Bai, C. E.; Hsieh, C. T.; Song, Z. M.; Wang, X. (2020). *Special Deals from Special Investors: The Rise of State-Connected Private Owners in China*. WP 28170. Cambridge: NBER. doi: 10.2139/ssrn.3743903.

Bertrand, A. (2022). How China Defeated Poverty. *American Affairs* 6 (1).

Boer, R.; Zhixiong L. (2015). Interpreting Socialism and Capitalism in China: A Dialectic of Utopia and Dystopia. *Utopian Studies* 26 (2): 309–323. doi: 10.5325/utopianstudies.26.2.0309.

Bremmer, I. (2010). *The End of the Free Market, Who Wins the War Between States and Corporations?* London: Penguin Books.

Brus, W.; Kowalik, T. (1983). Socialism and Development. *Cambridge Journal of Economics* 7 (3–4): 243–255. doi: 10.1093/cje/7.3-4.243.

Cai, J. (2022) Young and out of a Job in China: How Covid-19 is creating an Unemployment Crisis. *South China Morning Post*, August 30. https://www.scmp.com/news/china/politics/article/3190569/young-and-out-job-china-how-covid-19-creating-unemployment.

Chen, H.; Rithmire, M. (2020). The Rise of the Investor State: State Capital in the Chinese Economy. *Studies in Comparative International Development* 55: 257–277. doi: 10.1007/s12116-020-09308-3.

Cheung, T. M. (2009). *Fortifying China: The Struggle to Build a Modern Defense Economy*. Ithaca: Cornell University Press.

Dickson, B. J. (2008). *Wealth into Power: The Communist Party's Embrace of China's Private Sector*. New York: Cambridge University Press.

Evans, P. (1995). *Embedded Autonomy: States and Industrial Transformation*. Princeton, New Jersey: Princeton University Press.

Fan, J. P. H.; Morck, R.; Yeung, B. (2012). Translating Market Socialism with Chinese Characteristics into Sustained Prosperity. In: Fan, J. P. H.; Morck. R. (Eds.) *Capitalizing China*. Chicago: University of Chicago Press.

Fraser, N.; Jaeggi, R. (2018). *Capitalism: A Conversation in Critical Theory*. Cambridge: Polity Press.

Gabriele, A. (2020). *Enterprises, Industry and Innovation in the People's Republic of China*. Singapore: Springer Nature Singapore.

Galbraith, J. K. (1967). *The New Industrial State*. New York: Signet Book.

Galbraith, J. K. (1970). A Reply to Critics. In: Mermelstein, D. (Ed.) *Economics: Mainstream Readings and Radical Critiques*. New York: Random House.

Gerschenkron, A. (1962). *Economic Backwardness in Historical Perspective: A Book of Essays*. Cambridge, Massachusetts: The Belknap Press of Harvard University Press.

Gerschenkron, A. (1963). *The Early Phases of Industrialization in Russia: Afterthoughts and Counterthoughts*. London: Macmillan & Co.

Gilbert, S. (2017). Class and Class Struggle in China Today. *International Socialism*, 155.

Haggard, S. (2018). *Developmental States*. New York: Cambridge University Press.

Hall, P.; Soskice, D. (2001). *Varieties of Capitalism*. New York: Oxford University.

Harvey, D. (2005). *A Brief History of Neoliberalism*. Oxford: Oxford University Press.

Helleiner, E. (2020). The Diversity of Economic Nationalism. *New Political Economy* 26 (2): 229–238. doi: 10.1080/13563467.2020.1841137.

Jabbour, E; Gabriele, A. (2021). *China: O Socialismo do Século XXI*. São Paulo: Boitempo.

Jash, A. (2020). China's Military-Civil Fusion Strategy: Building a Strong Nation with a Strong Military. *CLAWS Journal*, Winter: 42–62.

Jessop, B. (2002). *The Future of Capitalist State*. Cambridge UK: Polity.

Johnson, C. (1982). *MITI and the Japanese Miracle: The Growth of Industrial Policy, 1925–1975*. Stanford, CA: Stanford University Press.

Kalecki, M. (1966) 1993. Introduction to the Theory of Growth in a Socialist Economy. *Collected Works of Michal Kalecki*, Vol. 3. Oxford: Clarendon Press.

Kalecki, M.; Kowalik, T. [1971] (1990). Observations on the 'Crucial Reform'. In: Osiatyński, J. (Ed.) *Capitalism: Business Cycles and Full Employment. Collected Works of Michał Kalecki*, Vol. 1. Oxford: Clarendon Press.

King, J. (2014). What Happened with Crucial Reform? In: Bellofiore, R.; Karwoski, E; Toporowski, J. (Eds.) *Economic Crisis and Political Economy. Essays in Honour of Tadeusz Kowalik*, Vol. 2. London: Palgrave MacMillan.

Knight, J. (2012). *China as a Developmental State*. WPS/2012–13. Oxford: Centre for the Studies of African Economies, University of Oxford.

Kohli, A. (2004). *State-Directed Development, Political Power and Industrialization in the Global Periphery*. New York: Cambridge University Press.

Kornai, J. (1980). The Dilemmas of a Socialist Economy: The Hungarian Experience. *Cambridge Journal of Economics* 4 (2): 147–157.

Lardy, N. (2018). *The State Strikes Back: The End of Economic Reform in China?* Washington: Peterson Institute for International Economics.

Li, Z.; Qi, H. (2014). Labour Process and the Social Structure of Accumulation in China. *Review of Radical Political Economics* 46 (4): 481–488. doi: 10.1177/0486613414537986.

List, F. [1841] (1904). *The National System of Political Economy*. Reprint, London: Longmans Green.

Lo, D. (2020). State-Owned Enterprises in Chinese Economic Transformation: Institutional Functionality and Credibility in Alternative Perspectives. *Journal of Economic Issues* 54 (3): 813– 83. doi: 10.1080/00213624.2020.1791579.

Losurdo, D. (2017). Has China Turned to Capitalism? Reflections on the Transition from Capitalism to Socialism. *International Critical Thought* 7 (1): 15–31. doi: 10.1080/21598282.2017.1287585.

Luxemburg, R. [1913] (2003). *The Accumulation of Capital*. London and New York: Routledge.

Majerowicz, E.; Medeiros, C. A. (2018). Chinese Industrial Policy in the Geopolitics of the Information Age: The Case of Semiconductors. *Revista de Economia Contemporânea* 22 (1): 1–28. doi: 10.1590/198055272216.

Marx, K. [1867] (2017). *O Capital*. Livro III. Reprint, São Paulo: Boitempo.

McKinsey. (2019). *China and the World: Inside the Dynamics of a Changing Relationship*. McKinsey Global Institute.

McNally, C. (2019). Theorizing Sino-capitalism: Implications for the Study of Comparative Capitalisms. *Contemporary Politics* 25 (3): 313–333. doi: 10.1080/13569775.2018.1553125.

McNally, C. (2020). Chaotic Mélange: Neo-liberalism and Neo-statism in the Age of Sino-capitalism. *Review of International Political Economy* 27 (2): 281–301. doi: 10.1080/09692290.2019.1683595.

Medeiros, C. A. (2008). Desenvolvimento Econômico e Ascensão Nacional: Rupturas e Transições na Rússia e na China. In: Fiori, J. L.; Medeiros, C. A; Serrano, F. (Eds.) *O Mito do Colapso do Poder Americano*. Rio de Janeiro: Record.

Medeiros, C. A. (2013). Padrões de Investimento, Mudança Institucional e Transformação Estrutural na Economia Chinesa. In: Bielschowsky, R. (Ed.) *Padrões de Desenvolvimento Econômico (1950–2008): América Latina, Ásia e Rússia*, Vol. 2. Brasília: Centro de Gestão e Estudos Estratégicos.

Medeiros, C. A.; Majerowicz, E. The "New Normal" of the Chinese Economy. *Economia e Sociedade*, (forthcoming), 2024.

Medeiros, C. A.; Trebat, N. (2017). Transforming Natural Resources into Industrial Advantage: The Case of China's Rare Earths Industry. *Revista de Economia Política* 37 (3): 504–526. doi: 10.1590/0101-31572017v37n03a03.

Medeiros, C. A.; Serrano, F. (1999) Padrões Monetários Internacionais e Crescimento. In: Fiori, J. L. *Estado e Moedas no Desenvolvimento das Nações*. Rio de Janeiro: Vozes.

Milanovic, B. (2019). *Capitalism, Alone*. London: Harvard University Press.

Naughton, B. (2017). Is China Socialist? *Journal of Economic Perspectives* 31 (1): 3–24. doi: 10.1257/jep.31.1.3.

Naughton, B. (2021). *The Rise of China's Industrial Policy: 1978 to 2020*. Ciudad de México: Universidad Nacional Autónoma de México.

Naughton, B.; Tsai, K. S. (2015). *State Capitalism, Institutional Adaptation, and the Chinese Miracle*. New York: Cambridge University Press.

NBS (National Bureau of Statistics). Annual Data. Accessed March 11, 2021. https://data.stats.gov.cn/english/easyquery.htm?cn=C01.

North, D. (1990). *Institutions, Institutional Change and Economic Performance*. New York: Cambridge University Press.

Orlik, T. (2020). *China: The Bubble that Never Pops*. London: Oxford University Press.

Pearson, M. (2015). State Owned Business and Party-State Regulation in China Modern Political Economy. In: Naughton, B.; Tsai, K. S. (Eds.) *State Capitalism, Institutional Adaptation, and the Chinese Miracle*. New York: Cambridge University Press.

Polanyi, K. [1944] (2001). *The Great Transformation: The Political and Economic Origins of Our Time*. Reprint, Boston: Beacon Press.

Qi, H.; Kotz, D. M. (2019). The Impact of State-Owned Enterprises on China's Economic Growth. *Review of Radical Political Economics* 52 (1): 96–114. doi: 10.1177/0486613419857249.

Ringen, S.; Ngok, K. (2013). *What Kind of Welfare State is Emerging in China?* WP 2013–2. Geneva: United Nations Research Institute for Social Development.

Robinson, J. (1966). *An Essay on Marxian Economics*. London: Macmillan.

Rodrik, D. (2020). China as Economic Bogeyman. *The Asean Post*, July 10. https://theaseanpost.com/article/china-economic-bogeyman.

Serrano, F.; Mazat, N. (2013). A Potência Vulnerável: Padrões de Investimento e Mudança Estrutural da União Soviética à Federação Russa. In: Bielschowsky, R. (Ed.) *Padrões de Desenvolvimento Econômico (1950–2008): América Latina, Ásia e Rússia*, Vol. 2. Brasília: Centro de Gestão e Estudos Estratégicos.

Sperber, N. (2019). The Many Lives of State Capitalism: From Classical Marxism to Free-market Advocacy. *History of Human Sciences* 32 (3): 100–124. doi: 10.1177/0952695118815553.

State Council. (2015a). *Made in China 2025*. Beijing: State Council.

State Council. (2015b). *China's Military Strategy*. Beijing: State Council.

Sweezy, P. (1970). Toward a Program of Studies of the Transition to Socialism. In: Mermelstein, D. (Ed.) *Economics: Mainstream Readings and Radical Critiques*. New York: Random House.

The Economist. (2020). Blown off Course: China Takes Aim at Its Entrepreneurs. *The Economist*, November 12. https://www.economist.com/business/2020/11/12/china-takes-aim-at-its-entrepreneurs.

The Economist. (2020a). The New State Capitalism: Xi Jinping Is Trying to Remake the Chinese Economy. *The Economist*, August 15. https://www.economist.com/briefing/2020/08/15/xi-jinping-is-trying-to-remake-the-chinese-economy.

Veblen, T. [1921] (2001). *The Engineers and the Price System*. New York: Batoche Books.

Wade, R. (1990). *Governing the Market: Economic Theory and the Role of the Government in East Asian Industrialization*. Princeton, New Jersey: Princeton University Press.

Wolfson, M; Kotz, D. (2010). Global Neoliberalism and the Contemporary Social Structure of Accumulation. In: T. McDonough, T.; Reich, M.; Kotz, D. (Eds.) *Contemporary Capitalism and Its Crisis: Social Structure of Accumulation Theory for the 21 Century*. New York: Cambridge University Press.

Xu, C. (2011). The Fundamental Institutions of China's Reforms and Development. *Journal of Economic Literature* 49 (4): 1076–1151.

Zeng, D. Z. (2012). *China's Special Economic Zones and Industrial Clusters: Success and Challenges*. Lincoln Institute of Land Policy Working Paper WP13DZ1: 1–44.

Zhao, Y. (2012). The Struggle for Socialism in China: The Bo Xilai Saga and Beyond. *Monthly Review* 64 (5): 1–17. doi: 10.14452/MR-064-05-2012-09_1.

Zheng, Y.; Pan, R. (2012). From Defensive to Aggressive Strategies: The Evolution of Economic Nationalism in China. In: D'Costa, A. P. (Ed.) *Globalization and Economic Nationalism in Asia*. London: Oxford University Press.

CHAPTER 2

The Trajectory of Chinese Developmentalist Action and Its Contemporary Challenges

Edemilson Paraná and Valéria Lopes Ribeiro

1   Introduction: Machiavelli in Beijing?[1]

> I compare luck to one of these impetuous rivers which, when irritated, flood the nearby plains, uproot the trees and the houses, drag lands from one point to the other: everyone flees away from them, yet eventually yield to their undertow, being powerless to stop them at any given point. Even so, nothing stops men from, after calmness having resumed, taking measures, building dams and dykes so that when the flood comes again the river flows through a canal, or its might become less free and harmful. Such is the case with Fortune, which shows its strength where it cannot find orderly Virtù ready to restrain it, and turns its might towards the points where it knows dams and dykes have not been erected to contain it.
> NICCOLÒ MACHIAVELLI

Even if it hasn't been written from its direct example, the excerpt above speaks directly to the millenary Chinese civilization. Its long-term Geo-History is trespassed by the repeated construction and destruction of restraints and dams to contain the overwhelming might of its waters, especially the great *Huang He* and *Yangatsè* rivers, which flow through large portions of its territory. The metaphor mobilized in *The Prince* to illustrate the duo *virtù* and *fortuna* – synonym of the meeting of the cleverness of human endeavor and the inescapable unpredictability of chance – could not, therefore, be more adequate for the purposes of our present reflection.

Since being published during the High Renaissance, the discoveries of Florentine thinker Niccolò Machiavelli have been, through many ages, reclaimed and contested over their startlingly resilient validity, which echoes

---

1   A modified version of this chapter was originally published in *Revista da Sociedade Brasileira de Economia Política*, n. 54 (set – dez 2019) in Portuguese language. We thank the journal editors for authorizing a revised publication.

throughout the most diverse matrixes of thought. Such is the stuff classics are made of. Machiavelli's works, with their power, complexity, and polysemic density, have transcended barriers of time, geography, culture, politics, and ideology in order to, centrally or laterally, take its place among the foundations of the great repertoire of Western thought.

Despite the obtuse interpretations his works have gained in certain circles, this master of politics continues, in the present, to "speak to us" (Althusser, 1999). It's precisely in order to listen to what Machiavelli's sophisticated political realism still holds for us regarding relevant matters of the present that we transport him, not without necessary adaptations, from Renaissance Florence to turbulent 21st century Beijing. In what manner could his formulations, received in light of contemporary problems and questions, contribute to an interpretation of the amazing Chinese development of the last two decades?

Without detracting from the long list of already undertaken successful interpretations, nuances, and incorporations of his thought[2] and, on the contrary, in open dialogue with some of those, the analysis exercise undertaken here appropriates freely its [dialectic] system [of a precarious encounter between] *virtù* and *fortuna*[3] to read the Chinese developmentalist action of the last decades, as well as some of its consequences – through the permanent tension between, or unpredictable combination of, social struggles and systemic-structural constraints, and the laborious (and risky) attempts to continuously utilize or reconfigure them in favor of given objectives.

In other words, and going back to Machiavelli's metaphor: what are the main Chinese dykes and canals that could contain the overwhelming currents of world economy and politics, and in which manner were they built?[4]

---

2 For a panoramic reassessment of some of those readings and interpretations, see Miguel (2015: 13–63).
3 *Virtù* and *fortuna* can be understood, respectively, as the strength, the power and the competence of men to perform or undertake well-succeeded actions in the world, on one hand, and the factors that are beyond their control, such as the chance conditions of good or bad luck showered upon them by fate, on the other. As explained by Miguel (2015: 45): "*Fortuna* and *virtú* are part of the same system and are far from being static categories. The innovations brought by men of virtù into history are also a source of uncertainty, meaning, they take part in fortuna. Each man of virtù, by acting in pursuit of his own interests, tries to re-shape the world in which he acts, making it more favorable to himself. That introduces a new element of discontinuity and uncertainty in the social environment: it's unpredictable also because, in it, the creative action of the political actors is manifested. For others, therefore, that action is an element of fortuna; it's legitimate to say that fortuna, in the end, is mainly the result of the non-coordinated actions of thousands of people who fight for their objectives".
4 There certainly is a full autonomy of politics in Machiavelli, seen as a self-explanatory dimension, moved solely by human weaknesses and strengths. The author, therefore, has not been led to acknowledge the relationships between the fate of princes, the forms of social organization of politics, and the movements of economic life, something that, keeping the

It is about reflecting, and therefore, returning to some milestones of its recent history, which is not only about the supposedly "political reins" of economic development, but – and at this point one follows Braudel's trail (1968) – also about interpreting such events through the lens of its adjacent structures and conjunctures.[5] In a broader sense, one will aim to investigate the tensions between transformation and continuity, and the imbrications of economy, politics, and society, in order to draw the complex and particular picture of the context in which Chinese developmentalist actions have taken place in the last decades.

Through this lens, it will be possible to perceive that such an agency, even if tethered to long-term and medium-term commitments, applies a certain prowess if summoned to show adaptive flexibility when faced with the fortunes and misfortunes of the global economy – as in a constant and innovative effort of "planned management of the unpredictable". Thus, the Chinese state has been shaping itself, in that regard, as an imposing "bamboo structure" – solid and, at the same time, adaptable to the movements of the adversities it is mobilized to overcome.

Relying on an immense potential consumer market, an extended, "disciplined", and relatively well-educated workforce, as well as a previously built socio-economic infrastructure,[6] the Chinese opening started in the late 1970s served the advancement of the so-called financial globalization (Chesnais, 1996, 2001). By, among other factors, helping make possible the reduction of global production costs (especially for corporations based in central industrialized countries) through the achievement of huge scale gains combined with high rates of exploitation of the workforce, China would eventually become the "factory of the world" – one of the newest (and favorite) frontiers in the process of trans-nationalization of capital. The Chinese urbanization process, which currently finds its summit in an astonishing real estate boom, keeps being one of the main levers of world growth after the 2008 financial crisis.

---

due parallels, we will aim to accomplish here. Our appropriation distances itself from the author's own formulations, in that particular point, by treating as systemically linked the economic and political practices, disposed in relative autonomy towards each other.

5   The debates of Fernand Braudel and the School of Annales regarding the Longue Durée in the historical process have an intriguing affinity with the notion of temporality mobilized in Chinese political rhetoric, which often means its actions as part of long historical processes. Quagio (2009) tells that in 1989, on the occasion of the 200th anniversary of the French Revolution, Deng Xiaoping was asked about the impact of this event on human history. "It's still too early to say," Deng would have replied.

6   For a reading of the Maoist legacy to the political economy of the reforms, see Nogueira (2011). For readings that emphasize the line of continuity between the Deng-era reforms and the Maoist revolution, see Wu Jinglian (2005; 2006) and Zheng Bijian (2005; 2006).

If China has, since then, played an important role in the process of financial and productive globalization in benefit of the repositioning of central capitalist countries (especially the United States) in the global structures of investment, production, and consumption, it's equally right to say that it has made wide use of this process. In the last three decades, besides reaching a high level of economic development and poverty reduction (Nogueira, 2015), China has been climbing the steps in the (technological) hierarchy of the new global value chains (Nogueira, 2015a), advancing in multiple levels regarding regional integration (Pempel, 2008; Nogueira, 2008), and therefore enhancing the international projection of its power and influence. This state of affairs has led the interstate capitalist system as a whole to go through a veritable "tectonic transformation" (Cintra; Filho and Pinto, 2015: 30).

If it makes any sense to admit, following Fiori (2013), that along this path capitalist development is mobilized in the service of the integrity and flowering of the millenary Chinese civilization (especially in the presentation, rhetoric, and action plans produced and undertaken by the Chinese Communist Party, the highest political authority in the country),[7] more than regarding the presence of *Adam Smith in Beijing*, title of a well-known book by Giovanni Arrighi (2008), it would be fitting to alternatively inquire about Machiavelli's specter haunting the headquarters of Chinese power. In other words: in what way does *The Prince*, consubstantiated in the figure of the party, "collective intellectual" and bearer of State authority, conceives and acts upon, with higher or lesser degree of success, the aforementioned directing (through governmental action) of the constraints and opportunities laid open by the transformations in global capitalism of the last decades?

It'll become clear that the exercise is not a fortuitous one. There are blatant parallels between Niccòlo Machiavelli's ideas and those of pragmatic Chinese philosopher Han Feizi,[8] who has been showing up with growing assiduity in the speeches of contemporary Chinese authorities (Mitchel, 2015). Indeed, some scholars (Franz-stefan, 2015; Kai, 2015; Mitchel, 2015) already ask themselves about a typically Machiavellian view of power implicitly or explicitly present in the recent actions of Chinese authorities.

---

7 Deng Xiaoping, for example, one of the main formulators of the ongoing reform and opening policy, is emphatic, on several occasions, regarding the directive that the country's development should be primarily at the service of its defense policy (Marti, 2007).
8 Han Feizi was an ancient Chinese philosopher of the Han era. Counselor to kings, he was one of the forerunners of the doctrine known as legalism. His writings deal with law, states and power. For more, see Cheng (2008).

Regarding the argumentative path of this work, after presenting in this introduction the basic set of tools mobilized in our analysis, we will proceed towards a brief discussion on the political horizon of Chinese actions in the last decades (their *leitmotiv*). Having done that, we will move on to an outline of the wider structural setup, as well as of the particular historical conditions in which Chinese developmentalist action is inserted. Finally, pointing towards the recent internationalization of Chinese economy and the projection of its political and economic power over the world stage, we will address some of the contemporary constraints and challenges faced by Chinese developmentalism.

2 From Mao to Deng: the Construction of a National Project

> One can only raise one's voice [in the global system] when one has plenty of money.
> DENG XIAOPING

The victorious 1949 revolution, the foundational moment of the People's Republic of China, holds, beyond its obvious communist content, a strong national component. Even if it represents the destruction of many of the millenary structures that had until then been typical of the great Middle Kingdom (Braudel, 1989), the revolution can additionally be understood as the beginning a process of national renewal after the end of a long process of disintegration and social instability. Thus, it shows up in the country's currently dominant narrative of self-representation as an important landmark of the enterprise of retaking the autonomy, integrity, and splendor typical of the millennial Chinese civilization.[9]

This imagination has certainly been mobilized in distinct forms since then, according to the waves of internal power struggles in each given phase (Bloodworth and Bloodworth, 2004). In any set of tonalities given to those images, however, it was undoubtedly about linking them to the painful ending of "the century of humiliation" (1829–1949), a period in which the most populous country in the world saw its fate being decided abroad, by the imperialist powers of the day – Japan, Russia, France, and especially England.[10]

---

9   According to an important intellectual member of the Chinese Communist Party (CCP), "the path of its development holds the essence of traditional Chinese culture for 5.000 years" (Wang, 2008: 199).

10 According to Cunha and Accioly (2009: 356): "In 1949, under the command of Mao Zedong, the communists imposed the task of recovering Chinese power. Since then, at

From popular revolt and seizure of power (1949), through Cultural Revolution (1966–1976), arriving to the reform and opening policies of the last decades (since 1978), the reconfiguration of the political structures, as well as the actions of promoting economic development, distinctly conceived in each one of those phases, have been invariably linked to the strategies and national defense policies, aiming to recover an hierarchically superior position in the international order (Wu Jinglian, 2005; 2006).

It's widely known that few other levers are as powerful to influence capitalist expansion than the entrepreneurial and proactive action of the State (Jessop, 1990; Mazzucato, 2014), especially when potentialized by focused war efforts (Medeiros, 2003). That is the conductive wire that goes through such and links such distinct periods as the Mao Zedong and Deng Xiaoping eras[11] – and without which we'd find it difficult to grasp the fundamental driver beyond those astonishing numbers charting Chinese development in the recent period: the search for an autonomous position in the chessboard of international geopolitics. It's precisely here, in consonance with this section's epigraph, that capital, army, and State power converge on the conformation of a radically "material" concept of power which will guide Chinese developmentalist action.[12]

---

various points, the desire to overpower Western powers was manifested. ... Even today Chinese leaders point out that the year 2050 will mark the fulfillment of Mao's promise about China catching up with the West, leaving behind more than a hundred years of defeat and humiliation. (Wu Jinglian, 2005; Zheng Bijian, 2005; 2006; Marbubani, 2005; Zwig e Jianhai, 2005; Hutton, 2007). This is the context in which some Sinologists suggest the proclamation of the republic and the communist revolution as the initial movements of national reaffirmation (Pinto, 2000; Fairbank and Goldman, 2008)". [Translation of all quotes originally written in Portuguese by the authors].

11 From one era to the next, the cognitive horizon of reading socio-economic reality through the lens of the typical tension between productive forces and social relations of production, in a conceptual blueprint of Marxist extraction, remains in dispute in Chinese politics. Deng and his followers manifest the need to overcome the previous period, fraught with class antagonisms in search for cultural transformations, in benefit of a new phase in which the accelerated development of productive forces is the top priority. They aim, thus, to establish the primacy of the development of productive forces instead of the primacy of class struggle, typical of the Maoist period. Those categories remain being activated as an element of rhetoric and political legitimation of the CCP among the people, albeit cautiously.

12 Differentiating a material vision from other relational vision regarding power, Miguel (2015: 22–23) points out that, in *The Prince*, Machiavelli "is stuck in a material vision of power as something that can be owned that is incarnated in some specific resources". In accordance with this section's epigraph, among so many other sentences and speeches, there is, in Deng Xiaoping and in many other Chinese authorities, an emphasis in an analogous vision of power. Such a typically realist vision, according to which only power controls power, is, in some fashion, part of the learning of the history of the "nation": the

Equally following that analytical path – the political and strategic nature of reforms – Fiori (2013) goes back to the 1950s, the moment of the so-called Sino-Soviet split, the beginning of the Chinese "great capitalist leap". To the contention of the Soviet threat along its borders through the "active defense" policy it would be added a bold political-diplomatic "offensive" of reapproximation with the U.S., uniting Mao and Nixon in the delimitation of an "horizontal line" (from the Middle East to Japan) that was meant to contain the Soviets.

For Kissinger (2011), given that the USSR was perceived as the main threat to its safety, China was reintegrated to the global economic circuit by means of an invitation by the U.S.

At this point, the aforementioned elective affinity between productive restructuring in central capitalism under financial globalization and Chinese economic opening gains its political-diplomatic content: a new wave of Western investments, especially from American provenance, was welcomed by the Chinese state as an opportunity to promote the strengthening of its defensive capability, to which the search for the activation of its economic development would be submitted.[13] That's when, in 1975, Zhou Enlai[14] proposes the "four modernizations program" (industry, agriculture, science and technology, armed forces), which would later give rise to the beginning of the great process of reform and opening – both implemented by Deng Xiaoping from 1978 on, after the "defeat" of the cultural revolution and the death of "great leaders of the nation", Mao Zedong and Zhou Enlai, in 1976.

---

long construction of the Great Wall, the historical conflicts with different peoples, among them the Mongols, and the historical Imperial China constant worrying about being subjugated by foreign armies, losing the integrity of its vast territory and population – all of these factors point towards that.

13 As observed by Pinto (2011: 24), "Beyond the Soviet blockade, that strategic partnership, on one hand, created one of the conditions for the start of the Chinese economic miracle: the inclusion of China in the market of goods and the market of capitals in the United States, which allowed for its exportation jolt and for Chinese access to American international financing. On the other hand, it allowed for the bigger and faster expansion of the American supranational economic territory, because it significantly potentialized 'the power of the dollar and of American government public debt bonds and the capacity for multiplication of its financial capital' (Fiori, 2008: 67). In other words, Chinese access to the American market was one of the most important elements in the process of financial globalization led by the United States".

14 Important leader of the Chinese Communist Party and Mao Zedong's right-hand man. From the foundation of the People's Republic of China (1949) until his death (1976), he occupied the position of Premier, accumulating the position of Foreign Minister from 1949 to 1958.

It is therefore in the service of a project of geopolitical ascension, widening of its regional influence and defense sphere, and search for ever growing economic, military, and technological autonomy that Chinese authorities will submit the country's initiatives towards economic opening. The main objective of such a development strategy is not to create a market economy, but to turn China into a modern, rich, and powerful country. The market mechanisms, therefore, appear as means, not as ends in themselves (Kroeber, 2011: 2).

Following that orientation, a set of reforms will take shape in continuous movements and several dimensions – politico-institutional, regulatory, economic-financial, socio-cultural, among others – whose specific aspects are not the focus of the present work, especially because they have been extensively explored by other scholars.[15] What should be highlighted, however, is the general (economic, social etc.) conditions and characteristics, as well as the political management, which made possible such a great leap in such a short time.

Following that train of analysis, one ought to observe the general characteristics that have anchored the model for developmentalist action under investigation here, in which, openly, "reform is the driving force, development is the objective, and stability is the prerequisite" (Weiguang, 2008). Without going deep into the meanderings of the institutional political structure of command in the country (see Saich, 2004), one ought to point out the main political directives for Chinese developmentalist action, verified in the official discourse, and in accordance with the most recent practice. Those are:

i) the option for accelerated development of productive forces as the central objective of State policies, alongside the search, when possible, for synchronization between productive forces and social relations of production, and for balance between superstructure and economic foundations;

ii) primacy of State property in economy, in coexistence with other pure or mixed property regimes, as a way to maintain a certain leeway for the political authorities in the conduct of the developmental process;

iii) planning, control, and gradualism in the implementation of policies, all sustained by experimentalism (a test of their effectivity in regional scale for posterior national application) and institutional innovations

---

15 To see panoramas and reconstructions of the policies and dynamics in the so-called "Chinese economic miracle", through different perspectives, see Medeiros (1999; 2006; 2011; 2013), Fairbank and Goldman (2006), Aglietta and Landry (2007), Lyrio (2010), Leão (2010; 2011), Pinto (2011), Kissinger (2011), Artus, Mistral, and Plagnol (2011), Keidel (2011), and Lardy (2011).

(search for new models and arrangements for the functioning of economic institutions in the scope of the so-called "Socialism with Chinese characteristics").

iv) maintenance of political and social stability, anchored in a project of national sovereignty conducted by the Party's leadership as representative of the nation, in detriment of the activation of the class antagonisms that were typical to the Cultural Revolution period;

v) promotion and strengthening of the Rule of Law and fighting against corruption.

Together, these five directives sum up the *official* line of the Chinese Communist Party, which in the last four decades has been put into expressions such as "harmonious society", "harmonious development", "scientific vision for development" or "scientific development", "pacific ascension", "construction of a moderately prosperous society in all aspects", among others. Thus, according to the directives that came to characterize the process of Reform and Opening, the great popular revolution, in the end, becomes "market socialism" or "Socialism with Chinese characteristics".

3 Communist China Meets Capitalist Globalization: the Configuration of the Sino-American Axis of Accumulation

In a relatively short period of time, China has gone from an agrarian and technologically "backwards" country to (contemporarily) an economic, military, and technological superpower. After three decades of accelerated growth, the country arrives in the second decade of the 21st century as the second biggest national economy, the biggest exporter of goods, the biggest producer of goods, the holder of the largest account surplus, and the owner of the biggest volume of international reserves in the world. According to Burlamaqui (2015: 278): "China has become the second economic superpower not by catching up with the West, but by actual leapfrogging".

Our enterprise aims to update and present additional elements to the discussion at hand. Thus, it certainly is unavoidable to take a look at the Chinese rise through the lens of their actions, options, and strategies in the configuration of a developmental model conducted by the State. It is equally unavoidable, however, to reflect upon the particular historical conditions which shape the structural frame at hand – which, at the same time, limit and stimulate the developmentalist action here reviewed.

In that regard, it may be fitting to start by outlining, once and for all, the fact that the Chinese take-off takes place in a symbiotic relationship with the phenomenon of globalization (financial liberalization, productive integration, and commercial opening) led by the trans-national enterprises from core capitalist countries – especially American, but also European, Japanese, South-Korean, etc. – as an active response to the depressive period in the world economy, and which finds in the oil crisis of 1973 an important landmark. From this point on, there are internal and external conditionals for the Chinese modernization process.

In the internal sphere, the political-diplomatic isolation, fruit of the Sino-Soviet severance, the tensions and hardships linked to the period of the Cultural revolution and, later on, the deaths of Mao Zedong and Zhou Enlai (1976) set the stage for the developmental strategy idealized by Deng Xiaoping and his followers, undertaken from 1978 on as "a kind of gigantic and very long NEP"[16] (Losurdo, 2004: 67) that bets on the development of productive forces, and not class struggle, as a central element for overcoming the preceding backwardness and political-economic isolation. On the international plane, the diplomatic approximation between China and the U.S. opens up the path for the country's inclusion in the American market of goods and in the American capital markets, giving commercial substance to the aforementioned symbiosis.

Starting from the deepening of the process of de-regulamentation and liberalization of markets in the 1980s, international investors searched for options of gains until then inaccessible and articulated an unprecedented expansion of the capital fluxes in the whole world (Chesnais, 1998). Such a process, later articulated through the constitution of a new and enlarged world financial system, is accompanied by the ongoing productive restructuring and delocalization, with the consequent migration of a considerable part of the productive plants from developed countries to Asia and, later, to Eastern Europe – a process that will find affinity with the simultaneous computer revolution and the accelerated development of information and communication technology (Paraná, 2016). At that moment, East Asia and China, in particular, demonstrated themselves to be able to supply cheap (and disciplined) labor, scale gains, and other competitive advantages to the great transnational companies – widening the frontiers for the expansion of global economy, led by the U.S. and under the direction of the renewed power of the dollar, now free from the gold standard.

Such a circuit of global accumulation contributed to the transformation of Asia into one of the main global centers for the production of industrialized

---

16   Making reference to the period under Lenin's direction in the USSR, NEP is the acronym by which the New Economic Policy (Novaja Ekonomičeskaja Politika) was known.

goods, and allowing China, then already one of the largest economies in the region, to activate the reaping of huge gains. That took place mainly through the slow and steady articulation of secondary chains of national and regional industries, which specialized in supplying parts, components, raw materials, and infrastructure, among other resources, making it possible to overflow some of that investment dynamic into new and relevant sectors of the Southeast Asia national economies. It's therefore in that manner that the Sino-Asian manufacturing cluster takes shape.

Through such transformations the configuration of a new international division of labor advances, moving along new global chains of production and value.[17] Those new commercial, productive, and financial flows have, on one extreme, developed capitalist countries, especially the U.S., and on the other, Southeast Asia countries, especially China.

That arrangement deepens itself and shows itself to be functional in regard to the new phase in the global economy, which resumes its growth and expansion, especially from the start of the 21st century on. On one pole, the U.S. – issuer of the global reserve currency, now free of the gold standard – expands credit, household debt, current account deficit, and, thus, its external liabilities. On the other pole, such liabilities find countries willing to attract foreign investments aimed at the enlargement of their productive capacity with growing competitiveness gains and low production costs. Adding to that, their own efforts towards industrial growth through high investment rates and the constant search for increasing the technological content of their exports.

That is certainly one of the main structural transformations originated in the process of financial and productive globalization in question: the new dynamic of capitalist accumulation is now led by the Sino-American axis,[18] not anymore by the triad formed by the U.S., Germany, Japan (Fiori, 2010; Pinto, 2010). Through that locomotive, the U.S., a kind of "minotaur" (Varoufakis, 2016), devourers of global surpluses, or "first degree spenders", grows while firmly anchored to high consumption, importing, and indebtment rates. It has China[19] and its development as its counterpart, with its low price exports, high

---

17 On the configuration of global production chains, see Sturgeon (2002) and UNCTAD (2013). To know more about the integration of China in the global productive chains, see Nogueira (2012, 2015b), Pinto (2015), Gouveia (2015), and Leão (2011).
18 For a detailed discussion of the constitution of the Sino-American accumulation axis, see Pinto (2011: 19–77).
19 According to Cintra and Martins (2013: 255): "in 2012, the deficit in international trade in goods by the United States totaled US$ 735.3 billion, of which US$ 315 billion was registered with China, representing 42.8% of the total. This means that almost half of the trade balance deficit in the United States stems from relations with the subsidiaries of

capital accumulation and investment, savings and reserve rates – which, in the end, bankroll American debt and increase the attractiveness of the American financial markets to capitals from all over the globe (right before the crisis, in the early 2000s, the U.S. was the destiny to more than 70% of the global capital outflows) – who fosters the overflowing of positive effects into other areas of the planet: Latin America, Africa, and even Europe. Thus, and at least until the 2008 crisis, several countries reaped commercial surpluses, which allowed for the accumulation of international reserves, a supposed reduction of external vulnerability, and even the concretization of policies aimed at stimulating production and employment. According to Varoufakis (2016), through such an arrangement the so-called twin American deficits (fiscal and commercial) have been for decades absorbing the surplus of goods and capitals from other countries, which produces a kind of "balanced imbalance", capable of flaunting for a long time an appearance of stability and sustained growth.

As pointed out by Pinto (2011: 36), "the trade currents between China and the United States, and between China and the world increased much faster than the global current". That's how the symbiosis between American financial globalization and the Chinese economic miracle, and the growth of the global economy along this axis in the last decades, have deepened the complementarities in the commercial, productive, and financial spheres between the two countries, and have shaped a new kind of "collaborative competition", or "competitive collaboration", something president Barack Obama himself characterized as an "amiable competition" (Rossi, 2010: A10).[20] The United States, naturally, has more power in this process. In this context, China is simultaneously debtor and creditor to the United States: debtor because of the high foreign American direct investments in Chinese territory, and creditor because of the accumulation of its sovereign reserves in the form of American Treasury bonds (Fiori, 2008; Tavares and Belluzzo, 2004).

The strategy of accumulating reserves through the purchase of U.S. Treasury bonds, therefore, makes China one of the main bankrollers of American deficits. In this position (high surpluses in current transactions, in the capital account, and in the financial account) the Chinese Central Bank is compelled to manage its exchange rate policy in a way that allows it to contain the entrance of capitals in the country, as a way to maintain the stability of

---

American companies abroad, which have shifted part of their productive structures to Asia, especially to China" (Whichard, 2003; Kregel, 2008a; Moran, 2011).

[20] In recent years, the "amiable" competition has been giving way to an open one, with the USA implementing a policy of open containment through commerce and diplomacy, aiming to restrain Chinese economic-technological development.

its currency in relation to the dollar – and maintain the competitiveness of its exports. Such a dimension of contact between Chinese exchange rate policy and US Treasury bonds leads to the existing tensions in the connections between these two economies.[21] The complexity of such relations, especially after (and because of) the 2008 crisis, has put on the table the question of the sustainability of global imbalances in a context of high supply of liquidity and low interest rates. The 2008 crisis can be read, in a way, as the crisis of that very arrangement – something that shall not be the focus of our present work.

Anyway, the bet of embracing, in its own manner, globalization through the constitution of an enormous program of Reform and Opening, with the widening of the economic spheres under the coordination of the markets, kept on being deepened by Chinese authorities, always in mediation with the constraints and openings that presented themselves at the moment. China, thus, advanced its project for reaching development (*virtù*) by seizing that window of reconfiguration of the global economy and its eventual opportunities (*fortuna*). In order to be able to do that, it aimed to (in general terms) articulate a competitive exchange rate, to raise the investments in education and R&D, to have active industrial and foreign commerce policies, high rates of investment and incorporation of technical progress in local companies through partnerships (joint ventures) with transnational companies, among other actions and strategies.

4   The Paradoxes of Recent Chinese Development: Pattern of Growth and New Challenges

One saw that the Chinese ascension has a structure and a conjuncture of its own. In that regard, we've shown that Chinese developmentalist action aims to adjust its *virtù* to *fortuna*, which can't be directly foreseen nor controlled. As in Machiavelli's metaphor (2008), we aimed to show how the Prince – enthroned in the authority of the party it directs and guarantor of the nation's political stability – has been building up its dams and contention devices for the convoluted economic and world politics monsoon that arrives from time to time. Entangled in this tricky combinatory puzzle, its command political apparatus

---

21   See what seems to be taking shape, gradually, as a substantive change in the relationship between the two countries since the arrival of Donald Trump to the presidency – a subject that will not be the object of our appreciation here. Moreover, beyond the financial sphere, as China has advanced through the global value chains, in many markets competition takes precedence over complementarity.

has been led to present, at the time, flexibility and resistance, something that has been reached through political-institutional gradualism and experimentalism, adjusted through the chasing of medium- and long-term goals. Rigid political control, in its turn, forces the consent of the disaffected. If hitherto that gigantic "bamboo structure" has been showing surprising economic results, it's certain that, in the rough dialectic of history, past success does not guarantee future success. Having already taken important steps, China is now called upon to deal with new challenges, which have been presenting themselves and piling up in the last decades even faster than China could reach its goals.

At least since the great 2008 crisis, and especially in the last years, the country has been facing several problems that are linked to its economy's accumulation pattern (Fang, Yang, and Meiyan, 2009), and thus the need to adjust it. The central goal for this transition is to reduce investment's share in the Gross Domestic Product (GDP) – especially in capital- and energy-intensive sectors, elevate household consumption, and widen social security and public services. Such measures are aimed at bestowing long-term sustainability and growth, and to reduce its external dependence. Along the way, problems will demand a solution – such as excess of installed industrial capacity (and the consequent accumulation of loss-making and idle companies), high leverage, growth in the debts of provinces and local governments, as well as of the debt service[22] itself, the relatively low rural development, the abysmal gap between rural and urban areas, the serious environmental damages, and the scarcity of natural resources, among others. Even if the government is apparently conscious of the hardships and has at its disposal a series of tools and resources that can be used to attempt a change in the growth pattern, that will not be an easy task, since there are enormous constraints.

One of the main constraints imposed on the continuity of Chinese growth and on the overcoming of its challenges certainly was the 2008 world financial crisis. The country felt the impact of the crisis, especially through a drop in the global demand for its exporting products; after that, it faced such challenges through a strong financial leveraging and the expansion of state investments, promoting what some defined as a "rebalancing". With lower (for Chinese standards) growth rates, which can be seen in Figure 2.1, the government has recently signaled its entrance in a new cycle of growth based on the expansion of consumption, the so-called "new normal".

---

22   The debt/GDP ratio went up to 247% in 2015, against 166% in 2007. Data from the CEICdata platform. See: https://www.ceicdata.com/pt/indicator/china/government-debt--of-nominal-gdp. Accessed 23 July. 2021.

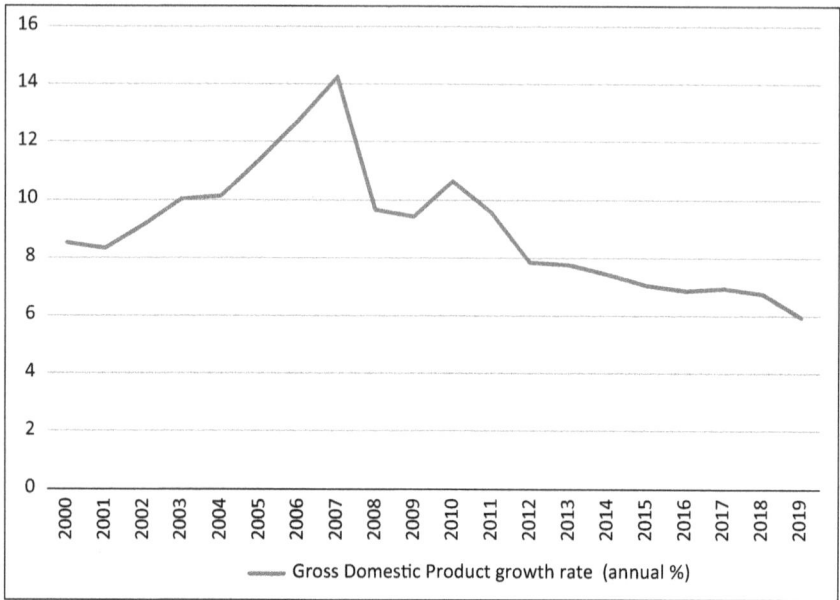

FIGURE 2.1 China – Gross Domestic Product growth rate (2000–2019)
SOURCE: WORLD BANK DATABASE, 2021

The Chinese new normal, in an effort to widen the technological process and the internal income, aims to add technological modernization and growth through internal consumption to the previous cycle – based on the investment expansion towards infrastructure and heavy industry, especially through large state investments, and on projects for urbanization and modernization.

In the new cycle, despite the directing of investments towards heating up of internal demand, China will not be able to do without the access to primary goods that characterized the previous cycle,[23] since the country's energy and arable base is still very restricted in view of its astonishing growth and size.

Oil is a significant example. Until the early 1990s, China was a big oil exporter, but later came to be the second largest importer in the world. The high demand had been linked not only to the expansion of industry and infrastructure, but

---

23 It's a well-known fact that the wide Chinese demand for primary resources – from raw materials to feed industries, such as iron ore and copper, to essential energetic resources such as oil – reached vertiginous heights in the first decade of the 21st century, and that that allowed for the expansion of exports from many peripheral countries and for the improvement of their macroeconomic framework. Such countries include Brazil, Venezuela, and many African countries.

also to the expansion of the number of cars, since the transportation sector was responsible for a third of the country's oil consumption (Blankendal, 2008).

Natural gas imports have also grown in the last years, despite coal remaining as the main component of the energy matrix. In 2019, coal amounted to 58% of China's total energy matrix; in 2018, it amounted to 59%. The second largest energy source is oil and other liquids, amounting to 20% of the total consumption in 2019. Despite the efforts to replace coal and oil, absolute consumption of coal in 2019 grew 1,1%. Consumption of crude oil, in its turn, increased by 6,8% compared to 2018 (National Bureau of Statistics of China, 2020). Clean energy sources still amount to a small fraction of the energy generated in the country: hydroelectric sources (8%), natural gas (8%), nuclear energy (2%), and other renewable energy sources (almost 5%) (EIA – U.S. Energy Information Administration, 2020).

Regarding food and agricultural resources, it's important to remember that the country has reduced arable area. According to the World Bank, in 2008 only 11% of all land in China was arable (World Bank Database, 2019). According to Medeiros (2013), available arable area per capita in the country, in 1993, was of the order of 0.08 hectares, one of the lowest in the world. That reality, added to the high rate of people living in the countryside and to the high proportion of agricultural jobs in the whole of Chinese employment (39%),[24] implicitly reaffirms, according to Medeiros (2013), the crucial challenge of the maintenance of a high number of people in the countryside (high rate of persons per parcel of land), besides the constant search for improvements in agricultural productivity. As highlighted by Zheng (2005), both Chinese arable areas and their mineral resources (despite being significant in absolute numbers) are relatively scarce when compared to the needs of Chinese productive structure. Also, according to that author, the amount of Chinese hydric resources per capita, for example, amounts to ¼ of the global average; while arable area per capita amounts to 40% of the global average. Thus, the increase in Chinese demand for primary resources must be related not only to conjunctural aspects, but to the material base of a country's internal supply of energy, mineral ores, and even arable land that is simply not enough to meet its demand.

Such constraints add up, since the 2008 crisis, to a conjuncture in which the drop in the global demand for Chinese exports promotes changes in the very growth pattern in the country and leads China towards a "rebalancing", or even to a new economic cycle. Lower growth rates, in their turn, like the ones seen

---

24 According to data presented by Majerowicz (2022), that proportion amounted to 22,9% in 2021.

during the period immediately after the crisis, cause the demand that drove the boom in commodity prices to start showing signs of exhaustion. (Wei, Xie and Zhang, 2016; Ocampo and Erten, 2013; Cintra, Filho, and Pinto, 2015).

Table 2.1 shows some indicators of the Chinese economy from 2000 to 2019, presenting data related to the Chinese GDP from the perspective of expenditure/consumption: household expenditure, government expenditure, Gross Fixed Capital Formation (GFCF), and exports and imports. One sees that even though there have been no drastic transformations since the 2000s, some changes do show up in the period after the 2008 crisis.

Between 2000 and 2008 there's a reduction of more than 10% in household consumption, from 46,7% to 35,3% of the GDP. Between 2008 and 2016, that consumption moderately recovered about 3%, reaching 38,7% of the GDP. In 2019, the share in consumption rises, even if modestly, to 39,2%, which could indicate some difficulty in reversing the expansion trajectory of household consumption. Despite the (modest) rise of consumption in that period, the

TABLE 2.1 China – GDP components from the expenditure perspective – share in GDP and annual growth rate (2000–2019)

	% of GDP				Growth rate (current US$)	
	2000	2008	2016	2019	2000–2008	2008–2019
Final consumption expenditure of households	46.7	35.3	38.7	39.2	14	13.2
Governmental final consumption expenditure	16.8	14.5	16.4	16.8	16	13.9
Gross fixed capital formation	33.6	42.3	42.6	43.3	19.9	13.9
Exports of goods and services	20.9	32.6	19.6	18.5	25.4	7
Imports of goods and services	18.5	25	17.3	17.3	24.1	9.19

SOURCE: WORLD BANK DATABASE, 2021

rhythm of expansion remained at 14% from 2000 to 2008 and at 13,2% from 2008 to 2019.

It is certainly not possible to state that there's a substitution of investment by consumption as the prime mover in Chinese growth, since, as can also be seen in Table 2.1, gross fixed capital formation remains high (43,3% in 2019), even if growing at the lighter rate of 13,9% per year between 2008 and 2019. In China, historically, there has been a strong correlation between investment and GDP growth, and this variable has been perceived as the main engine of growth since the establishment of the People's Republic (Medeiros, 2013). Since 2008, the investment share of the GDP remains high, well above 40% of the GDP, and more than 45% between 2010 and 2014 (World Bank Database, 2021).

In addition to the variables of investment and consumption, another interesting point in Table 2.1 refers to foreign trade. After 2008, there's a palpable drop in the share foreign trade had in the GDP and in the rhythm of expansion of exports (7,0% between 2008 and 2019, compared to a growth rate of 25,4% between 2000 and 2008). In the case of imports, the growth rate was also smaller (9% between 2008 and 2019, compared to 24% between 2000 and 2008). The data then shows that, in net terms, foreign trade contributed relatively little to GDP growth, much less than investment.

The new and interesting data, which appears in the analysis of the profile in current Chinese investment, is that the latter has been accompanying other important expenditures, such as research and development (R&D). OECD data shows that China already is the current second biggest investor in R&D in the world, only behind the U.S. Spending in this segment went from US$ 150 billion in 2008 to almost US$ 400 billion in 2015. At this pace of expansion, it is possible that China will overtake the U.S. as the largest investor in this segment. Currently, the U.S. spends around US$ 460 billion on R&D (OECD, 2017).

This reality of the Chinese growth pattern also signals the fact that a new process of technological catching up may be underway in the country. There's a strong preoccupation with industrial and technological modernization. The share of industry in Chinese GDP has been falling after a long period of expansion: in 2008 it amounted to 47%, decreased to 41% in 2015, and further dropped to 39% in 2019. In its place there has been an expansion in services, which can be analyzed as part of a process of complexification of the Chinese economy, with a strong expansion in activities such as e-commerce and more complex industries related to the so-called Industry 4.0 (World Bank Database, 2019). China has recently launched the *Made in China 2025 strategy*", the country's new industrial program. It foresees the modernization, until 2025, of industry and the development of its more advanced sectors – such as the ones linked to green services and technology, or linked to the next generation of IT, robotics, space equipment, aviation, and biomedicine.

As suggested in the OECD report (2015) titled *Trade in value added: China*, a significant structural change took place in the country in the last two decades. From an exporter of low added value products, such as textiles, the country has become a major exporter of high technology products. Besides, in many sectors, that change was accompanied by an increase in domestic value added, which reflects a great ability to move up the value chains. In 2008, domestic value added to Chinese exports amounted to 68,33%; in 2014, it went up to 70,65% (OECD, 2015).

Certainly, even after the crisis, there was no interruption of the investments in infrastructure. Investment in railroads, high speed train systems, and expansion of the internet throughout the country are going on at full throttle. According to Dic Lo (2016), expansion in investment took place based on the expansion of government spending – even though the central government debt is now smaller in comparison to the period that followed the Asian crisis in the 1990s. According to the author, other new financing mechanisms were expanded, with a wide variety of financial innovations, besides local government spending. Such financial and monetary expansion can become a long-term complicator for the Chinese economy.

It's important to highlight that monetary expansion via diversification of financial instruments and local government debt does not signal at all a process of financial expansion to the detriment of industry. The profit rate in manufacturing in China has not dropped since the late 1990s (Lo, 2016a). Chinese growth continues to be based on productive expansion and increased labor productivity, which reflects a model that the author calls "Golden Age", in reference to the post-World War II productive expansion cycle in the central capitalist countries. Also, in the post-2008 period, one perceives a productive expansion added to an increase in productivity – less due to the direct use of labor supply and more due to an increasingly capital-intensive model (*ibidem*).

In addition, there is an improvement in living standards and in the ability to generate jobs, despite the continued income inequality. One highlight is the importance of the efforts (or concessions through demanding) in the last years by the government in order to expand the universal health care system and strengthen the unions, which help increase working class's living standards and bargaining power, with potential effects in wage growth. Figure 2.2 shows the expansion of nominal wages from 2003 to 2013:

As evident, although the wage level has started from a very low point, there has been an increase in the last few years, including after 2008. It is worth mentioning that China has a wide diversified and complex labor market,

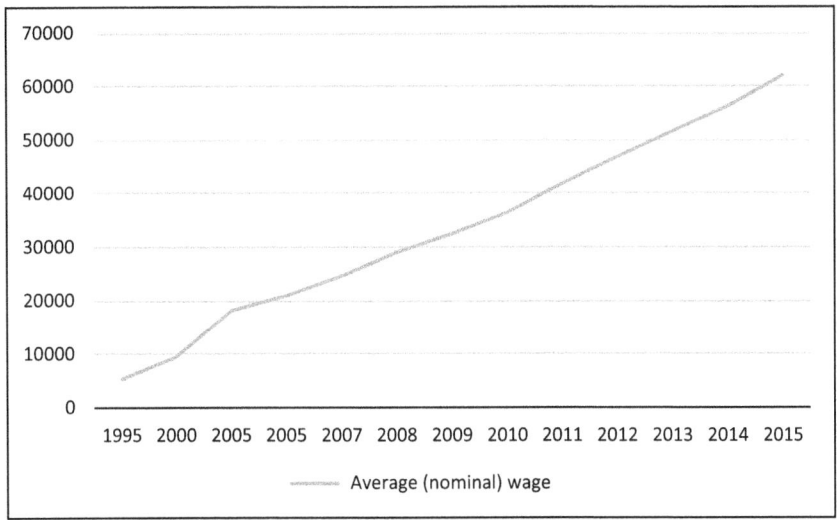

FIGURE 2.2   China – Average (nominal) wage of employed persons in urban unities (1995–2015) (yuans)
SOURCE: NATIONAL BUREAU STATISTICS OF CHINA, 2017

especially in urban centers. In the mid-1990s, for example, after the end of the *danwei*[25] and the privatizations, and after mass layoffs in the public sector, there has been an expressive growth of informal labor in urban areas. Despite the increase in the minimum wage for registered workers, there has also been an increase in wage inequality between formal and informal workers, meaning those who work without an urban residence registration (Nogueira, 2011).

A consequence of the wage increase is the increase in production costs, pointed out as a contributing factor to the transference of parts of industrial production to areas near to China, in Asia, which had lower wages. According to Pinto (2015), the process of transference of stages, phases, or specific tasks in Chinese industrial production to other Asian economies can be understood through its relationship with the "China plus one" strategy.

Chinese foreign direct investment (FDI) in the region has been deepening the regional links in the global productive chain even further. Having the

---

25   As highlighted by Nogueira (2011), until the 1990s the *danwei* represented a series of benefits granted to urban dwellers employed in State-run companies, in a model very close to the one found in welfare States. Among those benefits were the guarantee of lifetime employment, social security, subsidized housing, free healthcare, access to subsidized food, and primary and secondary school for one's children.

Chinese economy as its articulating axis, it is fairly easy to see changes that allow for the reduction of costs in the transaction of international operations. Thus, there is an increase in the interdependence of Asian countries, which reinforces the processes of fragmentation and relocation of global value chains.

The expansion in Chinese external investments, not only in Asia but in the whole world, represents a big change in the country's development strategy in the period after the 2008 crisis. In 2016, Chinese FDIs already amounted to US$ 217 billion, almost reaching the U.S.[26] (OECD Data, 2017).

According to Cintra and Pinto (2017), one of the central elements in the internationalization strategy for Chinese capital has been the support for the realization of large-scale infrastructure projects through what has been called "infrastructure diplomacy" (Kroeber, 2015: 3). A highlight is the "Silk Road Economic Belt" announced in 2013 by president Xi Jinping.[27]

It is worth mentioning that, over the course of more than 30 years, China has been on the receiving end of a growing amount of external investment, absorbing a total of more than US$1 trillion in FDI between 1979 and 2010 (Shambaugh, 2013). After the consolidation of economic growth, the situation was reversed and the Chinese advanced by projecting their own foreign investment, with Chinese enterprises expanding to many parts of the world while supported by a substantial volume of accumulated reserves. It is an important change, for it signals a more active posture towards the diversification of its assets and a greater disposition to expand outwards, be it as part of a strategy of diversifying its accumulated reserves, be it as part of a political strategy of national affirmation on a global scale.

In 2009, the volume of Chinese reserves amounted to US$ 2,4 trillion. In 2014, they already amounted to US$ 3,9 trillion. In 2016 there was a drop to US$ 3,1 trillion, due to some constraints imposed by the Chinese government. In 2020, the reserves amounted to US$ 3,3 trillion (World Bank Database, 2021).

---

26   Which can help explain or contextualize some of the recent tensions observed in international geopolitics.
27   The project's objective is an extremely ambitious one: it aims to promote radical changes in all of Central Asia, contributing both to internal integration in China and integration between China and its neighbors. The idea is to create a large set of (road, rail, and maritime) infrastructure projects that will link China to Europe, crossing 21 countries. The plan counts with a financial institution of its own, created to help finance such operations: the Asian Infrastructure Investment Bank (AIIB). China, the leader in that initiative, initially invested US$ 40 billion in the bank (Miller, 2014). To Cintra and Pinto (2017: 296), that is something in the proportions of a "new Marshall Plan, the initiative that made possible the rebuilding of European economies after World War ii, only now it involves 3 billion people scattered throughout dozens of countries".

It is a well-known fact that a good portion of Chinese reserves is used in the purchase of U.S. Treasury bonds. As highlighted by Pinto (2010), in 2001 the Chinese owned only US$ 78,6 billion in Treasury bonds, 7,6% of the total. There's been a significant growth in the weight of China as the holder of these titles, around 1.375%: in 2010, Chinese owned 26% of all American bonds, which amounted to more than US$ 1 trillion. From 2011 on, the Chinese kept on buying those papers, and in June 2017 they owned what amounted to US$ 1,146 trillion in American bonds.

It is noteworthy that, between 2011 and 2017, the pace of growth of the bonds held by the Chinese decreased considerably compared to the pre-crisis period. The average growth rate was 0.12%, highlighting the fact that there was, in 2016, a sharp drop in the purchase of bonds by the Chinese, as Japan took the lead as the largest holder. In October 2017, the Chinese share in total bonds fell to 18.7%, a much smaller share compared to the almost 30% it held in previous years (Department of the Treasury, 2017).

Simultaneously with the process of expanding Chinese FDI and diversifying its reserves, the country has been mobilizing strategies to internationalize its currency, encouraging its use in foreign trade, especially at the regional level, in order to reduce its global dependence on the dollar (Cohen, 2012). The reason for that is that the more Chinese national companies manage to settle their transactions and their investments abroad in their own currency, the less the Chinese Central Bank will be forced to make deposits in the American financial system. Thus, "the internationalization of the renminbi stems from the emergence of China as an economic and commercial power (not as a financial power)" (Cintra and Pinto, 2017: 393).

Within the scope of a clear "movement towards financial globalization" (Cintra and Filho, 2015: 477), the objective is to promote a "controlled internationalization" of the renminbi in trade and finance, in order to adjust to the advance of financial and productive globalization, counteracting the asymmetries of the international monetary system that end up conditioning the scope and degrees of freedom of Chinese domestic and foreign policies (Cintra and Pinto, 2017). In this way, the government has been seeking to carry out reforms in the national financial markets and, little by little, opening its capital account, as a way of strengthening Chinese finances for the country's new phase. It is something that poses enormous challenges, since it requires changes in the current axis of its macroeconomic model, characterized, as seen, by the exchange rate, interest rate, bank loan market and public debt managed by the government.

In addition to a series of gradual transformations in the national financial system, the initiatives launched so far to gradually connect the domestic financial system with the international one are fundamentally focused on creating an offshore renminbi market in Hong Kong and on trying to transform Shanghai into a major capital (stocks and bonds) market – a kind of new financial capital of Asia.[28] Linked to such initiatives, the renminbi is rapidly internationalizing. At the end of 2016, 57 countries were already using the renminbi in more than 10% of their payments with China and Hong Kong, and the currency has already become the fifth most used currency in the world (SWIFT, 2016). In 2015, the renminbi was included in the basket of currencies that make up the Special Drawing Rights (SDR), a kind of complementary currency asset managed by the IMF – something that was received as recognition of its growing importance.

In any case, there are many risks for an economy with a high rate of investment based on credit, such as the Chinese one, when slowing down and, simultaneously, deepening the internationalization of its financial system. Therefore, it is likely that the Chinese government will remain cautious, avoiding a complete and abrupt financial liberalization, which has been happening so far.[29] Defending the hypothesis that the "internationalization of the renminbi and Chinese banking institutions faces major constraints, given the nature and (internal and external) challenges of the country's development process", Cintra and Martins (2013: 212–13) maintain that, for the time being, this process is basically a defensive strategy.

It should be remembered, as previously mentioned, that the regional and international insertion of the Chinese economy is directly related to productive

---

28 Cintra and Pinto (2017: 387) also list other initiatives such as: "i. international renminbi trade clearing treaties with fourteen financial centers (Hong Kong, Macau, Taiwan, Singapore, London, Frankfurt, Seoul, Paris, Luxembourg, Doha, Toronto, Sydney, Kuala Lumpur and Bangkok); ii. Authorization of nine specific quotas of RMB Qualified Foreign Institutional Investor – RQFII, which allows foreign institutional investors to use offshore renminbi funds to invest in the Chinese capital market and the interbank bond market; iii. currency swap agreements with 30 central banks; iv. acting as a lender of last resort for countries with difficult access to the international financial market – Venezuela and Ecuador (Global Risk Insights, 2015; Ostroukh, 2015); and v. an independent payment system for renminbi operations". McNally (2020: 10) also highlights: "the establishment of onshore oil futures contracts denominated in RMB with trading open to foreigners. ... Other initiatives include the bond and stock connect programs between Hong Kong and Chinese markets in Shenzhen and Shanghai; incorporating Chinese equities and bonds into global indices, such as MSCI indices; the China-Japan cross-border investment scheme; the Shanghai-London stock connect based on depositary receipts; and, on a more macro-level, the BRI and AIIB".

29 Cintra and Pinto (2017: 390): "in an unprecedented way, which makes the process more difficult and not very predictable, [China] seeks to internationalize the renminbi with controls on the capital account. That is to say, restricting the full convertibility of the currency or building a limited convertibility".

and financial globalization led by the U.S. and, therefore, within the scope of the global monetary system dominated by the flexible dollar. We have also seen that its development model is characterized by relative domestic control of the currency and the banking system, which function under special conditions. This ends up greatly restricting its ability to transfer monetary and banking capital beyond its borders (Cintra and Martins, 2013). In this way, the country remains tied, in terms of exchange rate policy and the accumulation of reserves, to the policies and external pressures of developed countries led by the U.S. Given that large asymmetries persist in the international monetary and financial order, with great dominance of the flexible dollar, it is most likely that in the medium term the renminbi will play a relatively restricted role as a regional currency (Eichengreen and Kwai, 2014).

In any case, much seems to indicate that, despite all these challenges and constraints characteristic of the new framework, Chinese authorities will continue to seek ways to ensure, within the scope of the reforms, that the financial system, as well as other dimensions, will remain focused on promoting its global goals of economic and social growth and development. Whatever the new strategic direction, however, the paradoxes of accelerated Chinese growth will continue to cry out for direction.

5   Final Considerations

We saw that China strategically conditioned, through the political action of the State, the massive foreign investment it received to an autonomous national development project.[30] This strategy materialized through state planning (rearticulated amid the political changes the country went through),

---

30   It is not surprising how the CCP bureaucracy in control of the People's Republic since 1949 has been conceiving and adjusting its broader development strategy, deeply imbued as it is with debates and formulations (inside and outside the Marxist camp) about imperialism, dependency, and the constraints and open possibilities for the development of countries located on the periphery of the capitalist world-system. The great questions of the political-intellectual environment of the post-war period and of the Chinese revolutionary period (the decolonization of the global South, the revolts and national liberation revolutions, the dependent State) would continue, from one generation to the next, to be thought over, revised and re-elaborated by the intellectuals and leaders of the Party in charge of the State, always in the light of new challenges. Wang Weiguang (2008: 211), then Executive Vice President of the Chinese Academy of Social Sciences (CASS), says that "some famous [Brazilian] academic works were translated by our intellectuals and published by Cass Publishing Houses, such as Desenvolvimento Econômico Latino-Americano ["Latin American Economic Development"], by Professor Celso Furtado,

maintenance of large spheres of economic decision under state control (especially in strategic and base sectors), relative control of macroeconomic prices (wages, interest, exchange rate), high investment in infrastructure and urbanization, in addition to accelerated technological incorporation, adaptive absorption of organizational practices and Western institutional models, always focused on generating local innovation and subject to pre-established objectives. This, combined with other factors, enabled the country to grow economically and, in many ways, increase the income, educational level and quality of life of a considerable portion of its population, activating a gigantic and powerful consumer market – in addition to the consequent strengthening of its economic and political position in the international system. On the other hand, the advanced process of proletarianization of the population has been intensifying the contradictions with the country's ruling classes, which pushes the political and social environment in the direction of new concessions.

Virtù and *fortuna*. If the relative success of applying this strategy (*virtù*) is undeniable in terms of what it was proposed, especially taking into account the difficult balance between limitations and opportunities linked to the structural framework of the world economy in recent decades (*fortuna*), it would not be prudent to ignore its numerous missteps and distortions: the serious environmental degradation, the growing social and regional inequalities[31] and the great weight of economic power in the conduct of politics, the consequent corruption spread across different levels and spheres of the state apparatus, the dead-ends and tensions characteristic of the lack of popular participation in political life inside and outside formal institutions, the poor working and living conditions of a large part of the population, the lack of social assistance, the accelerated process of expropriation and real estate speculation, among many other problems. In some cases, such problems are even accepted openly and publicly by government authorities, which have even been preparing plans, measures and policies to mitigate them, with greater or lesser success.

Therefore, the contradictions of accelerated Chinese growth to be faced in the next period are not residual. In the troubled context of 21st century capitalism, the need for an adjustment or "soft landing" towards a development model anchored in domestic consumption and improving the quality of life of the population, for greater weight for services,[32] for technology-intensive

---

Imperialismo e Dependência ["Imperialism and Dependency"], by Professor Theotônio dos Santos, etc".

31 For an overview of growing inequalities in China, see Nogueira (2015).

32 Nogueira (2015a: 60–61) informs that, despite great international pressure, China has been very cautious in opening up its services sector. In this way, "The State has maintained a central (when not outright dominant) role in the main branches of services that are also

sectors, and for spheres more directly driven by market dynamics clashes with the need to constitute a deeper and more complex financial market (a more active presence in the international game of financial globalization), and with the consequent loss of political discretion over certain economic decisions that this gives rise to – which may reinforce, in turn, the deceleration of growth. Added to this is the huge and growing demand for energy and natural resources, the necessary adjustment of the country's multidimensional (class, gender, regional etc.) inequalities, and, even, more objective directions for commercial insertion and internationalization of the Chinese currency and capital around the world.

More than that, in recent years, the process of economic inclusion of ever-increasing portions of the population is one of the foundations of the political legitimacy of the CCP's authority and leadership (something that, as we have seen, was fundamental in China's development trajectory). What will the slowdown in growth entail in terms of this political dynamic – whether in relation to the masses of workers and peasants or the country's new business elites? What will be the consequences for China of such clashes regarding the complex equations entangled in the (national and international) dispute for economic and political power?

The Western world has a lot to learn from ancient Chinese history and its recent experience, in many different areas. There are, however, as seen, numerous questions still to be answered. When it comes to the exuberant "Middle" civilization and the dialectic relationship between openness and closure that it has maintained over the centuries with the rest of the world, it is always advisable to go back, review, and reanalyze. China's place in the history of our time remains open.

References

Aglietta, M.; Landry, Y. (2007). *La Chine vers la Superpuissance*. Paris: Economica.
Althusser, L. (1999). *Machiavelli and Us*. London, New York: Verso.
Arrighi, G. (2008). *Adam Smith em Pequim: Origens e Fundamentos do Século XXI*. São Paulo: Boitempo Editorial.

---

productive links (such as in the financial and telecommunications sectors, in which four banks and three State-owned operators dominate the market), and has stimulated the development of correlated national firms, especially in the case of telecommunications equipment".

Artus, P.; Mistral, J.; Plagnol, V. (2011). *L'Émergence de la Chine: Impact Économique et Implications de Politique Économique*. Paris: Conseil d'Analyse Économique.

Blankendal, N. (2008). *China's Energy Supply Security: The Quest for African Oil*. Msc Political Science Thesis (International Relations). International School for Humanities and Social Sciences University of Amsterdam.

Bloodworth, D.; Bloodworth, C. P. (2004). *The Chinese Machiavelli: 3000 Years of Chinese Statecraft*. London: Transaction Publishers.

Braudel, F. (1968). *La Historia y las Ciencias Sociales*. Madrid: Alianza.

Braudel, F. (1989). O Extremo Oriente. In: *Gramática das civilizações*. São Paulo: Martins Fontes.

Burlamaqui, L. (2015). As Finanças Globais e o Desenvolvimento Financeiro Chinês: Um Modelo de Governança Financeira Global Conduzido pelo Estado In: Cintra, M. A. M; Filho, E. B. S.; Pinto, E. C. (Eds.). *China em Transformação: Dimensões Econômicas e Geopolíticas do Desenvolvimento*. Rio de Janeiro: IPEA, 277–334.

Cheng, A. (2008). *História do Pensamento Chinês*. São Paulo: Vozes.

Chesnais, F. (1996). *A Mundialização do Capital*. São Paulo: Xamã.

Chesnais, F. (1998). Introdução geral. In: Chesnais, F. (Org.). *A Mundialização Financeira: Gênese, Custos e Riscos*. São Paulo: Xamã, 11–36.

Chesnais, F. (2001). Nova Economia: Uma Conjuntura Específica da Potência Hegemônica no Contexto da Mundialização do Capital. *Revista da Sociedade Brasileira de Economia Política*, 9: 53–85.

Cintra, M. A. M.; Martins, A. R. A. (2013). O Papel do Dólar e do Renminbi no Sistema Monetário Internacional. In: Cintra, M. A. M.; Martins, A. R. A. (Eds.). *As Transformações no Sistema Monetário Internacional*. Brasília: IPEA, 211–321.

Cintra, M. A. M.; Filho, E. B. S.; Pinto, E. C. (2015). Introdução. In: Cintra, M. A. M.; Filho, E. B. S.; Pinto, E. C. (Eds). *China em Transformação: Dimensões Econômicas e Geopolíticas do Desenvolvimento*. Rio de Janeiro: IPEA, 15–41.

Cintra, M. A. M.; Filho, E. B. S. (2015). O Sistema Financeiro Chinês: A Grande Muralha. In: Cintra, M. A. M.; Filho, E. B. S.; Pinto, E. C. (Eds). *China em Transformação: Dimensões Econômicas e Geopolíticas do Desenvolvimento*. Rio de Janeiro: IPEA, 425–490.

Cintra, M. A. M.; Pinto, E. C. (2017). China em Transformação: Transição e Estratégias de Desenvolvimento. *Revista de Economia Política*, 37 (2): 381–400.

Cohen, B. J. (2012). The Yuan Tomorrow? Evaluating China's Currency Internationalization Strategy. *New Political Economy*, 17 (3): 361–371.

Cunha, A.; Acioly, A. (2009). China: Ascensão à Condição de Potência Global: Características e Implicações. In: Cardoso, J.; Acioly, L.; Matijascic, M. (Eds.). *Trajetórias Recentes de Desenvolvimento*. Brasília: IPEA.

EIA – U.S Energy Information Administration. (2020). EIA *Analisys Coutries, China.* Country Analysis Executive Summary: China. https://www.eia.gov/internatio nal/content/analysis/countries_long/China/china.pdf.

Eichengreen, B.; Kawai, M. (2014). Issues for Renminbi Internationalization: An overview. *ADBI Working Paper Series*, n. 454, January. Accessed July 23, 2021. http://www.relooney.com/NS3040/000_New_476.pdf.

Fairbank, J. K.; Goldman, M. (2006). *China: Uma Nova História.* Porto Alegre: LP&M.

Fang, C.; Yang, D.; Meiyan, W. (2009). Crise e Oportunidade: Resposta da China à Crise Financeira Global. *Revista Tempo do Mundo*, 1(1).

Department of the Treasury. *Federal Reserve Board Data*, 2017. Accessed July 22, 2021. https://www.federalreserve.gov/data.htm.

Fiori, J. L. (2008). O Sistema Interestatal Capitalista no Início do Século XXI. In: Fiori, J. L.; Medeiros, C. A.; Serrano, F. (Eds.). *O Mito do Colapso do Poder Americano.* Rio de Janeiro: Record, 173–277.

Fiori, J. L. (2010). Brasil e América do Sul: o Desafio da Inserção Internacional Soberana. In: Acioly, L.; Cintra, M. A. M. (Eds.). *Inserção Internacional Brasileira.* Brasília: IPEA, v. 1.

Fiori, J. L. (2013). Sobre o Desenvolvimento Chinês. *Valor Econômico*, March 27.

Franz-stefan, G. (2015). Why We Should Study China's Machiavelli? *The Diplomat*, January 22. Access July 23, 2021. http://thediplomat.com/2015/01/why-we-sho uld-study-chinas-machiavelli/.

Gouveia, E. M. (2015). Relações Econômicas entre China e Malásia: Comércio, Cadeias Globais de Produção e a Indústria de Semicondutores. In: Cintra, M. A. M.; Filho, E. B. S.; Pinto, E. C. (Eds.). *China em Transformação: Dimensões Econômicas e Geopolíticas do Desenvolvimento.* Rio de Janeiro: IPEA, 81–127.

Jessop, B. (1990). *State Theory: Putting the Capitalist State in Its Place.* Cambridge (UK): Polity.

Kai, J. (2015). Are China's Leaders Disciples of Machiavelli? *The Diplomat*, February 10. Accessed July 23, 2021. http://thediplomat.com/2015/02/are-chinas-leaders-discip les-of-machiavelli/.

Keidel, A. (2011). China Economic Developments, Prospects and Lessons for the International Financial System. In: BRASIL. Ministério das Relações Exteriores. *Brasil e China no Reordenamento das Relações Internacionais: Desafios e Oportunidades.* Brasília: Fundação Alexandre de Gusmão, MRE.

Kissinger, H. A. (2011). *Sobre a China.* Rio de Janeiro: Objetiva.

Kroeber, A. (2011). The Renminbi: The Political Economy of a Currency. *Foreign Policy*, September 7.

Kroeber, A. (2015). The Never-ending Slowdown. *China Economic Quarterly*, November.

Lardy, N. R. (2011). *Sustaining China's Economic Growth after the Global Financial Crisis.* Washington: Peterson Institute.

Leão, R. P. F. (2010). *O Padrão de Acumulação e o Desenvolvimento Econômico da China nas Últimas Três Décadas: Uma Interpretação*. 2010. Dissertação (Mestrado). Instituto de Economia, Universidade Estadual de Campinas, Campinas.

Leão, R. P. F. (2011). A Articulação Produtiva Asiática e os Efeitos da Emergência Chinesa. In: Leão, R. P. F.; Pinto, E. C.; Acioly, L. (Eds.). *A China na Nova Configuração Global: Impactos Políticos e Econômicos*. Brasília: IPEA, 115–164.

Lo, D. (2016). Developing or Under-developing? Implications of China's 'Going out' for Late Development. *SOAS Department of Economics Working Paper*, n. 198, London. Accessed July 22, 2021. https://www.soas.ac.uk/sites/default/files/2022-10/economics-wp198.pdf.

Lo, D. (2016a). China Confronts the Great Recession: 'Rebalancing' Neoliberalism, or Else? In: Arestis, P.; Sawyer, M. (Eds.) *Emerging Economies During and After the Great Recession*. London: Palgrave Macmillan UK.

Losurdo, D. (2004). *Fuga da História?* Rio de Janeiro: Revan.

Lyrio, M. C. (2010). *A Ascensão da China como Potência: Fundamentos Políticos Internos*. Brasília: Fundação Alexandre de Gusmão, MRE.

Majerowicz, E. (2022). The Industrial Reserve Army and Wage Setting in China. *Bulletin of Political Economy*, 16 (1): 21–56.

Maquiavel, N. (2008). *O Príncipe*. São Paulo: Martins Fontes.

Marti, M. E. (2007). *A China de Deng Xiaoping*. Rio de Janeiro: Nova Fronteira.

Mazzucato, M. (2014). *O Estado Empreendedor: Desmascarando o Mito do Setor Público vs. Setor Privado*. São Paulo: Portfolio Penguin.

Medeiros, C. A. (1999). China: entre os Séculos XX e XXI. In: Fiori, J. L. (Ed.). *Estados e Moedas no Desenvolvimento das Nações*. Petrópolis: Vozes, 379–411.

Medeiros, C. A. (2003). The Post-war American Technological Development as a Military Enterprise. *Contributions to Political Economy*, 22 (1): 41–62.

Medeiros, C. A. (2006). A China como um Duplo Polo na Economia Mundial e a Recentralização da Economia Asiática. *Revista de Economia Política*, 26 (3): 381–400.

Medeiros, C. A. (2011). A China e as Matérias-primas. In: Brasil. Ministério das Relações Exteriores. *Brasil e China no Reordenamento das Relações Internacionais: Desafios e Oportunidades*. Brasília: Fundação Alexandre de Gusmão; MRE. Accessed July 23, 2021. http://funag.gov.br/loja/download/905-Brasil_e_China_no_Reordenamento_das_Relacoes_Internacionais.pdf.

Medeiros, C. A. (2013). Padrões de Investimento, Mudança Institucional e Transformação Estrutural na Economia Chinesa. In: Bielschowsky, R. (Ed.). *Padrões de Desenvolvimento Econômico (1950–2008): América Latina, Ásia e Rússia*. Brasília: CGEE, v. 2, 435–489.

McNally, C. A. (2020). Chaotic Mélange: Neo-liberalism and Neo-statism in the Age of Sino-Capitalism. *Review of International Political Economy*, 27 (2), 281–301.

Miguel, L. F. (2015). *O Nascimento da Política Moderna: de Maquiavel a Hobbes*. Brasília: Editora Universidade de Brasília.

Miller, T. (2014). A Dream of Asian Empire. *Gavekal Dragonomics*, december.

Mitchel, R. (2015). Is 'China's Machiavelli' Now Its Most Important Political Philosopher?, *The Diplomat*, January 16. Access July 23, 2021. http://thediplomat.com/2015/01/is-chinas-machiavelli-now-its-most-important-political-philosopher/.

National Bureau Statistics of China, 2017. Access July 22, 2022. https://data.stats.gov.cn/english/easyquery.htm?cn=C01

Nogueira, I. (2008). A Política Regional da China e os Processos de Integração na Ásia. In: *Conferência Nacional de Política Externa e Política Internacional – III CNPEPI*. Brasília: Fundação Alexandre de Gusmão, 289–326.

Nogueira, I. (2011). *Desenvolvimento Econômico, Distribuição de Renda e Pobreza na China Contemporânea*. Tese (Doutorado) – Instituto de Economia da Universidade Federal do Rio de Janeiro, Rio de Janeiro.

Nogueira, I. (2012). Cadeias Produtivas Globais e Agregação de Valor: A posição da China na Indústria Eletroeletrônica de Consumo. *Revista Tempo do Mundo*, 4 (3).

Nogueira, I. (2015). Desigualdades e Políticas Públicas na China: Investimento, Salários e Riqueza na Era da Sociedade Harmoniosa. In: Cintra, M. A. M.; Filho, E. B. S.; Pinto, E. C. (Eds.). *China em Transformação: Dimensões Econômicas e Geopolíticas do Desenvolvimento*. Rio de Janeiro: IPEA, 237–273.

Nogueira, I. (2015a). Políticas de Fomento à Ascensão da China nas Cadeias Globais de Valor. In: Cintra, M. A. M.; Filho, E. B. S.; Pinto, E. C. (Eds.). *China em Transformação: Dimensões Econômicas e Geopolíticas do Desenvolvimento*. Rio de Janeiro: IPEA, 45–79.

Ocampo, J. A.; Erten, B. (2013). The Global Implications of Falling Commodity Prices. Access December 24, 2018. https://www.project-syndicate.org/commentary/china-s-growth-slowdown-and-the-end-of-the-commodity-price-super-cyle-by-jose-antonio-ocampo-and-bilge-erten.

OECD. *OECD Data*. 2017, 2018. Access July 23, 2021. https://data.oecd.org/.

OECD. (2015). Trade in Value Added: China In: *OECD-WTO. Trade in Value Added*.

Paraná, E. (2016). *A Finança Digitalizada: Capitalismo Financeiro e Revolução Informacional*. Florianópolis: Insular.

Pempel, T.J. (2008). A China e o emergente regionalismo Asiático. In: *A Política Regional da China e os Processos de Integração na Ásia*. Conferência Nacional de Política Externa e Política Internacional – III CNPEPI. Brasília: Fundação Alexandre de Gusmão, 267–288.

Pinto, E. C. (2010). O Eixo Sino-americano e a Inserção Externa Brasileira: Antes e Depois da Crise. In: Acioly, L.; Cintra, M. (Eds.). *Inserção Internacional Brasileira*, v. 2. Brasília: IPEA.

Pinto, E. C. (2011). O Eixo Sino-americano e as Transformações do Sistema Mundial: Tensões e Complementaridades Comerciais, Produtivas e Financeiras. In: Leão, R. *et al. A China na Nova Configuração Global: Impactos Políticos e Econômicos*. Brasília: IPEA.

Pinto, E. C. (2015). A Integração Econômica entre a China e o Vietnã: Estratégia *plus One*, Investimentos e Cadeias Globais. In: Cintra, M. A. M.; Filho, E. B. S.; Pinto, E. C. (Eds.). *China em Transformação: Dimensões Econômicas e Geopolíticas do Desenvolvimento*. Rio de Janeiro: IPEA, 81–125.

Quagio, I. (2009). *Olhos Abertos: a História da Nova China da Morte de Mao à Crise Econômica*. São Paulo: Francis.

Rossi, C. (2010). Como fica o Brasil diante do G2?, *Folha de São Paulo*, January 22, A10.

Saich, T. (2004). *Governance and Politics of China*. New York: Palgrave Macmillan.

Shambaugh, D. (2013). *China Goes Global: A Partial Power*. Oxford University Press.

Sturgeon, T. (2002). Modular Production Networks: A New American Model of Industrial Organization. *Industrial and Corporate Change*, 11 (3): 451–496.

Swift. (2016). *More than 100 Countries are Now Using the RMB for Payments with China and Hong Kong*. Brussels, October 27. Accessed July 23, 2021. https://www.swift.com/news-events/press-releases/more-100-countries-are-now-using-rmb-payments-china-and-hong-kong. Access in: July 23, 2021.

Tavares, M. C.; Belluzzo, L.G. M. (2004) A Mundialização do Capital e a Expansão do Poder Americano. In: Fiori, J. L. (org.). *O Poder Americano*. Rio de Janeiro: Vozes.

UNCTAD. (2013). *Global Value Chains and Development: Investment and Value Added Trade in the Global Economy*. Geneva: UNCTAD. Accessed December 24, 2018. http://unctad.org/en/pages/newsdetails.aspx?OriginalVersionID=411.

Varoufakis, Y. (2016). *O Minotauro Global: A Verdadeira Origem da Crise Financeira e o Futuro da Economia Global*. São Paulo: Autonomia Literária.

Wei, ShangJing; Zhuan, Xie; Zhang, Xiaobo. (2016). From 'Made in China' to 'Innovated in China': Necessity, Prospect, and Challenges. *NBER Working Paper* n. 22854, November.

Weiguang, Wang. (2008). A Reforma, a Abertura e a Rota do Desenvolvimento Chinês. In: *Conferência Nacional de Política Externa e Política Internacional – III CNPEPI*. Brasília: Fundação Alexandre de Gusmão, 187–212.

World Bank Database (2019). Access July 22, 2021. https://databank.worldbank.org/home.aspx

Wu, Jinglian. (2005). *Understanding and Interpreting Chinese Economic Reform*. Mason: Thomson.

Wu, Jinglian. (2006). Does China Need to Change its Industrializations Path? In: Gill, I.; Huang, Y.; Kharas, H. (Eds.). *East Asian visions*. Washington: World Bnk.

Zheng, Bijian. (2005). China's Peaceful Rise to Great Power Status. *Foreign Affairs*, Council of Foreign Relations, New York, 84 (5).

Zheng, Bijian. (2006). The Internal and External Environments of China's Development over the Next Five Years. In: Gill, I.; Huang, Y.; Kharas, H. (Eds.). *East Asian visions*. Washington: World Bank.

CHAPTER 3

The State and Domestic Capitalists in China's Economic Transition

Isabela Nogueira and Hao Qi

Over the past four decades, China has undergone a transition from a planned economy to a market economy.[1] This transition has given rise to not only a great transformation of the working class but also the formation of a domestic capitalist class, one which is particularly entwined with state structures. What role has the state played in the formation of this new class? What has been the impact of this new class on the state? How has this state-bourgeoisie relationship evolved within the dynamics of class conflicts, contradictions, and regimes of accumulation?

At the beginning of this transition, the state firmly controlled the economy via the central planning system. While private firms play a crucial role in the present-day economy, a state presence remains via state-owned enterprises, a financial system dominated by a few giant state-owned banks, and a land ownership system largely controlled by local municipal governments. In fact, fiscal revenue as a share of GDP has significantly increased since the mid-1990s (Naughton, 2017; Piketty, Yang, and Zucman, 2017). Therefore, China appears a puzzle, since it has witnessed both the rise of new capitalists and a continued significant economic role for the state.

The existing literature emphasizes the specificity of the Chinese political economy in terms of the relation between the state and emerging domestic capitalists. These scholars explicitly or implicitly depict the Chinese state as a developmental state. They posit that the state has adequate capacity to maintain control over domestic capitalists (So, 2003; Dickson, 2008; McNally and Wright, 2010; van der Pijl, 2012, 2016; Yao, 2010, 2011). The guiding assumption is that, in pursing their economic interests, new capitalists seek to participate in the state and to establish interpersonal relationships with government officials, rather than seek an alternative political regime. It is noteworthy that

---

[1] A modified version of this chapter was originally published in *Critical Asian Studies*, vol. 51, n. 4, 2019. We thank the journal editors for authorizing a revised publication. In this chapter, the state refers to the whole political structure consisting of both the central government and local governments.

these studies mirror the Chinese Communist Party (CCP) official ideology of "Socialism with Chinese characteristics" in that they all contend that capitalists function as controllable instruments for achieving the party-state's fundamental goal, be this economic development or a particular version of socialism.

For critical approaches such as Marxian political economy, the dynamics of capital accumulation are vitally entangled with political power. On the one hand, the state provides the regulatory, legal, and repressive framework for private ownership, contracts, and competition to occur; it also tries to contain crises, reduce uncertainty on the return of capital, and guide the accumulation of capital in varied forms (Brunhoff, 1978). On the other hand, the state depends on the accumulation of capital for its functioning, both through the collection of taxes and the more abstract relationship between the accumulation of wealth and increased state capacity. Generally speaking, capital-labor conflicts, capitalist competition (both domestic and international), and the contradictions generated by accumulation not only shape the state, but also are shaped by the state (Jessop, 2008; Cox, 1981).

In this chapter, we examine the changing patterns of the relationship between the Chinese state and China's domestic capitalist class by using a Marxian political economy methodology. In doing so, we provide an account of the dialectical relationship between the Chinese state and this emerging class. Our argument has two parts. First, we argue that the formation of a domestic capitalist class is a two-way movement in which the state interacts, conflicts, and compromises with new economic elites and prototype capitalists. This two-way movement remains a prominent feature of the relationship between the state and the new class in present-day China. Second, the state-class relationship in China has been continuously affected by capital-labor conflicts and contradictions within the regimes of accumulation. As a result, the state-class relationship has undergone a transition from what we call a "great compromise" to a "strained alliance."

This chapter contributes to the existing literature in two ways. First, we investigate the two-way movement between the Chinese state and the country's domestic capitalist class in both the formation and transformation of this new class, arguing the state has shaped and been shaped by this new class. In so doing, we challenge the conventional wisdom that the Chinese state is a developmental state, strictly controlling the new capitalist class. Second, we identify the historical trajectory of the changing patterns of the relationship between the state and the new class, placing this in the context of capital-labor conflicts and contradictions within changing regimes of accumulation. In addition, we analyze the relations between each faction of the new class and the state, since different factions in different contexts share some interests or have potential conflicts with the state. We identify three factions of the new class, according to the characteristics of their regimes of accumulation: a low-road faction of capitalists, whose accumulation mainly depends on cheap labor and cheap land,[2] an innovation faction, whose accumulation mainly depends on high labor productivity and technological innovation, and a finance faction, whose accumulation mainly depends on financial speculation.[3]

The chapter is outlined as follows. In the first section, we review the existing literature and present our approach. Following this, we offer an overview of the historical stages and factions of China's new capitalist class. This is followed by a discussion of the relationship between the state and the capitalist class in the process of primitive accumulation. This is the stage of what we call "great compromise." The fourth section discusses the interactions between the state and the capitalist class by focusing on the background of the state's indigenous innovation policies and responses to an accelerated process of financial expansion. This is the stage of what we call "strained alliance." We conclude with a discussion of future implications of this two-way movement.

1 Literature Review

A significant part of the existing literature suggests that the Chinese state maintains strict control over its new class of domestic capitalists. Both for Bruce Dickson, who calls this class "red capitalists," (Dickson, 2008) and Alvin So, who describes the emergence of a "cadre-capitalist class," (So, 2003) the Chinese state has created capitalists from its own ranks or co-opted emerging capitalists. Both authors discuss the disproportionate participation of entrepreneurs in the political structures of local and central government, as well as the enrichment of the families of traditional political elites at all levels. In the same vein, Kees van der Pijl has argued that the state has anticipated in and guided class formation, leading to a "contained capitalist class" disinterested in a broader process of political and economic liberalization (van der Pijl, 2012; van der Pijl, 2016). Christopher McNally and Teresa Wright argue that the CCP has been successful in co-opting emerging capitalists with the benefits of privatization and subjective bonds of reciprocity, making the Chinese bourgeoisie deeply dependent on the party-state apparatus for links that range from personal material interests to affective ties (McNally and Wright, 2010). Yao

---

2 Including low environment costs.
3 Details about the factions will be discussed in Section 3.

Yang argues that the Chinese government has been neutral since the beginning of the reform era in the sense that it does not endorse any particular interest group and has been able to repress the interests of any such group for its own purpose; this disinterested government approach sets economic growth as its main goal in order to maintain political legitimacy (Yao, 2010, 2011).

To a large extent, these scholars depict China as a developmental state – an autonomous, rational actor endowed with a talented bureaucracy and a long-term and coherent view of economic development. A developmental state is more than a state pursing economic development because it also implies that the state is able to maintain its autonomy and control an emerging class of private entrepreneurs (Evans, 1989). According to Elaine Hui, the Chinese state is, to varying degrees, treated by scholars as an actor that is free-standing from society, leaving state-society relations secondary, if not marginalized. Thus, whenever social and economic interests emerge in these analyses, the state is perceived as standing above sectoral interests and as being able to mediate these (Hui, 2017).

While there is no doubt that this literature captures important characteristics of the state-capitalist class relationship at certain stages of history, there has been a lack of analysis of the dynamics of this relationship. More importantly, these studies tend to depict the formation of a certain pattern of state-class relations as an outcome of the actions of a powerful authoritarian state. This approach downplays the impact of the new class and class struggles on the state.[4] Put differently, the literature underscores the specificity of the state but ignores the historical conditions and social relations that have given rise to this specificity. That said, some scholars have analyzed the diversity of the roles of the Chinese state and interactions between local state actors and private entrepreneurs, emphasizing the power of capitalists and their impact on local authorities (Howell, 2006; Ong, 2012; Hui, 2017; Heberer and Schubert, 2019; Zhang, 2019). However, these studies tend to neglect changing patterns over time.

We view the Chinese state as a social relation. We argue that the state is continuously affected and shaped by class relations in society. The political and the economic orders, despite their formal institutional separation, should be structurally coupled to produce a relatively unified historical bloc (Jessop, 2008: 25). In a typical capitalist society, the modes of exercising state power are the result of complex social relations which are historically determined by the

---

4 See Fine (2013) and Chang (2013) for a comprehensive evaluation and critique of missing class relations in the developmental state literature.

forms that capital assumes (Jessop, 2008). In contrast to the current literature, this chapter highlights the dialectical nature of the relationship between the Chinese state and the new capitalist class. This relationship should be understood as a historical process conditioned by class relations and contradictions within capital accumulation. The state has played an active role in the formation and transformation of the new class, whereas this formation and transformation in turn has affected and shaped the state.

To sum up, while the current literature mostly marginalizes the impact of the new class on the state, our "two-way movement" hypothesis explicitly acknowledges it. Second, while the current literature tends to emphasize a single type of relation between the state and the new class, we suggest the state-class relationship is an evolving outcome of a complex historical process involving major class relations and contradictions of accumulation.

2 Historical Stages and Capitalist Factions

The reform era that began in 1978 can be divided into three stages: from 1978 until 1991, the initial stage of market reform; from 1992 to 2008, which ended with the most recent global financial crisis; and from 2009 to the present.

In order to visualize the stages, we have measured the shares of the state (the central government, local governments, and SOEs), private capital, and labor in the primary distribution of the net value added in the corporate sector (non-financial corporations and financial institutions). This net value is the sum of employee compensation, taxes on production (less subsidies), corporate taxes, the after-tax profits of state-owned enterprises, and the after-tax profits of private enterprises (see Figure 3.1). Due to data availability, we are able to show the dynamics between 1992 and 2020. It is worth noting that each point in the data series reflects the relative power of the actor as well as minor factors such as economic fluctuations, thus it can only roughly reflect the power relations.

As Figure 3.1 illustrates, labor's share significantly declined between 1992 and 2008, while private capital's share rose from 4.8 percent to 17.3 percent and the state's share – the sum of the governments' share and state-owned enterprise's share – rose from 30.6 percent to 38.9 percent over this period. The post-2009 period saw a mild recovery of labor's share and fluctuations in the shares of private capital and the state. These trends roughly correspond to the historical facts about power relations among the state, private capital, and labor throughout the three stages of the reform era.

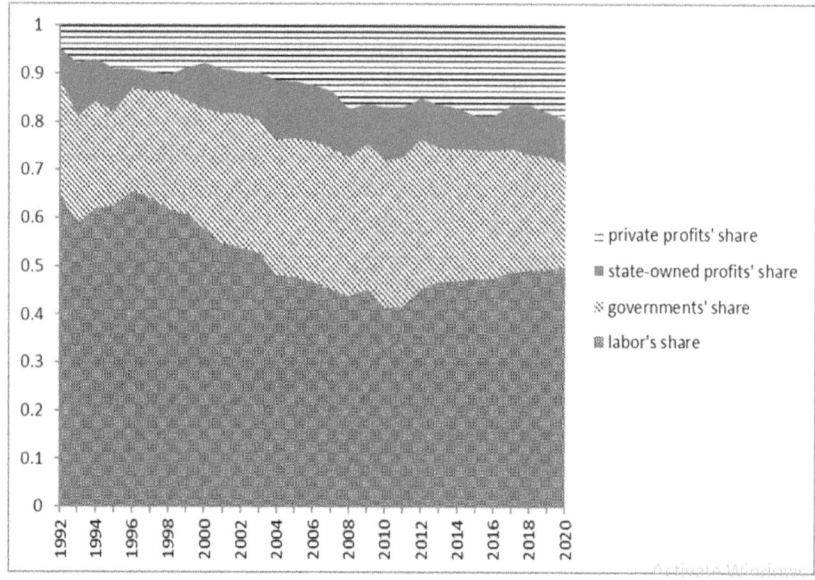

FIGURE 3.1 Distribution of net value added in the corporate sector, 1992–2020
SOURCE: THE AUTHORS' CALCULATION AND ESTIMATION BASED ON FLOW OF FUNDS ACCOUNT TABLES IN DATA OF FLOW OF FUNDS PUBLISHED BY THE NBS (2008) AND THE *CHINA STATISTICAL YEARBOOK* 2012–2021

Reforms during the first stage focused on the provision of incentives and the formation of a market economy that would coexist with the planning system.[5] During this period urban workers employed at SOEs still had access to various welfare programs and enjoyed job security. Rural-to-urban migration was rare, and peasant workers were mostly employed in township and village enterprises (TVEs), as well as foreign-funded enterprises in special economic zones (SEZs). The state and collectives owned the vast majority of productive wealth. However, this stage saw the emergence of new elites who accumulated wealth from price reforms.

During the second stage, a domestic private capitalist class emerged, along with primitive accumulation in the form of massive privatization of state-owned and collective assets and the expropriation of land. The state-capital relationship during this stage was a "great compromise:" the state allowed the

---

5 The data for an alternative measure – the share of employee compensation in total gdp – is available for this period, which increased from 49.7 percent in 1978 to 50.1 percent in 1992, signifying that reforms during the first stage did not erode labor's interests. See Qi (2014).

rise of capitalists on the condition that it maintained a crucial role in the economy. Labor's power was substantially reduced by massive layoffs and an increase in the number of migrant workers to urban areas. Increases in the shares of private capital and the state were at the expense of workers.

The third stage roughly corresponds to what we label a "strained alliance," although the adjustment of state-capital relations started as early as the mid-2000s. By a strained alliance, we mean that internal and external contradictions imposed pressure on the relationship between private capital and the state, reducing their common interests and intensifying the conflicts between them. Since the mid-2000s, wages have grown substantially and labor unrest has noticeably increased, undermining the profits of private capital. Externally, while a large portion of domestic capitalists initially achieved prosperity through export-oriented industries, the outbreak of the global financial crisis in 2008 made some of these industries unprofitable and unsustainable. Economic growth slowed down, and the economy entered the stage of a so-called "new normal," as rising wages, unstable export markets, and an economic slowdown have driven an increasing number of domestic capitalists to engage in financial speculation.

In addition to these three temporal stages, we identify three factions of domestic capitalists in China, according to their regime of accumulation: the low-road faction, the innovation faction, and the finance faction. Table 3.1 summarizes these factions and corresponding regimes. It is noteworthy that there is no hard boundary among factions because capital can simultaneously belong to two or more factions or move from one faction to another. What we emphasize are the different interests associated with different regimes of accumulation rather than a precise method to classify individual capitalists.

We call a particular group of domestic capitalists the "low-road faction" because their accumulation of wealth has centered on cheap labor and cheap land.[6] These capitalists comprised the majority of China's private entrepreneurs in the 1990s. A significant proportion of them concentrated in labor-intensive export-oriented industries and were deeply engaged in the global value chain. They shared common interests with the state in terms of creating jobs and promoting economic growth; however, the corresponding regime

---

6 "Low road" is a concept initially describing the accumulation regime of an economy, which we use to characterize a capitalist faction. As David Gordon explains, "the 'low road' relies on conflict and insecurity, control and harsh worker punishments, and often features relatively stagnant or even declining real wage growth" (Gordon, 1996: 44).

of accumulation intensified capital-labor conflicts due to its reliance on low wages and harsh management practices, which in turn has generated conflicts between the state and this faction (Pun and Huilin, 2010; Smith and Pun, 2018; Howell and Pringle, 2019).

In the context of rising wages, labor unrest, and an economic slowdown after 2000, two additional factions emerged. Since the mid-2000s, the state has supported indigenous innovation in order to restructure the low-road accumulation regime and lessen the economy's dependence on cheap labor and cheap land. In contrast to the low-road faction, accumulation by the innovation faction depends on technical innovation and improved labor productivity. While it is far from dominating China's capitalist class, this faction has achieved remarkable growth due to the state's supportive policies and the expansion of domestic markets.

Another faction that emerged as a result of the economic slowdown is the finance faction. Faced with rising wages and diminished global market conditions, domestic capitalists have increasingly engaged in speculative activities, feeding bubbles in the stock market. Similar to what has occurred in the United States since the 1990s, a crucial reason for financialization is the decline in the profitability of capital accumulation (Kotz, 2015). The finance faction of capitalists in China not only generates instability and insecurity due to speculation in major financial markets, it also provides incentives for private entrepreneurs to withdraw capital from accumulation and jeopardize economic and employment growth. Therefore, the response by the state has been to repress this faction and impose more regulations.

TABLE 3.1 Factions of domestic private capitalist class

Classifications	When emerged	Characteristics of the accumulation regime
Low-road faction	Early 1990s	Reliance on cheap labor and cheap land and export-oriented
Innovation faction	Mid-2000s	Technological innovation and high labor productivity
Finance faction	Late 2000s	Financial market speculation

3   The Great Compromise

Economic privatization formed part of a compromise between the state and new elites whose rise was a result of the reforms in the first stage of the reform era. These new elites were businessmen who accumulated private wealth by taking advantage of the then-dual price system and personal connections with officials.[7] This new class included SOE managers and state officials who accumulated considerable private wealth by taking advantage of their positions. Compared to the old political elites, these new elites were significantly more responsive to monetary incentives. While the planning system was retained, market reforms dramatically transformed the incentives that guided the behavior of people, especially those in power, which made operation of the planning system increasingly difficult.[8] Monetary incentives in turn increasingly commercialized society and mobilized people to engage in market activities, which in turn made further marketization imperative.

The dual price system, which was established in 1984, was aimed at providing SOEs with more incentives for the production of industrial materials. This system allowed SOEs producing industrial materials to sell outside-plan goods at market prices as long as they fulfilled their in-plan quotas. The resulting gap between market prices and planning prices created not only production incentives for state companies but also rent-seeking opportunities for individuals, as enterprises were able to divert in-plan goods to the market sector. An influential study estimates that the amount of rents was thirty percent of national income in 1988 (Hu, 1989).

The dual price system offered an historical opportunity for new elites to accumulate private wealth by utilizing political and economic connections. Specifically, it was the officials of the Material Supply Bureau (MSB) who were responsible for the in-plan allocation of industrial materials (Li, 2001). Businessmen with connections to high-level officials were able to purchase in-plan goods at planning prices by pressuring or bribing MSB officials. They were also able to purchase outside-plan goods from SOEs at prices higher than planning prices but lower than market prices. SOE managers in many cases used revenue from selling outside-plan goods to fund bonuses or welfare funds for their workers. In contrast to self-employed entrepreneurs who

---

[7] We note that the new elites are not from below in the sense of "capitalism from below" as examined by Byres (2009) and Yan and Chen (2015.) While the elites were not from below, they had different goals than the state.

[8] SOE managers could bargain with planners for reducing the output quota so that they could increase the goods supplied to the market.

became rich by producing and selling goods in the market, these new elites accumulated wealth mainly through market speculation with the assistance of political power and bribes. This kind of corruption, known as *guandao* (official profiteering), provided a way to convert political power into private wealth (Sun, 2004).

Guandao reveals the fundamental contradiction in the accumulation regime in the 1980s. This contradiction lies in the impact of market incentives on the capacity of the state, reflected by the relative decline in the taxes and profits controlled by the state that could be used for government expenditure and accumulation. The 1980s witnessed a substantial decline in the share of profits and taxes in the net value added of SOEs (Qi, 2018). Fiscal income as a share of the national income declined from 30.8 percent in 1978 to 14.3 percent in 1991.[9] The reforms were designed to generate incentives in the incremental part of output. However, once market incentives mobilized new elites, SOE managers, and state officials, resources were diverted to the market and converted into private income in various forms such as the rents captured by new elites and bribes captured by SOE managers and officials (Qi, 2018). As a result, the shares of profits and taxes captured by the state were reduced.

The formation of this new class had a substantial impact on the state. As increasingly more output was allocated through the market, new elites gained more economic power and the state's fiscal capacity declined (Wang and Hu, 1993).[10] The decline in the state's capacity in China was the cause of the limited fiscal support provided by the state to SOEs in the early 1990s and later the insolvency of some of these enterprises.

By the end of the 1980s, the state confronted problems associated with the emerging elites, including corruption and social injustices. In 1988, concerned with these problems, the state initiated a radical reform to liberalize prices, in part to eliminate *guandao*. However, this failed because it induced panic buying and social unrest (Zhang, 2016: 563). Among those participating in the 1989 social movement were the new elites who had gained great benefits from the economic decentralization policies of the 1980s (Wang, 2011: 31). After the government repressed the social unrest in June of 1989, leaders in favor of economic and social stability and more cautious policies dominated policy making at the central level. Between 1989 and 1991, some high-level officials and businessmen who had engaged in *guandao* were investigated and arrested (Li, 2001). However, this short-lived anti-corruption movement failed to repress

---

9   Authors' calculation, using data from the *China Statistical Yearbook* (2018).
10   A fall in the state's fiscal capacity also happened during Gorbachev's economic reforms in the USSR. See Kotz and Weir (1997: 73).

the new elites, in part because even relatives of some key leaders reportedly engaged in *guandao* (Meisner, 1996: 326). Following the demise of the Soviet Union, Deng Xiaoping hoped that economic growth through further marketization reforms would bolster the party-state. In 1990, Deng explicitly said, "Why do the people support us? Because over the last ten years our economy has been developing ... if the economy stagnated for five years or developed at only a slow rate ... this would be not only an economic problem but also a political one" (Vogel, 2011: 668). In his famous southern tour at the beginning of 1992, Deng clearly sent signals to other leaders, including those in favor of stability, announcing that "whoever is against reform must leave office" (Vogel, 2011: 673). Following his southern tour, state officials were encouraged to establish companies and engage in market activities. This was the start of a "great compromise" between the state and the new elites. This compromise constituted the background for the privatization of state-owned and collective enterprises as well as a symbiotic relationship between local government officials and private entrepreneurs. But this did not mean that new elites could challenge the party or state politically. In the late 1990s, restructuring of the state-owned sector led to the consolidation of strategically positioned state-owned enterprises that could control the nodes of accumulation, play a crucial role in technological progress, carry out counter-cyclical macro policies, and secure natural resources from abroad. SOEs that remained in business slashed their social and worker responsibilities and focused on strategic industries such as energy, chemicals, steel, telecommunications, and banking. This alliance between a private capitalist class and state power reveals a dialectical relation between politics and economics. A political compromise partially was a result of economic contradictions in the 1980s, while economic shifts such as marketization and privatization in the 1990s were premised on a political compromise and the particular structure of the state's political power.

3.1 *Primitive Accumulation and the Low-Road Faction*

While *guandao* gave the new elites an opportunity to accumulate wealth through market speculation, it did not enable them to dominate production and thus form a capitalist class. It was the privatization of SOEs and TVEs (township and village enterprises) in the mid- and late 1990s and later the expropriation of rural land that allowed private entrepreneurs to dominate production and thus control investments and employment. Privatization of public assets and land expropriation are forms of primitive accumulation that involve "the historical process of divorcing the producer from the means of production" (Marx, 1976: 875). Similar to *guandao*, privatization and expropriation converted political power into private wealth and led to the emergence of the new capitalists – former managers of state-owned and collective firms, local officials, and manufacturers, and real estate speculators, who captured rents from land expropriation by making use of their symbiotic relationships with local government officials.[11]

Inaugurated with the slogan "grasp the large and let the small go" (*zhuada fangxiao*), privatization entailed a broad and diverse reorganization of the ownership structure of the enterprise sector, leading to the emergence of a domestic capitalist class and the strategic positioning of large SOEs. Newly privatized firms achieved rapid growth by taking advantage of formerly public assets and technologies while downsizing their workforces and disciplining their workers that remained with unemployment threats. For these new capitalists, privatization occurred via a process that often resembled a transfer of assets rather than a sale. The beneficiaries were insiders with deep connections, often ex-factory managers or local officials. Generally, these insiders were able to affect the pricing of assets because of insider information about particular assets or their personal connections with local government officials, which resulted in asset losses, debt forgiveness, and subsidized credit for investors who lacked their own sufficient capital. There have been many cases of former SOE managers or local officials who did not pay anything out of pocket but became owners of privatized enterprises by means of loans to be paid with future profits (Lau, 1999; Li and Rozelle, 2004; Chen, 2006; McNally and Wright, 2010).

The large-scale expropriation of rural land was a second and powerful mechanism for primitive accumulation. Through the expropriation and commodification of rural land, capitalists gained a considerable share of the rents distributed to rural collectives – the original landlords. Although rural land is owned by rural collectives in China, local governments have the right to expropriate a certain amount in the name of the public interest. At the turn of the twenty-first century, the country went through an "epidemic" of expropriation, fueled by both the expansion of the housing market (inflated by rapid urbanization and speculation) and the fiscal needs of local governments (Riskin, 2008). Case studies show that fiscal revenue from land expropriation accounted for between thirty percent and sixty percent of total revenue at the municipal level in the mid-2000s (Tao *et al.*, 2010). An estimated seventy million farmers had lost their land by 2006 in return for "grossly inadequate" compensation (Riskin, 2008). Case studies that have attempted to measure the national mean value of compensation suggest that compensation to farmers

---

11   Note that these capitalists were not necessarily the new elites, although some of the new elites became well-known private entrepreneurs in the 1990s. See Sun (2004).

has been between one percent and ten percent of the price paid by those who received the grant of land (Tao *et al.*, 2010; Zhou, 2008; Guo, 2003). The country's arable land had shrunk to 1.827 billion mu by the end of 2008, only slightly above the 1.8 billion mu (120 million hectares) the government has set as the minimum needed for national food security.[12]

Privatization and the expropriation of land contributed to the formation of the low-road faction of private capitalists, whose accumulation mainly depends on access to cheap labor and cheap land. Layoffs after privatization of SOEs and the explosion in the number of landless migrants dramatically expanded the country's reserve army of labor while local governments' strategies for attracting investment prepared the conditions for cheap land.

While the compromise was a prominent feature at the central state level, the relationship between the state and private capital at the local level was more symbiotic. The central government pursued both social stability and economic growth whereas local officials, faced with meeting promotion incentives, tended to solely focus on economic growth. Especially since tax reforms in 1994, local government officials have sought to overcome budgetary constraints in a number of ways, including using their control over the conversion of rural land as a way to increase off-budget income and attract investments to their regions.[13] This difference has made the state-capital relationship more clientelist at the local level (Ong, 2012). On the one hand, private industrial investors are able to push local governments to expand the spatial possibility of accumulation via land expropriation and infrastructure building, pressuring them to provide lower labor standards, land costs, and environmental standards. Real estate developers have kept a significant share of the ground rent generated through local governments' infrastructure building that has contributed to urbanization and population concentration. On the other hand, both industrial investors and real estate developers have helped local governments to maintain solvency. In the early 2000s, to attract investments, local governments tended to individually negotiate with investors instead of holding public bids. In extreme cases around the Pearl River Delta, the price paid for land was virtually zero (Tao *et al.*, 2010). Moreover, given local governments' pursuit of

---

12 Source: *China Statistical Yearbook* 2009.
13 The legislation governing urban land ownership is distinct from rural land. In rural areas, there has been no concentration of land partly due to the collective regime. In cities, the real estate market functions the same as in most capitalist countries. Urban land is owned by the state, but private ownership is permitted in the case of urban real estate, which today is exchanged according to market rules. Anything that is built on urban land by private interests is classified as private property.

economic growth and urbanization, the annual land conversion quotas determined by the central government have been explicitly ignored (Zhou, 2008).

A comparison of real estate profits and net land transfer income shows some characteristics of the symbiotic relationship in which domestic capitalists achieve profits and local governments generate fiscal income from land transfers. From 1998 to 2015 (last data available), the gross land transfer income to local governments rose from 50.8 billion yuan to 3078.4 billion.[14] Local governments need to spend a significant part of their land transfer income on preliminary infrastructure construction and to a lesser extent compensation for land expropriation; thus, only the net land transfer income can be treated as gains by the local state. Figure 3.2 compares the growth of local governments' net land transfer income to that of real estate enterprises' profits from 2000 to 2015. The data show that the profits of real estate enterprises have grown more rapidly than has the net land transfer income of governments. The result has been a distorted system of urban land expropriation that benefits real estate developers and industrial entrepreneurs, alleviates local budget constraints, but places the cost of rapid urbanization on ex-peasants, which in turn coerces the landless to sell their labor power.

4   Strained Alliance

The rise of the low-road faction corresponded to the formation of an investment-led and export-led regime of accumulation. Export producers were the most important players in this regime, while the restructured state-owned sector also played a crucial role. With the support of the state-dominated banking system, SOEs and local governments carried out massive investments, particularly in infrastructure, which significantly promoted and stabilized economic growth under the regime. Favorable domestic conditions and the restructuring of global capitalism made China a world factory. However, this investment-led and export-led regime had contradictions which arose from both internal class conflicts and external constraints. Internally, this regime intensified social unrest while increasing wages for migrant workers threatened the sustainability of the regime. Externally, China's domestic capitalists were located at the lower end of the global value chain due to technological disadvantages, which also challenged the sustainability and profitability of the regime.

---

14   Sources: various issues of *China Fiscal Yearbook* and *China Land and Resources Statistical Yearbook*.

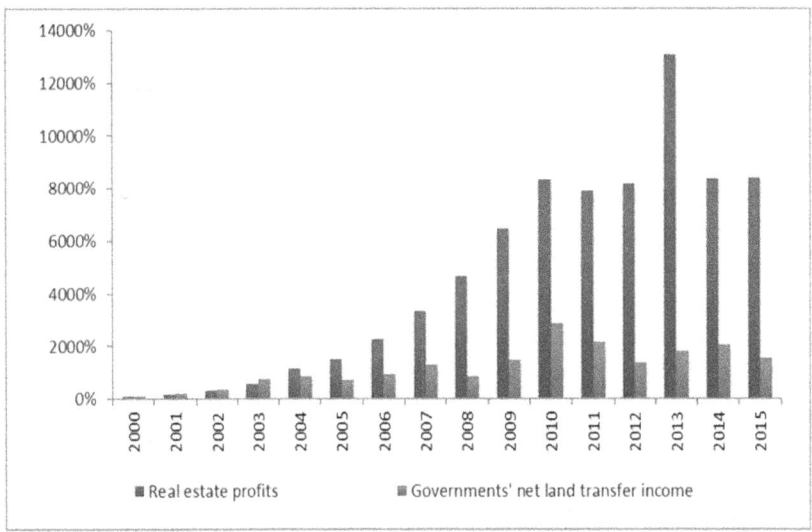

FIGURE 3.2   Growth of real estate profits and net land transfer income, 2000–2015 (2000 = 1)
Notes: Real estate profits are the profits of real estate enterprises. Governments' net land transfer income comprises total land transfer income less land transfer costs. Land transfer costs comprise governments' expenditures for the compensation of land acquisition and preliminary infrastructure construction. All values are in nominal terms. Both values in 2000 are set to 1. The Ministry of Finance does not report land transfer costs between 2000 and 2007. We thus have estimated the ratio of net land transfer income to land transfer income based on a linear trend and then calculated net land transfer income and land transfer costs using this estimated ratio
SOURCE: REAL ESTATE PROFITS AND BUILDING COSTS DATA COME FROM THE *CHINA STATISTICAL YEARBOOK* 2016. LAND TRANSFER INCOME AND LAND TRANSFER COSTS DATA COME FROM THE WEBSITE OF THE MINISTRY OF FINANCE

First, privatization and land expropriation led to social unrest, especially among laid-off workers and landless peasants. Due to reforms in the state-owned sector, about fifty million jobs were lost between 1995 and 2003 (Chavance, 2017), leading to a reserve army of laid-off workers and an explosive increase in job informality (Lee, 2016). Laid-off state employees spontaneously took to the streets, strongly anchored in the Maoist discourse of socialist rights and public ownership of the means of production. These protests of despair were also caused by the accelerated commercialization of public services, especially health and education, and the dismantling of *danwei* (work units), the former socialist system of urban social protection.[15] On the side of the landless peasants, over the course of the 2000s, conflicts over land were the main cause of mass incidents, due to the historical relationship between land use and social protection.[16] This social unrest demanded a more sustainable regime of accumulation to contain internal conflicts.

Second, since 2004, the rapidly growing export sector in coastal regions has experienced a labor shortage, leading to substantial increases in the wages of migrant workers (Lu, 2012). While there was a large reserve army of labor in both rural and urban areas thanks to demographic reasons and institutional shifts, labor processes in the export sector, characterized by long hours, high intensity, and low pay, meant that only some workers out of the reserve army met the needs and accepted such working conditions. As labor shortages continued, the struggles of migrant workers also increased, backed by stronger bargaining power.[17] The disadvantage of Chinese capitalists in the global value chain has restricted their capacity to absorb wage raises, making the export-led regime unsustainable.

Lastly, the state's "Trade Market for Technology" (TMFT) strategy failed. The TMFT strategy was promoted by the central government in the 1980s and 1990s as a replacement for the Maoist self-reliance strategy for technological progress. While no national leaders opposed introducing foreign technologies, there was a debate within the CCP leadership in the early 1980s about whether the self-reliance strategy should be abandoned. Supporters of introducing foreign technology dominated the state at the time; as a result, some crucial projects such as the Shanghai Y-10 aircraft were abandoned (Lu, 2006). The strategy adopted then was to encourage the transfer of advanced technologies by establishing joint ventures and allowing foreign firms to enter the domestic market and keep some monopoly (Lazonick and Li, 2012). However, this strategy failed to bring about sound technological transfers because these joint

---

15 This vacuum in social protection was only seriously addressed in the second half of the 2000s, after intense conflicts and varied mobilizations promoted by members of the precarious working class.

16 Equal distribution of land among the rural population has been the main social protection mechanism in the countryside since the end of the communes. But universal access to land in rural areas is an impediment to the formation of a landless poor class, as is the pattern in so many underdeveloped countries, and is the main guarantee of subsistence for rural workers in the absence of a social protection system. Not only do migrants return to their land when they lack work in cities, old and sick people find some form of protection against extreme poverty and destitution by having land rights. See Riskin (2008).

17 The number of labor disputes reported by the government increased by fourfold from 2000 to 2008. For more information, see the *China Statistical Yearbook*.

ventures typically only manufactured products and did not participate in any research and development activity (Lu, 2006; Zhou and Liu, 2016). The transformation of the global production network also made technology transfer ineffective. Criticism of the state's science and technology strategy arose from intellectuals. They were concerned that China's dependence on an unsuccessful technology transfer approach would jeopardize not only the sustainability of growth, but also economic independence and national security.

Given internal conflicts and external constraints, a consensus arose within the CCP that the party's political legitimacy had to be rebuilt and the social costs arising from the unleashed expansion of capitalism reduced (Wang, 2008; Hui, 2017). Since the mid-2000s, these contradictions and the consensus within the party have led to a re-adjustment of the relationship between the state and the new-born capitalist class, leading to what we call a stage of "strained alliance."

The state's initial strategy was to initiate systematic support for indigenous innovation, seeking to summarize a broad set of policies to stimulate innovation and the formation of global Chinese brands and technologies. As the evidence below shows, both state-owned companies and the innovation faction of private capitalists greatly benefited from this support. This strategy should be regarded as the state's response to the external constraints and internal contradictions mentioned above. While it is undeniable that these policies were associated with China's catching up with advanced countries in technologies and the state's pursuit of economic independence, they also reflect the state's motivation to reduce the economy's reliance on cheap labor.

These policies gained momentum in 2006 when the *Zizhu Chuangxin* ("Indigenous Innovation") program was launched by the Hu Jintao and Wen Jiabao administration.[18] This program set up a national plan involving several ministries in ambitious megaprojects. The indigenous innovation program adjusted the relationship between the state and domestic capitalists, requiring that the expansion of private capital takes into account political legitimacy and social conflicts. This program, along with the concept of a "Harmonious Society" proposed by the Hu-Wen administration and the "Common Prosperity" program proposed by President Xi Jinping, signaled that the new class should contribute to rebuilding the state's political legitimacy. The pursuit of technological progress has persisted under the current administration. It is interesting

---

18   This program further developed into the *Zhongguo Zhizao* 2025 ("Made in China 2025") program in 2015, which is believed by some analysts to be the real target of Donald Trump's trade war against China. Cf. Dodwell (2018).

to note that a significant proportion of private entrepreneurs invited by the symposium held by Xi Jinping in 2018 came from high-tech industries.

While the Indigenous Innovation program relied heavily on restructured SOEs, it supported private firms in a selective manner, revealing the state's tendency to adjust the regime of accumulation. Two instruments have been widely used as innovation policies based on domestic demand: public procurement and the choice of technical standards, both much contested by international competitors. Equivalent to 3.5 percent of GDP in 2016, government procurement was quickly perceived as an instrument for boosting national brands (Ministry of Finance of P.R.C., 2017). A main beneficiary of the program was Lenovo, a private company with a state-owned history. The choice of technical standards by the state has often been used in the telecommunications sector to support Chinese firms. Both Huawei and ZTE, two major Chinese telecommunication companies, were favored by the government's decision to select the V5.1 standard, used in switching systems for large capacity telephone exchanges and jointly developed by these two firms.[19] As most foreign firms did not produce systems under this standard, the expansion of domestic brands was significant until competitors from outside managed to adapt (Zhao et al., 2007; Nogueira, 2015). The third-generation mobile phone standard is a telling example of the cooperation between SOEs and the innovation faction. From the mid-2000s onwards, there have been reports of pressure from Chinese manufacturers for protecting indigenous technology via, for example, technical standards for mobile phones. In 2009, the government selected TD-SCDMA as the technical standard for third-generation mobile phones, after intense disputes between domestic state-owned operators, foreign manufacturers, and domestic private manufacturers (Lee, Mani, and Mu, 2012). The standard was developed by Datang, a SOE that had suffered from competition with foreign manufacturers (mainly Motorola and Nokia) and domestic operators but was supported by domestic manufacturers. In 2009, 3G TD-SCDMA was adopted nationally and accompanied by a national support program that provided domestic manufacturers with access to credit and subsidies (Gao and Liu, 2012; Nogueira, 2015).

Repressing the finance faction is the second part of the re-adjustment of the relationship between the state and the new capitalist class, and also is evidence of increased tensions in this relationship. This faction includes capitalists who speculate in major financial markets such as the stock market via commercial

---

19   Huawei is a private-owned company and ZTE is a state-owned but private-operated company.

banks, financial holding companies, investment funds, and insurance companies that they own or control. The rise of the finance faction has constituted a crucial part of the financial overdevelopment that took place when China's industrial sector lost momentum as the global economy was trapped in the 2008 Great Recession. The state stimulus package in 2009 and 2010 effectively postponed an economic slowdown in the PRC but finally lost momentum as the package dramatically increased the leverage of both local governments and SOEs, which gave rise to the significant expansion of a shadow-banking sector (Ehlers, Kong, and Zhu, 2018). The economic slowdown discouraged private non-financial investments. The annual real growth of private non-financial investment was minus 2.3 percent in 2017 – the lowest rate since the mid-1990s. Meanwhile, private capital in the financial faction increasingly concentrated and engaged in speculative activities that could threaten the overall financial stability and security.

This faction raised capital through the financial institutions that they own or control. Baoneng's hostile takeover of Vanke – one of China's largest real estate developers – is a well-known example. In 2015, as a private financial services conglomerate, Baoneng raised 26.2 billion yuan to buy Vanke stock, using asset management plans (AMP) issued by a financial company owned by Baoneng. The majority of the funds used for the takeover came from a few commercial banks, particularly China Zheshang Bank. This joint-stock commercial bank provided Baoneng with 13.3 billion yuan, which ultimately came from the bank's wealth management products (WMP) sold to households, especially rich ones (Hua, 2017). In 2018, Baoneng cashed out Vanke's stocks and harvested the profits. The speculative activities of this finance faction powered by the development of new financial products such as AMP and WMP not only disturbed the order of the stock market but also fed the bubble in 2014 and 2015.

One of the features that most strongly distinguishes China's accumulation regimes from other economies is its relative independence in relation to financialization (Lo, 2016). Financialization, which has affected the rhythms and modes of accumulation in many countries since the beginning of neoliberalism in the 1980s, has not penetrated the Chinese economy in the same way. For the most part, this is because of a state-controlled financial system in which the state imposes limits on short-term capital flows and speculation (Vermeiren and Dierckx, 2012). However, the finance faction, together with foreign interests, are the ones pushing for the opening of China's capital account. In March 2017, during the Fifth Session of the Twelfth National People's Congress, executives from the financial and civil construction sectors openly criticized capital controls for hindering Chinese acquisitions abroad, which demonstrates the two-way movement between state forces and capitalists' interests (Bloomberg News, 2017). So far, Chinese financial expansion has maintained relative autonomy in relation to the power of the U.S. dollar. But internal and external pressures are strong, and China's outflow of capital in 2016 showed its vulnerability to unregulated speculative movements. From 2015 to 2016, during a period of limited financial liberalization, China lost almost half a trillion dollars in international reserves, bringing total reserves down to below USD three trillion for the first time since 2011 (Tsui *et al.*, 2017; Chen, 2017). Since then, the government has imposed more stringent regulations on overseas investments by private capital. Tycoons such as Wanda Group and HNA Group have had to reduce their overseas investments due to these regulations.

Likewise, a wave of multi-pronged regulatory crackdown has hit a dozen of giant private techs since late 2020, including Alibaba, Baidu, ByteDance, Didi, Meituan and Tencent, and also major companies from sectors such as private education and gaming. Although there are several motives behind the regulatory crackdown, it is clear that leaders in Beijing do not want technology and educational sectors dependent on IPOs in the U.S. and on complex international financial vehicles in order to gain markets. Similarly, Chinese leaders do not want these sectors to be subject to U.S. regulatory maneuvers or to represent strategic vulnerabilities amid to a cyber or data control conflict that may take different forms.

The social tension generated by this fracture within the capitalist class is reflected in domestic struggles. Since President Xi Jinping's anti-corruption campaign began in 2012, thousands of corrupt officials have been arrested and punished, as well as some capitalists and officials who have made a fortune in the financial system. Wu Xiaohui, a member of the finance faction with strong ties to former high-level officials, was arrested in June 2017. Wu Xiaohui's holding company, Anbang Insurance Group, is one of the largest in the country, and has been notable for its billion-dollar purchases of luxury hotels around the world. In November 2016, Wu tried to close a Manhattan hotel deal with Jared Kushner, the son-in-law and adviser to U.S. President Donald Trump (Haas, 2017). This case is just one glaring example of the connections of a faction of Chinese capitalists with international capital, which the current Chinese leadership is trying to contain via intense internal struggle.

5 Conclusion

We have shown how the formation and transformation of a capitalist class and its factions is intertwined with the dominant accumulation regime. In

TABLE 3.2 Relationship between the Chinese state and the domestic private capitalist class

	Privatization and land expropriation	Low-road faction	Innovation faction	Finance faction
Contradictions of the accumulation regime	Accumulation by dispossession Inducing social unrest among laid-offs and landless peasants	Reliance on cheap labor and cheap land, inducing labor unrest and peasants' struggles. Unsustainable due to rising wage and global economic downturn	Conflict between domestic capital and foreign capital in technology transfer and monopoly power	Financial instability and insecurity due to speculation and demands for financial liberalization. Undermining incentives for capital accumulation
State-domestic private capital relation	Great Compromise	Great Compromise	Strained Alliance	Strained Alliance
State's forces	Deng's Southern tour and push for marketization	State's pursuit for legitimacy through promoting economic growth	Economic independence in technological progress and releasing labor unrest	Economic independence in financial expansion
Capitalists' forces	Rise of new elites as a result of the 1980s reform	Manufacturing capitalists' pursuit for profits and competitiveness in global markets	Moving up in the global value chain	Rise of the finance faction in the context of economic slowdown

the period of a "great compromise," the state responded to pressure to reform the economy and strengthen the strategic positioning of the remaining SOEs. Likewise, the expropriation of peasants' land and the explosion of investments in housing and infrastructure greatly facilitated the emergence of China's first billionaires and paved the way for investment-led growth. In the period of "strained alliance," the conflicts generated by primitive accumulation were partially cooled by the rhetoric of a "harmonious society" and systematic state support for indigenous innovation. However, the factional basis of China's capitalist class, rapidly accelerated by financial expansion, generated new pressures on the state. The state responded by intensifying its repressive apparatus through, among other things, the anti-corruption campaign of President Xi Jinping (Table 3.2).

We reject the claim that the state firmly controls the new capitalist class. In our view, the seeming autonomous power of the Chinese state can only be fully understood by taking into account the historical trajectory of social relations. The state's autonomy is a legacy of the 1911 Revolution and class struggle that led to the foundation of the PRC. While the state in the reform era abandoned some of the goals of the earlier Maoist regime, it has retained the goals of economic development and enhanced living standards in order to maintain political legitimacy and to contain social conflicts. This autonomy is also the result of a gradualist path of reform. In contrast to a more radical path that led to economic recession and political rebuilding in Russia, the gradualist path assumed by the Chinese government and Chinese Communist Party has enabled the historical trajectory to play the role of generating persistent effects during the reform era. This also means an analysis of contemporary Chinese political economy should regard the state as a social relation with historical dynamics, rather than reducing the state to either a neutral supra-class or a servant of the capitalist class.

References

Bloomberg News. (2017). China's Capital Control Trigger to Backlash after Scrapped Deals. *Bloomberg News*, March 7. Accessed March 14. https://www.bloomberg.com/news/articles/2017-03-07/china-s-capital-controls-trigger-a-backlash-after-deals-thwarted.

Brunhoff, S. de. (1978). *The State, Capital and Economic Policy*. London: Pluto Press.

Byres, T. J. (2009). The Landlord Class, Peasant Differentiation, Class Struggle and the Transition to Capitalism: England, France and Prussia Compared. *Journal of Peasant Studies* 36 (1): 33–54.

Chang, D. (2013). Labour and the 'Developmental State': A Critique of the Developmental State Theory of Labour. In: Fine, B.; Saraswati, J.; Tavasci, D. (Eds.) *Beyond the Developmental State: Industrial Policy Into the 21st Century*, 85–109. London: Pluto.

Chavance, B. (2017). Ownership Transformation and System Change in China. *Revue de la régulation* 21 (Spring). Accessed June 4, 2018. http://journals.openedition.org/regulation/12298.

Chen, F. (2006). Privatization and Its Discontents in Chinese Factories. *The China Quarterly* 185: 42–60.

Chen, L. (2017). Containing Capital Outflows. *Gavekal*, February 15. Accessed May 2, 2018. https://research.gavekal.com/.

Cox, R. W. (1981). Social Forces, States and World Orders: Beyond International Relations Theory. *Millennium: Journal of International Studies* 10 (2): 126–155.

Dickson, B. J. (2008). *Wealth into Power: The Communist Party's Embrace of China's Private Sector*. New York: Cambridge University Press.

Dodwell, D. (2018). The Real Target of Trump's Trade War Is 'Made in China 2025'. *South China Morning Post*, June 17. Accessed July 2. https://www.scmp.com/business/global-economy/article/2151177/real-target-trumps-trade-war-made-china-2025.

Ehlers, T.; Kong, S.; Zhu, F. (2018). Mapping Shadow Banking in China: Structure and Dynamics. *Bank for International Settlements Working Papers* (701).

Evans, P. B. (1989). Predatory, Developmental, and Other Apparatuses: A Comparative Political Economy Perspective on the Third World State. *Sociological Forum* 4 (4): 561–587.

Fine, B. (2013). Beyond the Developmental State: An Introduction. In: Fine, B.; Saraswati, J.; Tavasci, D. (Eds.) *Beyond the Developmental State: Industrial Policy into the 21st Century*, 1–32. London: Pluto.

Gao, X.; Liu, J. (2012). Catching up Through the Development of Technology Standard: The Case of TD-SCDMA in China. *Telecommunications Policy* 36c (7): 531–545.

Gordon, D. M. (1996). *Fat and Mean: The Corporate Squeeze of Working Americans and the Myth of Managerial "Downsizing"*. New York: Martin Kessler Books.

Guo, B. (2003). Political Legitimacy and China's Transition. *Journal of Chinese Political Science* 8 (1–2): 1–25.

Haas, B. (2017). Chinese Tycoon Reportedly Caught up in Sweeping Corruption Crackdown. *The Guardian*, June 14. Accessed June 20. http://www.theguardian.com/world/2017/jun/14/chinese-tycoon-reportedly-caught-up-anti-corruption-crackdown-wu-xiaohui-anbang.

Heberer, T.; Schubert, G. (2019). Weapons of the Rich: Strategic Behavior and Collective Action of Private Entrepreneurs in China. *Modern China* 45 (5): 471–503.

Howell, J. (2006). Reflections on the Chinese State. *Development and Change* 37 (2): 273–297.

Howell, J.; Pringle, T. (2019). Shades of Authoritarianism and State – Labour Relations in China. *British Journal of Industrial Relations* 57 (2): 223–246.

Hu, H. (1989). '1988 Nian Zhongguo Zujin Jiazhi De Gusuan' [An Estimate of the Value of Rent in China in 1988]. *Jingji Shehui Tizhi Bijiao* [*Comparative Economic Systems*] 5: 10–15.

Hua, S. (2017). *Wanke Moshi Kongzhi Quan Zhizheng Yu Gongsi Zhili* [*The Mode of Vanke: The Battle Over Control and Corporate Governance*]. Beijing: Dongfang Press.

Hui, E. S. (2017). Putting the Chinese State in its Place: A March from Passive Revolution to Hegemony. *Journal of Contemporary Asia* 47 (1): 66–92.

Jessop, B. (2008). *State Power: A Strategic-Relational Approach*. Cambridge: Polity Press.

Kotz, D. M. (2015). *The Rise and Fall of Neoliberal Capitalism*. Cambridge, MA: Harvard University Press.

Kotz, D. M.; Weir, F. (1997). *Revolution from Above: The Demise of the Soviet System*. New York: Routledge.

Lau, W. K. (1999). The 15th Congress of the Chinese Communist Party: Milestone in China's Privatization. *Capital & Class* 23 (2): 51–87.

Lazonick, W.; Li, Y. (2012). China's Path to Indigenous Innovation. Working paper.

Lee, C. K. (2016). Precarization or Empowerment? Reflections on Recent Labor Unrest in China. *The Journal of Asian Studies* 75 (2): 317–333.

Lee, K.; Mani, S.; Mu, Q. (2012). Explaining Divergent Stories of Catch-up in the Telecommunication Equipment Industry in Brazil, China, India and Korea. In: Malerba, F.; Nelson, R. R. (Eds.) *Economic Development as a Learning Process: Variation Across Sectoral Systems*, 21–71. Northampton, MA: Edward Elgar.

Li, H.; Rozelle, S. (2004). Insider Privatization with a Tail: The Screening Contract and Performance of Privatized Firms in Rural China. *Journal of Development Economics* 75 (1): 1–26.

Li, W. (2001). Corruption During the Economic Transition in China. University of Virginia Working Paper.

Lo, D. (2016). Developing or Under-developing? Implications of China's 'Going Out' for Late Development. London: School of Oriental and African Studies Department of Economics Working Paper No. 198.

Lu, F. (路风). (2006). *Zouxiang Zizhu Chuangxin* [*Towards Indigenous Innovation*]. Guilin: Guangxi Normal University Press.

Lu, F. (卢峰). (2012). Wage Trends among Chinese Migrant Workers: 1979–2010. In Chinese. *Zhongguo Shehui Kexue* [*Social Sciences in China*] 7: 47–68.

Marx, K. (1976). *Capital*, Volume 1. London: Penguin Books.

McNally, C. A.; Wright, T. (2010). Sources of Social Support for China's Current Political Order: The 'Thick Embeddedness' of Private Capital Holders. *Communist and Post-Communist Studies* 43 (2): 189–198.

Meisner, M. (1996). *The Deng Xiaoping Era: An Inquiry into the Fate of Chinese Socialism 1978–1994*. New York: Hill and Wang.

Ministry of Finance of P.R.C. 2017. 2016 Nian Quanguo Zhengfu Caigou Jianyao Qingkuang [National Government Procument in 2016]. Accessed May 10, 2018.http://gks.mof.gov.cn/zhengfucaigouguanli/201708/t20170824_2683523.html.

Naughton, B. (2017). Is China Socialist? *Journal of Economic Perspectives* 31 (1): 3–24.

Nogueira, I. (2015). Policies to Promote the Rise of China in the Global Value Chains. In: Cintra, M. A. M; Filho, E. B. S.; Pinto, E. C. (Eds.) *China in Transformation: Economic and Geopolitical Dimensions of Development* (in Portuguese), 45–79. Brasilia: IPEA.

Ong, L. H. (2012). Between Developmental and Clientelist States: Local State-Business Relationships in China. *Comparative Politics* 44 (2): 191–209.

van der Pijl, K. (2012). Is the East Still Red? The Contender State and Class Struggles in China. *Globalizations* 9 (4): 503–516.

van der Pijl, K. (2016). Le transnational et le national dans la formation de la classe capitaliste. *Actuel Marx* 60 (2): 75–89.

Piketty, T.; Yang, L.; Zucman, G. (2017). Capital Accumulation, Private Property and Rising Inequality in China, 1978–2015. *NBER Working Paper* No. 23368.

Pun, N.; Huilin, L. (2010). Unfinished Proletarianization: Self, Anger, and Class Action among the Second Generation of Peasant-Workers in Present-Day China. *Modern China* 36 (5): 493–519.

Qi, H. (2014). The Labor Share Question in China. *Monthly Review* 65 (8): 23–35.

Qi, H. (2018). 'Distribution According to Work': An Historical Analysis of the Incentive Systemin China's State-Owned Sector. *Review of Radical Political Economics* 50 (2): 409–426.

Riskin, C. (2008). Property Rights and the Social Costs of Transition and Development in China. *Economic & Political Weekly* 43 (52): 37–42.

Smith, C.; Pun, N. (2018). Class and Precarity: An Unhappy Coupling in China's Working Class Formation. *Work, Employment & Society* 32 (3): 599–615.

So, A. Y. (2003). The Changing Pattern of Classes and Class Conflict in China. *Journal of Contemporary Asia* 33 (3): 363–376.

Sun, L. (2004). *Zhuanxing yu Duanlie [Transformation and Rupture]*. Beijing: Tsinghua University Press.

Tao, R.; Su, F.; Liu, M.; Cao, G. (2010). Land Leasing and Local Public Finance in China's Regional Development: Evidence from Prefecture-Level Cities. *Urban Studies* 47 (10): 2217–2236.

Tsui, S.; Wong, E.; Chi, L. K.; Wen, T. (2017). The Tyranny of Monopoly-Finance Capital: A Chinese Perspective. *Monthly Review* 68 (9): 29–42.

Vermeiren, M.; Dierckx, S. (2012). Challenging Global Neoliberalism? The Global Political Economy of China's Capital Controls. *Third World Quarterly* 33 (9): 1647–1668.

Vogel, E. F. (2011). *Deng Xiaoping and the Transformation of China*. Cambridge, MA: Harvard University Press.

Wang, H. (2011). *The End of the Revolution: China and the Limits of Modernity*. London: Verso Books.

Wang, S. (2008). The Great Transformation: Two-way Movement in China Since the 1980s. *Zhongguo Shehui Kexue* [*Social Sciences in China*] 1: 129–148.

Wang, S; Hu, A. (1993). *Zhongguo Guojia Nengli Baogao* [*Report on China's State Capacity*]. Shenyang: Liaoning People's Press.

Yan, H.; Chen, Y. (2015). Agrarian Capitalization Without Capitalism? Capitalist Dynamics from Above and Below in China. *Journal of Agrarian Change* 15 (3): 366–391.

Yao, Y. (2010). The End of the Beijing Consensus: Can China's Model of Authoritarian Growth Survive? *Foreign Affairs* 2: 2–5.

Yao, Y. (2011). *Zhongguo Daolu De Shijie Yiyi* [*World Significance of China's Road*]. Beijing:Peking University Press.

Zhang, C. (2019). Asymmetric Mutual Dependence between the State and Capitalists in China. *Politics & Society* 47 (2): 149–176.

Zhang, S. (2016). *Zhongguo Jingjixue Fengyun Shi* [*The History of Chinese Economic Studies Part I Volume 2*]. Singapore: World Scientific.

Zhao, Z.; Huang, X.; Ye, D.; Gentle, P. (2007). China's Industrial Policy in Relation to Electronics Manufacturing. *China & World Economy* 15 (3): 33–51.

Zhou, F. (2008). Creating Wealth: Land Seizure, Local Government, and Farmers. In: Davis, D. S.; Feng, W. (Eds.) *Creating Wealth and Poverty in Postsocialist China*, 112–125. Stanford, CA: Stanford University Press.

Zhou, Yu; Liu, X. (2016). Evolution of Chinese State Policies on Innovation. In: Zhou, Y.; Lazonick, W.; Sun, Y. (Eds.) *China as an Innovation Nation*, 33–67. Oxford: Oxford University Press.

PART 2

China's Global Expansion and the Technological Dispute

CHAPTER 4

Recent Chinese Expansion: State, Capital and Accumulation on a Global Scale

Valéria Lopes Ribeiro

1   Introduction[1]

Four decades ago, between the end of the 1970s and the beginning of the 1980s, China began a long process of economic opening with profound changes in its social structure and impacts throughout the world. The Chinese industrialization process of the last decades, allied to urbanization and modernization, allowed the country's economic growth and the leading of China to the position of one of the largest economies in the world[2] through the maintenance of the leadership of the Chinese Communist Party (CCP).

The consolidation of economic growth coincided with the wide insertion of the country in international capitalism, starting in the late 1970s, through a process of economic opening and transformation of the socialist model inaugurated with the victory of the Chinese Revolution of 1949.

From this period, with the creation of the People's Republic of China, the implementation of a project of national ascension and construction of socialism began through a series of policies aimed at industrialization, mainly regarding base and military industries, which were fundamental to consolidate the foundations of Chinese development. According to Anderson (2018), it was a revolutionary process that, in opposition to what took place in the USSR, gradually undermined the supremacy of the adversary in terms of force and control of consent, broke the state monopoly and rooted the socialist project at the very beginning among the base strata of the population, thus ensuring a unique and lasting degree of social penetration.

---

1 I'd like to thank Professor Esther Majerowicz for her careful reading and her comments on the draft version of this chapter. Any errors and omissions are the sole responsibility of the author.
2 In 2019, China's GDP was US$22.526 trillion in Purchasing Power Parity (PPP) terms at constant 2017 prices and US$23.460 trillion in PPP at current prices. In the case of the US, GDP in PPP at constant prices was US$ 20.524 trillion, and in terms of PPP at current prices, US$ 21.374 trillion. (World Bank, 2020).

After about three decades since the founding of the People's Republic of China under the command of Mao Zedong, in the late 1970s the country entered a period of rupture, with the death of Mao and the rise of Deng Xiaoping to the post of greater leadership within the Party. At that point, Deng articulated within the CCP the implementation of a proposal already discussed since the mid-1960s, the so-called Four Modernizations (Agrarian, Industrial, Defense, and Science and Technology). The Chinese socialist regime would undergo profound changes and the rupture of a way of life that had been built since the creation of the People's Republic. Among the measures around the Four Modernizations, the following stand out: the dismantling of the commune regime, even though land in the countryside remained State property; the end of the state regime of social protection, which guaranteed rights to workers in the countryside and especially in the cities through the free and universal provision of education and health; a process of property diversification which accompanied the end of the monopoly of state and collective property and the beginning of privatizations; and also the trade opening, which came through the country's rapprochement with the US and made way for the insertion of Chinese economy in Asian and global production chains.

This economic transition took place through the maintenance of the CCP's political power and the State's control over the economy, but in a context of opening and international integration, shaping the path of economic growth via investments, mainly state-owned, exports, technology imports and attraction of direct foreign investment.

Thus, the Chinese trajectory since Deng Xiaoping represented the victory of a political line present within the CCP, which defended the development of the productive forces as priority, as opposed to the development of production relations. This polarization was already present in the mid-1960s and would prove to be an important dimension of the events of the Cultural Revolution. At that time, the dispute around the deepening of the construction of socialism, through practices that went beyond the development of the productive forces, took on the contours of a profound criticism of state bureaucracy, which led to broad popular mobilization and efforts towards political control by the base (Badiou, 2020; Bettelheim, 1979; Motta, 2013).

Deng's ascension to the post of Great Leader in China consolidates, in a certain way, the victory of the Chinese option for the development of productive forces, to the detriment of the advancement of production relations. Based on a profound critique of the period of the Cultural Revolution, the veteran leaders of the CCP will form the hegemonic political force that will fight against the so-called "leftist tendencies". As Souza (2018) states, making a reference to the book *Brief History of the Communist Party of China*, after the death of Mao the CCP built its vision of China from a general tone of (careful) criticism of the theory and practice of the "cultural revolution"[3] and of Mao Zedong's methods, which "are completely wrong". Mao's ideas about socialism are deemed "utopian, disconnected from reality" (Oficina, 1994 *apud* Souza, 2018: 31).

According to Bettelheim (1979: 179), "at the end of 1976, a new course took shape, corresponding to the victory of a revisionist line and the existing bourgeoisie within the Party". From then on, Deng Xiaoping will successfully materialize the vision that, in order to overcome the crisis situation and move towards modernization and prosperity, China should follow the direction of reforms and economic opening.

Thus, throughout the 1980s, reforms went full steam ahead, with the dissolution of communes, the creation of Special Economic Zones and the privatization of some sectors of the economy, all of which introduced advances and also contradictions in Chinese society. At the end of the decade, faced with what could be presented as a new internal dispute and social split – the protests in Tiananmen Square –, Deng again articulated his vision within the Party through the so-called "great commitment" (Marti, 2007). On that occasion, through an alliance with the internal (mainly coastal) elites and the Army, Deng defended the continuity of the opening project and the further development of the productive forces by maintaining the political model centered on the leadership of the CCP (Marti, 2007).

From this perspective, the trajectory of expansion and economic growth in China in recent decades can be seen as the expression of the construction of a path that, although based on the permanence of the centrality of the State, also represents a rupture, rather than a continuation, with the formerly prevalent socialist model.

Thus, contrary to what claims Losurdo (2004) – for whom Deng Xiaoping's reforms are a new national pact that reunites the internal classes (bourgeoisie and proletariat) in defense of the anti-colonial struggle and in favor of nationalism and socialism –, the economic reforms and the movement to resume relations with the United States represented a political option that certainly led China towards the affirmation of a national project, but also towards a break with the construction of socialism and towards the country's increasing integration to international capitalism.

It is a fact that the nationalist project of modernization has come to fruition over the last few decades in China. Since the 1980s, the country has

---

3 All English translations of direct quotations of texts originally written in Portuguese were done by the author.

been able to grow at significant rates, lift thousands of people out of poverty, increase GDP per capita, expand its technological base, and achieve national sovereignty simply unimaginable for most Western peripheral economies in the context of neoliberalism, thus fulfilling a national development project.

As Amin (2013) points out, recent Chinese state capitalism was built in pursuit of three objectives: to build a modern, integrated and sovereign industrial system; to manage the relationship between such system and the small rural production; and to control China's integration into the world system, dominated by the generalized monopolies of the imperialist triad (United States, Europe and Japan). According to the author, and also as advocated by the CCP, the pursuit of these three priority objectives has made possible the progress on the long road to socialism (Amin, 2013).

However, at the same time, according to Amin (2013), this search undertaken by China strengthens trends that may lead to the abandonment of the socialist possibility in favor of pure and simple capitalist development. For Amin, this conflict is inevitable and has always been present: rather than defining whether China is socialist or capitalist, he argues, the fundamental question is to analyze how China's concrete choices have favored one path or the other (Amin, 2013). In this perspective, it is essential to understand recent China through a consideration of its advances (mainly in the construction of national sovereignty) and its efforts in economic development via the State; but one should also consider the deep contradictions derived from the political choice for modernization through insertion in international capitalism using (domestic and foreign) capital.

In his *"On the correct treatment of contradictions among the people"* (1957), Mao Zedong reflects on the contradictions of Chinese society in the quest for socialism, stating that they would be part of the process. The contradictions between the bourgeoisie and the workers, as much as they were antagonistic, could assume a non-antagonistic character, consistent with the project of the construction of socialism.

It is necessary, however, to consider that Mao was writing in a specific context: one in which, unlike the current one, the dispute between capitalism and socialism was concrete, and China organized in its own way the advancement of socialist construction via industrialization, collectivized agricultural production and expansion of workers' rights. It was a trajectory that used to remain coherent with the strengthening of labor emancipation and the reduction of the role of the bourgeoisie and private interests.

In the current period, as Amin suggests, despite modernization, China has not started to reorganize work around the axis of the socialization of the economy (Amin, 2013), as precognized by the Maoist construction of socialism. Contrary to this effort, according to Souza, the process of reforms and opening led to a situation in which

> There is a more general process of structuring the plurality of Chinese and foreign capital within the Chinese economy. Beyond the surface of the market and the phenomenon of economic growth, it is necessary to understand the essence and depth of the growing rooting of all the extensive and multiple determinations characteristic of the domination of capital, with the recrudescence of the division of society into social classes.
> SOUZA, 2018: 22

In this sense, the challenge of understanding the process of recent Chinese economic growth and its external projection requires the analysis of the relations between the State and market/capital, which have been guiding this process since the economic opening and shaping internal transformations related to the expansion of the space allowed to private capital, in addition to the insertion in international capitalism.

As Nogueira (2018) pointed out, in recent decades the Chinese accumulation regime was based on the use of mechanisms aimed at the concentration of capital in the hands of domestic capitalists, who established a close relationship with the Party-State. The State itself intended to leverage this domestic capital and use it for the benefit of material expansion and the development of the productive forces; at the same time, this process meant that the internal capitalist class began to exert a strong influence over the course of accumulation, prioritizing its own interests. Through this lens, Nogueira (2018) highlights the idea that the Chinese State is not detached from the concrete struggles of classes in formation and transformation, and that it is essential to understand how the capitalist class acts internally, whether via privatizations, land expropriations, support for the technological modernization of domestic capital, or the opening of the financial system.

The acceleration of economic growth in China, initiated by the economic opening through capital accumulation and expansion of space for private capital under state supervision, made the country achieve large-scale growth. In recent years, this trajectory of ascension based on industrialization and modernization has reached a level from which China has projected itself into the world, in a process that is already widely perceptible, whether through the expansion of investments and financial flows throughout the globe or in the deepening of the diplomatic and political relations it establishes.

Since the beginning of the 21st century, and especially in its second decade, China has been expanding its investments abroad through companies interested in expanding consumer markets, always focused on the search for essential natural resources and on technological acquisition. This external projection occurs in parallel with the increase in institutional mechanisms that facilitate this process and the strong financial leverage from banks and institutions. More recently, the country launched a large-scale investment plan called the *Belt and Road Initiative*.

In a demonstration that Chinese socialism was entering a new era, one marked by overcoming internal challenges and the intention of projecting the Chinese model outward, at the Nineteenth Communist Party Congress in 2017, President Xi Jinping stated that

> The system and culture of socialism with Chinese characteristics has been constantly developing, expanding the avenues towards modernization for developing countries, providing completely new options for countries and nations who wish to accelerate their development while maintaining their own independence, and contributing Chinese wisdom and the Chinese plan to solve the problems of mankind.
> XI JINPING, cited in LIMA, 2017

According to Lin Chun (2018), this CCP posture forwards the idea that the country has a global strategy, one based on the assumption that everyone could follow the path of socialism, in a kind of global optimism in the name of spreading its own brand of socialism. However, for the author, the projection of the Chinese model comes up against deep contradictions linked to the country's subordination to the logic of capitalism. Thus, what is currently presented as Chinese "globalism" actually represents a complete rupture with the socialist and anti-imperialist revolutionary internationalism that was present during the Maoist period.

According to Chun (2018), during the Maoist period, the Chinese external projection had two fundamental dimensions: defending national sovereignty based on ethnic equity and solidarity; and supporting countries in the third world socialist field. Tenets such as overcoming unequal capitalism and defending revolutionary nationalism were inscribed in this foreign policy, so that Chinese nationalism was not detached from the realignment of post-war global politics: it was nationalist and intrinsically internationalist (Chun, 2018).[4]

According to Chun (2018), after the fall of the USSR, China isolated itself, and the nationalists who took the lead of the Party broke with the class nature characteristic of the third world version, allying themselves with the United States and abandoning the internationalist nationalist project and third world countries.

In this sense, recent Chinese "globalism" is part of the idea of abandoning the anti-imperialist struggle and of the project of inserting China into global capitalism as a new space for capitalist accumulation and exploitation. Decades since the opening, Chinese "globalism" is only the deepening of this strategy through the opening of capital, privatizations, and the projection of its own capital in the world.

The controversies related to the Chinese rise and its external projection lead to several questions, such as: how does Chinese external projection reflect the current moment of capital accumulation in the country and State/capital relations?

After four decades of growth, China faces a new stage of its internal accumulation, related both to the limits of growth at higher rates and to the challenge of transitioning towards an economy based on innovation. This current stage is also characterized by the increasing presence of interests represented by

---

[4] The history of the People's Republic of China's foreign policy is marked by its non-alignment with the main powers, the U.S. and the USSR. Although supported by the USSR in the early years of the Revolution, China pursued an independent foreign policy based on its own principles. In 1955, the country took part in the Bandung Afro-Asian Conference, defining from then on the guidelines and principles of its foreign policy: mutual respect for territorial integrity and sovereignty between states; non-aggression between states; non-interference in the internal politics of States; equality and mutual benefit among States; and peaceful coexistence (Wang, 2018 *apud* Santos, 2020). In 1961, when the Bloc of Non-Aligned Countries, or Non-Aligned Movement, was formed, China was present through Zhou Enlai (PRC), defending the fight against colonialism, racism and hegemonism, and supporting the peaceful resolution of international conflicts and the self-determination of peoples (Santos, 2020). Although founded on the idea of non-intervention, in practice China was on the side of third world countries. According to Chun (2018), "China was visibly among the progressive countries across all three continents, extending its support to struggles ranging from Congolese independence, and the Algerian revolution, to the construction and financing of TAZARA, the only long-distance railway in sub-Saharan Africa, which connected Tanzania and Zambia and was completed in the early 1970s. In fact, China maintained a broad aid program and friendly diplomacy with third world countries, offering subsidies, interest-free loans and construction, training and services projects which involved technology transfer, especially in agriculture. China's international conduct was an example of an alternative practice to the relationship between the first and third world". (Chun, 2018: 389).

private capital, which in turn has also been influencing the country's external projection. It is by understanding the characteristics of this new stage of accumulation that one can understand the way in which China has been projecting itself externally in its relationship with the various countries of the world.

In this chapter, we seek to advance in the analysis of the Chinese accumulation process through the investigation of the characteristics of the current stage of growth and the analysis of the relationship between State and Capital, seeking to understand how these issues have been influencing the way China projects itself externally.

As Jessop (2002) suggests, the form taken by capital accumulation depends on the relationship between State and the market, that is, the relationship between the political and the economic, which influence each other in determining the paths of capital accumulation. For Jessop, "several relevant social class struggles shape the ways in which the various contradictions and dilemmas of capital come to be expressed in specific conjunctures" (Jessop, 2002: 17). In this sense, the State cannot be taken as an autonomous and monolithic entity, but rather as a sphere in dispute, in which interests and social classes determine and influence decision-making.

As Bastiaan van Apeldoorn (2017) suggests, in the analysis of foreign policy it is necessary to empirically examine how state agents are embedded in a broader field of forces and how they are particularly related to the general class structure, through which the connection between State and capital, beyond mere structural interdependence, must be seen as intrinsically related. Class is thus seen as the causal link between the process of capital accumulation and concomitant interests. National interests are political constructs that serve a particular social purpose, making it imperative to analyze how decision-makers are operating across a wide field of social forces (van Apeldoorn, 2017).

As Poulantzas points out, there is a complex and intrinsic relationship between the capitalist State and the bourgeoisie in which the State does not directly represent the economic interests of the dominant classes, but their political interests. This complex relationship with the bourgeoisie will also shape the action of States at the international level, whether in the metropolises or dependent countries (Bugiato, 2014).

It is important to point out that the role of the State in conducting accumulation processes in China is unquestionable. Furthermore, the Chinese state is the result of a historical formation that is largely different from that of Western countries. Even so, from the moment China enters international capitalism, expanding the use of capital and transforming the social relations of production, the State must be understood in its relationship to the processes of accumulation and to its internal interests. It's not possible to avoid an interpretation based on the analysis of State/capital relations.

It is also important to point out that, as China deepens its insertion in international capitalism, it is also inserted in a context of interstate disputes marked by the search for, and affirmation of, national powers. This reality also shapes China's own decisions regarding its strategy of national affirmation and accumulation.

Faced with the various dimensions of the subject in question, namely, the process of expansion of China in the world, in this chapter we analyze a specific dimension, namely, the relationship between Chinese external projection and the current moment of capital accumulation in the country. We will also try to investigate how the relationship between State and capital influences the external projection through a dialectical relationship in which strategic and class interests seem to be increasingly intertwined.

2   Political Economy and the Growth Cycle

Since 2001, in the Tenth Five-Year Plan, a growth cycle has been affirmed in China, driven by investments in infrastructure and the expansion of heavy industry, in addition to the increase in the automobile industry and the consumption of automobiles in the domestic market. This growth cycle was marked by the continuity and expansion of state investments, the urbanization process, and civil construction (Ribeiro, 2013; Medeiros, 2013).

Through this cycle, the Chinese economy was able to grow at 10.37% per year in the first decade of the 21st century, with an average GDP per capita growth rate of 9.72% per year (WorldBank, 2021). In 2001, the share of GDP in terms of industry added value was 44.7%; services represented 41.2%, and agriculture, 13.98% (World Bank, 2021). In 2006, heavy industry represented 70% of Gross Industrial Product, while light industry represented 30% (NBS, 2016).

In this cycle, the country added thousands of workers and expanded China's share of global manufacturing output, continuing the growth trajectory driven by Deng Xiaoping's reforms.

It was also during this cycle that the country started increasing the use of primary resources, from raw materials for industry, such as iron ore and copper, to essential energy resources, such as oil. The country lived with the structural imperative of accessing primary goods, to the extent that the expansion of growth depended on these resources, even though China had an important base of natural resources of its own. Based on this imperative, the Chinese government and state-owned companies approached many regions that had ample resources, such as Latin America and Africa, and the interest in access to primary and energy resources stimulated the import and expansion of direct investments in several countries.

It is through these characteristics linked to the specific cycle of growth that one must understand the Chinese external projection of the first decade of the 21st century, materialized in the expansion of imports and foreign investments, with state-owned companies playing a fundamental role – the so-called "big SOEs" ("state-owned enterprises") – in fields such as oil, mining and construction (Shambaugh, 2013).

Associated with this imperative linked to the Chinese material base, a policy was designed to support the expansion of companies: the "Going Out" strategy. In 2001, Chinese Vice Premier Wu Bangguo officially announced the strategy, and in the same year Premier Zhu Rongji, in his political address to the People's Congress, officially used the term "going global" to outline a strategy for Chinese companies. Since then, Chinese officials and think tanks have come to recognize the relationship between *Yinjinlai* [引进来], literally meaning 'inviting in' (foreign direct investment coming in) and *Zouchuqu* [走出去], or 'going global' (foreign direct investment going abroad)", as part of the modernization course that the country had been undertaking (Power et al., 2012: 101).

The going out strategy is largely related to the reform that Chinese companies have been going through since the 1990s, as part of the transition from a planned economy to a market economy. In this context, the idea was for state-owned companies to become more modern, with clearly established property rights, clearly defined responsibility and authority, in addition to the separation between company management and government (Qian and Wu, 2000 *apud* Power et al., 2012. This reform process was accompanied by the privatization of some state-owned companies, the smaller ones, in a process that gained strength from 1995 onwards (Cao et al., 1999 *apud* Power et al., 2012), initially through experiments by local governments in some provinces such as Shandong, Guangdong and Sichuan (Power et al., 2012).

Throughout the process of modernization and privatization of companies, many state-owned companies went through difficulties, had their profits reduced and contracted loans that they could not repay, facing the challenges of inserting themselves in a more open economy. From then on, the "going out" strategy was related to the search for strengthening these companies, making them internationalized in a context of modernization and privatization.[5]

---

5   As stated by Power et al. (2010), in 2002, the government began to select the 'national champions' among state-owned companies, those that would be globally competitive and strategic for the country's economic growth. These large companies enjoyed a host of government

Almost twenty years after the beginning of the process of expansion of Chinese companies and almost forty years since the beginning of the opening of the country, China has undergone important transformations. Although it is not a consensus that the country entered on a new cycle of growth, it is possible to identify important changes that have been influencing the way China projects itself externally.

In sectoral terms, China is now primarily a services and industrial economy, with industry's share of GDP in value-added terms accounting for 38.9% in 2019, services accounting for 53.9% of GDP, and agriculture accounting for only 7.11% (World Bank Database, 2020).

Despite the expressive growth of China in the last decades, more recently one of the remarkable changes has been the drop in the rate of annual growth of the Chinese GDP. Between 2000 and 2010 the GDP average was 10% per year, but from 2016 on this rate dropped to around 6% per year.

According to Shambaugh (2016), several factors converged to this slower growth, such as: excess debt from the credit-fueled stimulus program; industrial overcapacity; the inefficient allocation of capital by state-owned banks; and the slow recovery of China's partner countries after the 2008 crisis.

For Naughton (2018), the period of strong expansion that China went through, which can be called an economic miracle, was linked to the interrelation of some characteristics such as: the population available to compose the necessary workforce; the rapid structural change that moved workers from agriculture to activities in industry and urban services; the high investment rates that promoted infrastructure and industrial incentives; and the open economy to drive growth based on manufacturing exports. But, according to Naughton (2018), this miracle could not last forever. It would end when structural and demographic conditions were exhausted, for different reasons, such as the transformation from a traditional rural economy to a more modern urban economy, a process that led most workers to transition to non-agricultural work.[6] After that point, growth may slow down (Naughton, 2018).

Thus, China would currently be at a "structural turning point" (Naughton, 2018), which follows the exhaustion of the previous rapid growth cycle and in which the country faces the need to transition from a high-growth model to a high-quality model.

---

benefits, including information-sharing networks, domestic tax breaks, cheap land, diplomatic support, and low-interest financing from state-owned banks.

6 Migration from the countryside to China's cities peaked during the period 2005 to 2010. Migration between provinces reached a staggering 11 million per year during this period (Naughton, 2018).

The end of the miracle in China is, therefore, the result of structural changes such as: the slowdown in the growth of the labor force – also marked by the decline of the economically active population in China; the decrease in rural-urban migration; the maturity of domestic industry and the abundance of saturated markets (Naughton, 2018). All these structural changes lead to the need to move from a manufacturing economy based on the production of final goods to the production of articles with high technological content, which requires a recalibration of domestic investment: to move it away from infrastructure and heavy industry and towards an economy based on "soft innovation" and increased consumption (Naughton, 2018).

These structural changes linked to a new pattern of growth, or at least to an exhaustion of the previous one, lead, in turn, to changes in China's global economic projection.

During the miracle period, foreign trade assumed centrality, as China expanded the production of manufactured goods for export (using the ample labor supply) and the imports of natural resources, broadly integrating itself into the global economy.

While business relationships remain critical, as internal transformations begin to shape growth, external interaction also changes. According to Naughton (2020), two fundamental domestic changes have altered the way China relates to the global economy: the change in the labor market, associated with rising wages, which are causing a loss of competitiveness in Chinese labor-intensive exports; and the increase in domestic savings available for international investment. The two are linked: changes in the labor market contribute to a change in the pattern of accumulation based on labor-intensive exports; the improvement in wages allows for an improvement in living standards, expansion of the middle class and greater accumulation of income and internal savings, which already represent 50% of internal income (Naughton, 2020).

The expansion of domestic savings was channeled into expanding reserves to maintain the low value of the Chinese currency, the Renminbi; but this policy becomes progressively ineffective, according to Naughton, as the labor-intensive export model runs out. Excess savings also create a surplus for investments abroad, which begin to play a growing role (not only through state-owned companies, but also through private ones) and are directed at different sectors, with Chinese companies seeking expertise abroad through mergers and acquisitions.[7]

---

7   This movement would imply a tendency, according to Naughton (2020), for China to advance more and more in the process of easing controls on capital flows and liberalization, coherently with the efforts to internationalize the currency, which started in the second decade of

The 2008 crisis represented a key moment in the Chinese accumulation process, to the extent that, given the drop in external demand, the government responded by expanding investments to get out of the crisis. Although it did obtain positive results in terms of economic recovery, the need to reduce dependence on investments in a context of internal structural changes was clearly perceived. China realized the importance of using its economic strength to achieve internal goals, via a model based more on innovation and consumption, through investments in modernization.

Thus, technological advancement appears as one of the great current challenges towards structural change (Naughton, 2018; Majerowicz and Medeiros, 2018). Even though the country has taken an important technological leap, this does not mean that most Chinese companies have acquired innovative capacity for more technologically sophisticated production, because although production originates in Chinese factories, the production process is still significantly based on in foreign technology.[8]

In addition, China faces a challenge already faced by other economies, including Asian ones such as Japan and South Korea: the middle-income trap, that is, the difficulty in moving towards a high-income economy status, which requires capacity techniques, better institutions and more innovation (Naughton, 2018).

The Chinese government appears to be committed to this challenge. In the Twelfth Five-Year Plan of 2011 and in the Third Plenary Session of the CCP, in 2013, emphasis was placed on the need to continue reforms, advance the modernization of the economy and increase domestic consumption in order to make the economy less dependent on investment and exports and heavy industry (Shambaugh, 2013).

In fact, in the last decade, despite investment remaining always high as a proportion of GDP, it is possible to observe a greater convergence between the

---

the 21st century. But in recent years, the movement towards greater liberalization has been retreating, as the government perceives the risks of greater openness to growth. The currency internationalization process itself and the easing of capital controls receded. As of 2016, there has been a decline in Chinese foreign direct investment outwards after a long period of growth. This decrease, according to Naughton, is related both to a reaction by the Chinese government to block the strong leverage of private companies that invested abroad (see the next section of the chapter), as well as to the interruption of the liberalization process through stricter controls enforced by the government. (Naughton, 2020).

8 The country has been trying to overcome this limitation, increasing investments in Research and Development and filing 1.3 million patent requests, surpassing the sum of the USA (605,571), Japan (318,381), South Korea (208,830) and the European Union (159,358) (Souza, 2018).

rates of GDP expansion, investment, and household consumption, which signals the fact that household consumption begins to advance in parallel with investment. However, it is still too early to say that China promoted a transition to a consumption-centered economy, since investment remains an essential variable (see Chapter 2).

As Naughton (2016) suggests, during the period of strong structural change and rapid growth it was relatively easy to find productive investment projects. However, after the end of the miracle those could be more difficult to find, as some domestic markets are saturated (appliances, for example); infrastructure networks such as high-speed rails are completed; and the stock of innovations from developed countries that can be copied cheaply is depleted. None of these opportunities are completely exhausted, but investors are forced to be more selective and to look for more productive and profitable opportunities. More generally, the end of the growth miracle era reshapes the economic landscape in such fundamental ways that new approaches and policies are needed to sustain moderately rapid growth (Naughton, 2016).

Another fundamental change in the Chinese economy in recent years has been the expansion of the private sector in the economy. As mentioned earlier, since the early 1990s, as part of the process of modernizing state-owned companies, the government has promoted the "keep the big ones and let the small ones go" policy, which in practice led to a privatization process in China. At the Fifteenth Congress of the CCP in 1997, Jian Zemin declared that large and medium-sized companies should have the characteristics of ownership clarified by law, in order to effect the separation between the State and the management of companies (Souza, 2018).

According to Dougherty and Herd (2005: 8), the industrial added value of the private sector grew from 27.9% in 1998 to 53.3% in 2003. Almost half of this growth was due to individually owned companies. The list of the 100 largest private enterprises in China in 2006 increased to a minimum revenue level of 1.889 billion yuan, instead of 1.1 billion yuan in 2005 (ACFIC – All-China Federation of Industry and Commerce, 2019 *apud* Souza, 2018).

According to Milanovic (2020), Chinese private companies are many and large-scale. Their share of the top 1% of companies ranked by total added value grew from 40% in 1998 to 65% in 2007. The share rate of state-owned enterprises in the country's industrial production dropped from 50% in 1998 to 20% in 2015 (Zhang *apud* Milanovic, 2020). Investments in fixed assets by the private sector have increased considerably in recent years and represent 50% of the total in 2014, while state investments are below 35% of total investments (World Bank, 2018: 8).

As Souza (2018) states, despite the strategic importance of state-owned companies, over the years, since the opening, the State has ended up fulfilling the economic function of helping to increase private capital in the country through the "relative devaluation of the constant capital of investments due to the supply, by state-owned companies, of machinery, equipment, parts, inputs and energy, at advantageous prices, as if it were a State subsidy for other companies" (Souza, 2018). According to Milanovic (2020), the growth of the private sector and of a capitalist class in China was part of the government's strategy, in which the idea was not to limit the size of the private sector, but its political role, that is, the ability to impose their preferences in state policies.[9]

The transformations observed in contemporary China, whether of productive modernization or the growth of the private sector, were accompanied by an increase in inequality. Currently, China is a country with an inequality index of 50 Gini points, close to countries in Latin America. Despite the slight downward trend in inequality since 2009, it can be observed that since the beginning of the opening process, and even with the strong reduction in poverty, inequality has increased in China. According to Milanovic (2020), there is an increase in the share of private capital income in the total income, an aspect similar to that observed in Western countries such as the U.S. There is a growth in the share of capital income in the hands of the rich, with private wealth increasing from 100% of national income in 1980 to 450% of national income in 2015. According to the author, this is due to an expansion of privatization processes in recent years (including real estate) and the increased weight of investments in private sector shares due to the privatization of state-owned companies and the growth of new private companies.

---

[9] It is essential to consider that any analysis of the progress of the private sector in China must take into account the complexity of the issue of property in the country. It is difficult for a company considered to be private to be completely independent of the government, either because of the fact that it may be publicly traded and from then on rely on state shareholding, or because of the strong connections established between companies and the Party. Li (2014) highlighted how the CCP has, over time, incorporated among its members businessmen from different sectors, which expanded the space for internal disputes within the Party. We therefore understand that the private character must be thought of in order to consider all these issues. Even so, we are approaching the interpretation that, although the State's participation is broad, in recent decades there has been a fundamental diversification of property, which has opened space for the expansion of private appropriation of the surplus, even if always mediated by the State.

3 State, Classes, and Global Expansion

How do changes in the Chinese growth pattern influence the country's global projection? To what extent does this projection reflect the complex relationship between state and capital in China today? These are difficult questions to be answered, although they seem urgent both for understanding the internal contradictions of Chinese society and for interpreting the impact of the Chinese advance in the various countries that are increasingly related to the Asian giant.

As previously pointed out, according to Chun (2018), after the fall of the USSR, the nationalists who took the lead of the Chinese Communist Party broke the class nature characteristic of its third world version, allying themselves with the United States and abandoning the internationalist nationalist project and third world countries. In this sense, recent Chinese "globalism" is part of the idea of abandoning the anti-imperialist struggle and is part of the project of inserting China into global capitalism as a new space for capitalist accumulation and exploitation. Decades after the opening, "globalism" is, for the author, just the deepening of this strategy through the opening of capital, privatizations, and the projection of its own capital in the world.

Chun's (2018) view raises an important point about the discussion on China's foreign policy today, namely, the idea that contradictions in China are manifested externally, through the country's entry into a capitalist path.

An interesting example, according to Chun (2018), is the most recent Chinese expansion project, the Belt and Road Initiative (BRI), which is presented as a large project articulated by the Chinese government and aimed at expanding economic and cultural relations between countries around the land and sea belt in the pursuit of cooperation and mutual benefits. However, Chun (2018) points out that the various existing analyzes of the BRI lack a discussion of the class interests involved. The author asks herself: what would be the class content of the BRI? Is it in the interest of the Chinese government or the Chinese elite? And the governments and elites of the countries involved? (Chun, 2018).

It seems to us that a possible path in the investigation of the recent Chinese external projection and its relationship with the current stage of accumulation and the relations between State and capital in China is the more detailed analysis of Chinese investments in recent years, seeking to identify how they reflect the current accumulation stage and the increasing manifestation of private capital, whose objectives are aimed at capital accumulation. Another path is to analyze the Belt and Road strategy in addition to state strategic objectives, as a reflection of a certain process of capital accumulation, also with the presence, even on a smaller scale, of private interests.

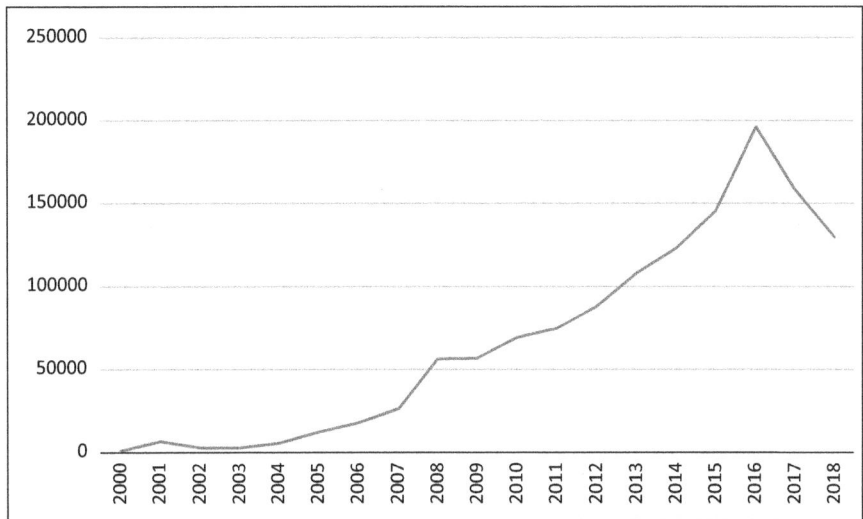

FIGURE 4.1 Chinese foreign direct investment (2000–2018), in billions of dollars
SOURCE: UNCTADSTAT (2020)

3.1 Chinese Investments

In the first two decades of the 21st century, Chinese foreign direct investment (FDI) abroad expanded considerably around the world. After China consolidated itself as one of the largest recipients of investments, in 2016, for the first time, Chinese FDI surpassed FDI received by the country from abroad. In 2005, the flow of Chinese FDI was US$ 12.26 billion, while in 2016 it was already at US$ 196.15 billion (Figure 4.1), which makes China the second country in terms of global investments, just behind the U.S. (US$ 299 billion) (UNCATD, 2020). In 2017, there was a drop in the volume of Chinese FDI, attributed to greater government control over high leverage (Naughton, 2020). Even so, Chinese FDI ranked third in the ranking of countries that invest the most, behind only the U.S. and Japan (MOFCOM, 2017).

In 2017, the bulk of Chinese investment (69.5%) was directed towards Asia, with Hong Kong alone accounting for 57.6% of FDI. Another 11.7% of FDI went to Europe and 8.9% to Latin America. It is important to consider that the Chinese databases do not detail the FDIs that go to Hong Kong and from there to other locations. According to data from the China Global Investment Tracker (CGIT, 2020), of total Chinese investments in the world between 2005 and 2019, 62% went to developing economies, including Asia, Sub-Saharan Africa, Middle East/North Africa and South America, while 37.87% of FDI went to advanced economies including Europe, North America and Australia.

In 2017, the number of investment projects via mergers and acquisitions of Chinese companies in the world was 431, reaching a total of US$ 119.62 billion in 56 countries. The volume of these mergers and acquisitions has been increasing every year. In 2005, the value of mergers and acquisitions was just US$ 6 billion; in 2016, mergers and acquisitions accounted for 44% of total outward investment, followed by foreign financing (MOFCOM, 2017).

Chinese investments are increasingly related to different activities and sectors, in addition to the traditional energy and mining sector, which characterized the early 2000s. In 2016, most FDI was linked to the trade-related services sector, such as leasing and business services, manufacturing (of raw chemicals, automotive, computers and electronic communication devices, pharmaceuticals, transportation equipment, among others), wholesale and retail trade, and financial industry. These sectors accounted for 81% of total FDI in 2017 (MOFCOM, 2017).

According to data from the China Global Investment Tracker (2020), in 2006, of the total Chinese FDI in the world, 45% were in the energy area. In 2018, although the energy sector was still important, its share of FDI fell to 23% of the total. That year, investment was more spread across several sectors, including the transport sector, which accounted for 31% of the total; the real estate sector, 6.48%; technology, at 4.5%; and others, at 7.9% (CGIT, 2020). Figure 4.2 shows the increase in total Chinese investments in the technology sector over the years.

It is known that state-owned enterprises have always occupied a central place in Chinese FDI in the world. However, over the years there has been a reduction in their participation (Lo, 2020; Rithmire, 2019; Power et.al, 2010). In 2008, state-owned enterprises accounted for 70% of Chinese FDI in the world. In 2018, this percentage dropped to 48%.

According to MOFCOM data, in 2017, of the total non-financial investments, investments by non-public companies represented 48.7% of the total, while public investments represented 51.3%. In the same year, of the total stock of external investments (Figure 4.3), 50.9% were carried out by non-state companies, while 49.1% were carried out by state companies (MOFCOM, 2017).

According to Lo (2020), the drop in the participation of state-owned companies partly meant an increase in the presence of so-called mixed-ownership shareholding companies, which represented, in 2018, 27% of FDI. This change reflects the reform in ownership of state-owned enterprises that has been taking place in China and a kind of division of labor between state-owned and non-state-owned enterprises. State-owned companies, which are larger and less profit-oriented, have their activities related to broader strategies, have

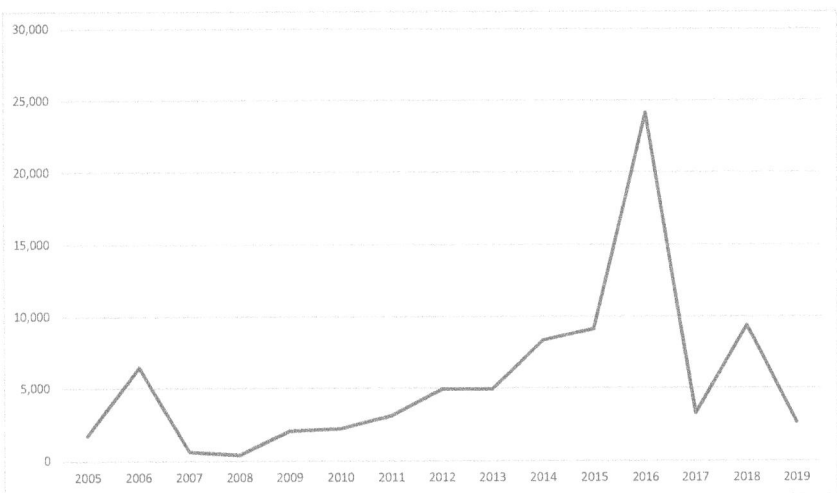

FIGURE 4.2   Chinese foreign direct investment in the technology sector (2005–2019), in millions of dollars
Note: The data presented corresponds to the China Global Investment Tracker (CGIT) database, which presents FDI data broken down by investment by company, sector and FDI-receiving country. These data allow us to measure the diversification of Chinese FDI in the world. There is, however, a discrepancy in the universe of total FDI from this base, with respect to FDI data from the UNCTAD base. CGIT data show a higher volume of investments. One reason that may explain this discrepancy is the incorporation by CGIT of Chinese investments that are directed to other countries, such as Hong Kong, before reaching their destination.
SOURCE: AUTHOR'S OWN ELABORATION FROM THE CHINA GLOBAL INVESTMENT TRACKER (2020)

strong state support and pave the way for the subsequent entry of non-state companies (Lo, 2020).

As Naughton (2020) states, private companies began to play a greater role in Chinese FDI, as there is greater diversification of investments. Investments in sectors such as finance and technology often appear to be more profitable compared to traditional sectors. For example, private companies seek expertise and access to technology abroad through acquisitions. The more diversified the investments are, the more the form of ownership changes. According to Naughton, since 2013 non-state enterprises account for ¾ of Chinese FDI in the United States.

Although non-state enterprises represent a wide range of distinct ownership types, many of which have state stock ownership, the decline of the state's monopolistic presence and the expansion of some form of private ownership

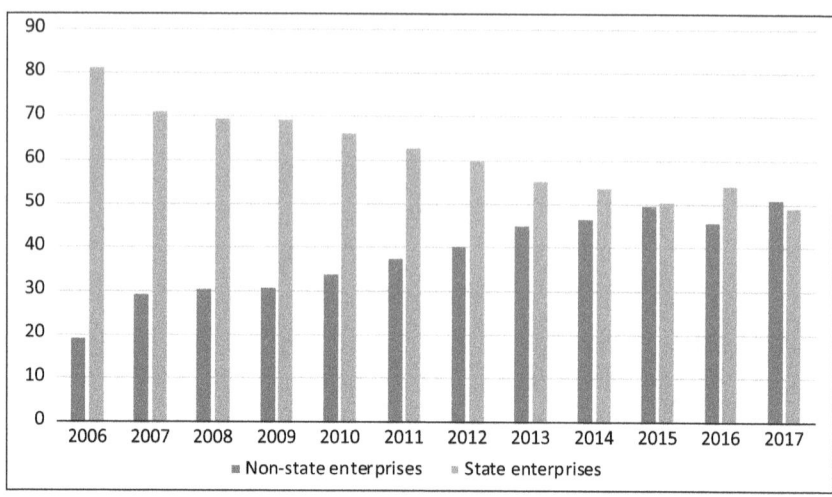

FIGURE 4.3 Chinese foreign direct investment (stock) – share of state and non-state enterprises in total (2006–2017)
SOURCE: AUTHOR'S OWN ELABORATION FROM THE MOFCOM (2017) DATA

is clear. According to Rithmire (2019), although state-owned enterprises still account for more than half of China's total foreign investment, the rise of non-state enterprises has been quick and substantial. Since the global financial crisis, several Chinese non-state companies are investing in the developed world, accelerating merger and acquisition (M&A) activities, as well as investments in industries ranging from culture and entertainment to health and education (Rithmire, 2019).

As pointed out by Power et al. (2010), the global expansion of Chinese companies increasingly involves small and medium-sized companies, which are seen as more dynamic and characterized by high flexibility and strong entrepreneurial spirit and work ethic.

Rithmire (2019) points out that most studies of China's global effort strongly emphasize the role of the state, reading Chinese FDI as sanctioned only by the state or focusing exclusively on SOE activities; but the rise of non-state enterprises has been swift and substantial. According to the author, it is possible to identify three types of Chinese domestic capital that have been making foreign investments: state capital, competitive or private capital, and what she calls "crony capital": private companies that enjoy a strong connection with the state.

While all seek internationalization, they do so for different reasons: state capital uses preferential access to domestic credit to expand political power and prestige internationally, as well as profits. Private or competitive capital seeks an internationalization strategy that follows what can be expected of elite companies anywhere in the world: markets for profit expansion, in addition to geographic areas in which they can enjoy a competitive advantage, such as lower costs, and acquisition of foreign technology or know-how. Crony capital seeks to expand its internal political influence, in addition to increases in profitability (Rithmire, 2019).

Table 4.1 shows some direct foreign investments made between 2005 and 2019 by some of the largest Chinese private companies, according to China Global Investment Tracker data. These companies were named in the list of the 500 largest private companies in China, according to the All-China Federation of Industry and Commerce (ACFIC) (Xinhua, 2019).

According to Xinhua (2019), in the list presented by ACFIC, Huawei leads the list of the largest private companies in China, with revenue of 721.2 billion yuan (US$ 102 billion) in 2018. Companies such as HNA Group, Suning, Amer International, Evergrande, JD.com, Country Garden, Hengli Group, Legend

TABLE 4.1 Foreign direct investments by selected Chinese private companies (2005–2019)

Enterprise	Projects	Amount (US$ bi)	Sector
HNA	38	49,670	Real estate, transportation, tourism, finance, others
Huawei	31	11,370	Technology
Alibaba	30	10,390	Technology, agriculture, finance
Tencent	15	16,920	Technology, entertainment, finance
JD.com	3	730	Transportation, others
Evergrande	3	1,950	Others
Country Garden e Country G. Holdings	6	1,680	Real estate
Legend	6	1,760	Agriculture, finance, energy
ZTE	9	3,070	Telecommunications

SOURCE: AUTHOR'S OWN ELABORATION USING CHINA GLOBAL INVESTMENT TRACKER DATA (2020)

Holdings, and Gome Holdings also make the list of largest companies, with revenues exceeding 18.59 billion yuan (Xinhua, 2019).

These large Chinese companies have been expanding their external insertion. Between 2005 and 2019, companies such as HNA, Huawei, Alibaba and Tencent invested more than US$ 88 billion (CGIT, 2020) promoting mergers and acquisitions and other investments in several countries. In 2005, according to CGIT data, these companies were not listed among companies that made investments abroad. More than ten years later, they invest in different regions, mainly in developed countries (Table 4.2).

The case of Huawei is an example of how the Chinese external projection reflects a complex and intertwined relationship between state and capital in the country today. Huawei has become the second largest smartphone company in the world, passing Apple and ranking second after Samsung (Colório, 2019). The company is known as the developer of 5G technology and its own operating system and has obtained strong state support to promote its internationalization, which has been stirring up the trade war between the United

TABLE 4.2 Selected Chinese private companies – foreign direct investment by regions, % of total invested (2006–2019)

Huawei		Alibaba	
Europe	44%	East Asia	52%
Sub-Saharan Africa	21%	West Asia	30%
West Asia	16%	USA	10%
East Asia	13%	Europe	7%
North America	5%	South America	1%
Australia	1%		
HNA		Tencent	
EUA	59%	Europe	57%
Europe	36%	USA	32%
West Asia	3%	West Asia	6%
South America	1%	East Asia	4%
Australia	1%	South America	1%

SOURCE: AUTHOR'S OWN ELABORATION USING CHINA GLOBAL INVESTMENT TRACKER DATA (2020)

States and China. At the heart of this dispute, as Majerowicz and Medeiros (2018) point out, is less a question of conquering markets for final goods and much more the dispute for the control of technical progress, with China seeking to access technology to produce integrated circuits (semiconductors), essential technology for the manufacture of electronic products and also for the development of new generations of weapons and war tactics. It is therefore a question of national security and sovereignty.

According to Rithmire (2019), the internationalization movement of Chinese companies is part of the technological advancement strategy, inserted in the China Manufacturing 2025 program. For the author, "the establishment of industrial funds for several target industries aimed to catalyze investment in technology, sometimes through foreign acquisition as a means of acquiring technology" (Rithmire, 2019: 19).

Chinese investments in technology via mergers and acquisitions have been contested by governments, especially in developed countries such as the United States. According to Khanapurkar (2019), most of the actions taken to deny China access to technology undoubtedly occurred in the domain of internal investments in search of technology. Following the announcement of the strategy "Made in China 2025" in 2015, Chinese investments in technology increased in the US and Europe, marking a watershed moment in those countries' perceptions of the threat of the Chinese innovation drive. Technology-seeking investments received more attention than other acquisition methods in the 2018 report prepared by the office of the United States Trade Representative (USTR) under section 301 of the US Commerce Act (Roach, 2018 *apud* Khanapurkar, 2019).

The United States Congress also passed the Foreign Investment Risk Review Modernization Act in an attempt to strengthen the Committee on Foreign Investment in the United States (CFIUS), the executive body responsible for screening domestic investments for national security risks. The change specifically targets China, requiring periodic reporting of its investment activity under the CFIUS purview, filling what was considered a major gap that had been exploited by China (Cornyn, 2017 *apud* Khanapurkar, 2019). In 2018, CFIUS blocked the acquisition of the American semiconductor testing company Xcerra by the Chinese company Hubei Xinyan (Kharpal, 2020 *apud* Khanapurkar, 2019). Also in Europe, albeit to a lesser extent, the leaders of Germany, France and the United Kingdom have been vocal about the sudden increase in Chinese acquisitions that followed the announcement of MIC 2025 (Jennen and Buregin, 2018 *apud* Khanapurkar, 2019) and promptly took steps to tighten investment regulations.

According to Rithmire (2019), Chinese private companies that have been promoting foreign investment generally operate based on their own objectives, often independently of the connections they establish with the State, seeking to open paths of profitability. But the author points out that companies included in what he calls "crony capital" promote internationalization processes through association with the State, through political connections, including to obtain resources and protection for their enterprises. Unlike competitive firms, these firms acquired their size and status through proximity to political elites, using influence in the Party to gain advantages, especially credit (obtaining low-rate financing), land, and the former assets of the socialist command economy. According to Rithmire (2019), in a large and decentralized economy such as China, this type of company exists at all levels of the political hierarchy, from local real estate magnates who obtain land at preferential prices and win construction contracts based on political connections, up to the national level.

These companies have been internationalizing in search of profitability, but mainly as a way to capitalize on domestic political advantages, using informal political connections and financing investments abroad in the form of mergers and acquisitions. The HNA Group itself is appointed as a "crony firm", in addition to Dalian Wanda Group, Fosun Group and Anbang Insurance. The four companies jointly carried out more than US$ 45 billion in foreign mergers and acquisitions in the period from 2001 to 2017, most of them in developed countries and in the period before the anti-corruption campaign created by Xi Jinping in 2013.

According to Rithmire (2019), the strong political connections of these companies have been the target of contestation by the government. In recent years, it has been common to observe cases in the press in which the government has condemned movements towards the internationalization of private companies, with the arrest of high-profile figures associated with these companies, restricting their access to credit and even nationalizing the company's assets.

According to Naughton (2020), the four private companies known for their strong political connection (Anbang Insurance, Dalian Wanda Group, Fosun Group and Hainan Airlines) suffered a block in their external acquisitions in the first half of 2017. The companies were investigated and forced to reduce leverage. The result of this pressure even helps to explain the 48% drop in outward FDI in 2017, combined with the effects of blockade measures in developed countries: "Although the reduction in foreign direct investment abroad in 2017 and 2018 was mainly driven by the Chinese domestic policy, restrictions on acquiring firms in Germany and the United States were a significant contributing factor" (Naughton, 2020: 130).

For Rithmire (2019), domestic policies blocking foreign investment have multiple logics: the CCP may be trying to restrict kleptocratic practices; trying to address what many consider dangerous levels of corporate debt; or trying to stop capital flight that puts the value of the RMB at risk. The CCP has adopted capital controls on investments in specific sectors and domestic regulation to combat business-class actors who use overseas investments to seek their own security and undermine the authority of the central state.

As one could observe, the profile of Chinese FDIs in the last decade reflects a greater complexity, both in terms of destination and sectors. The Chinese internationalization strategy seems to be strongly connected with the changes observed in the country's economy and the current stage of the Chinese growth pattern. The need to diversify investments and reach an economy based on innovation seem to influence Chinese foreign investment. The high participation of private companies strengthens the idea that the strategic interests of the State are combined with the interests of private capital.

The Party's recent condemnation movements and the blocking of private activities abroad certainly reveal the role of the Chinese State in the internationalization process, in addition to reflecting a political response to the blockades carried out by governments of developed countries such as the United States and those of Europe, which establishes an environment of increasing geopolitical disputes, strongly related to the technological race.

But the Party's own need to act more actively in controlling the movement of Chinese private capital that has been internationalizing happens precisely due to the existence of a concrete movement of advancement of Chinese capital in the world, which operates in a similar way to international capital, in search of profitability, access to technology and foreign markets. Thus, like other capitalist economies, internationalization responds to a movement of capital expansion, through a dialectic relationship between State and capital and in search of spaces of valorization.

In the case of China, the capacity of the State to shape this movement is quite high. Thus, faced with the risk that the internationalization process could interfere with the PCC's development strategy, there will always be a strong response. The case of blocking FDI, which is also related to a reluctance to broad financial liberalization, is an example (Naughton, 2020). But this capacity for action by the Chinese State does not imply a wide interruption of the process of capital accumulation, now on a global scale, nor the implementation of a model outside the logic of capitalism.

3.2 Belt and Road Initiative

In September 2013, in Kazakhstan, Xi Jinping announced the creation of the "Economic Belt of the Silk Road" Project, and in October, in Indonesia, the "Maritime Silk Road of the 21st Century". The two announcements were part of the launch of what became known as the great Chinese strategy of expanding investments and creating trade routes to connect the country to Europe, passing through different regions, in a kind of re-edition of the ancient Silk Road.

In 2015, the Ministry of Commerce, the Ministry of Foreign Affairs, and the National Commission for Development and Reform published the "Action Plan on the Belt and Road Initiative". In this document the Chinese government announces that

> The initiative to jointly build the Belt and Road, embracing the trend of a multipolar world, economic globalization, cultural diversity and greater application of IT, is designed to support the global free trade regime and open world economy, in the spirit of open regional cooperation. Its objective is to promote an orderly and free flow of economic factors, highly efficient allocation of resources and deep integration of markets; encourage countries along the Belt and Road to achieve economic policy coordination and carry out broader and deeper regional cooperation with higher standards; and jointly create an open, inclusive and balanced regional economic cooperation architecture that benefits all. The joint construction of the Belt and Road is in the interest of the world community. Reflecting the common ideals and pursuit of human societies, it is a positive effort to pursue new models of international cooperation and global governance and inject new positive energies into world peace and development.
>
> National Development and Reform Commission, 2015

From then on, the Silk Road Economic Belt – Belt and Road Initiative (BRI) – would open a new front for Chinese investments in the world in areas such as traditional infrastructure (transport, highways, railways, bridges, ports) and digital infrastructure (terrestrial and submarine fiber cable networks, satellite links):

> According to Shen (2018), the digital infrastructure – which includes terrestrial and submarine fiber optic cables and satellite links with Beidu – is a critical component of the Chinese strategy of internationalization through the Silk Road, through which China seeks to build a self-centered

transnational network infrastructure, aiming to "build a global information superhighway with China at its center".
China Telecom 2014 *apud* SHEN 2018: 2692
MAJEROWICZ, 2019: 26

According to Chinese government documents, all investments and projects would be aimed at promoting the sustainable development of countries along the Belt and Road, creating job opportunities, expanding the connectivity of the Asian, European and African continents and their adjacent seas, establishing partnerships between countries. The project would aim to "enhance cultural and personal exchanges, mutual learning between the peoples of the relevant countries, enabling them to understand, trust and respect each other and live in harmony, peace and prosperity". (National Development and Reform Commission, 2015).

According to the OECD, by 2018, 64 countries were involved in BRI projects (in addition to countries directly adjacent to the belts and routes, accounting for more than a third of the world's GDP and almost half of the population). Connectivity and cooperation will take place through 6 economic corridors: China-Europe; China-Mongolia-Russia; China-Central and West Asia; China-Pakistan, China-Indochina Peninsula; China-India, Bangladesh, Myanmar. It is estimated that BRI projects will add around US$1 trillion in external funds in the 10 years since 2017 (OECD, 2018).

Through these large corridors that create trade and distribution channels between China and other regions, hundreds of projects are distributed – mainly, but not only in infrastructure.

According to the OECD, among the objectives of the BRI, one can point out the search for the promotion of markets for Chinese products, solving problems of lagging industries, alleviating excess capacity, transferring activities abroad, creating demand and solving debt problems. Furthermore, the BRI would also fulfill part of China's objective to advance its position in value chains, as the expansion of companies can create external demand for materials and for Chinese technology and know-how (Figures 4.4 and 4.5).

The main sources of funding for BRI projects are Chinese development banks, mainly the China Development Bank (supporting 400 projects in 37 countries, totaling US$ 110 billion). Other sources include: the Bank of Industry and Commerce of China (involved in 212 projects worth about US$ 67 billion); the Bank of China (promoted US$ 100 billion between 2016 and 2018); China EximBank (support for 1000 projects in 49 countries, totaling around US$ 80 billion); China Construction Bank, China New Development Bank, and Asian Infrastructure Investment Bank. Investments also rely on a fund created

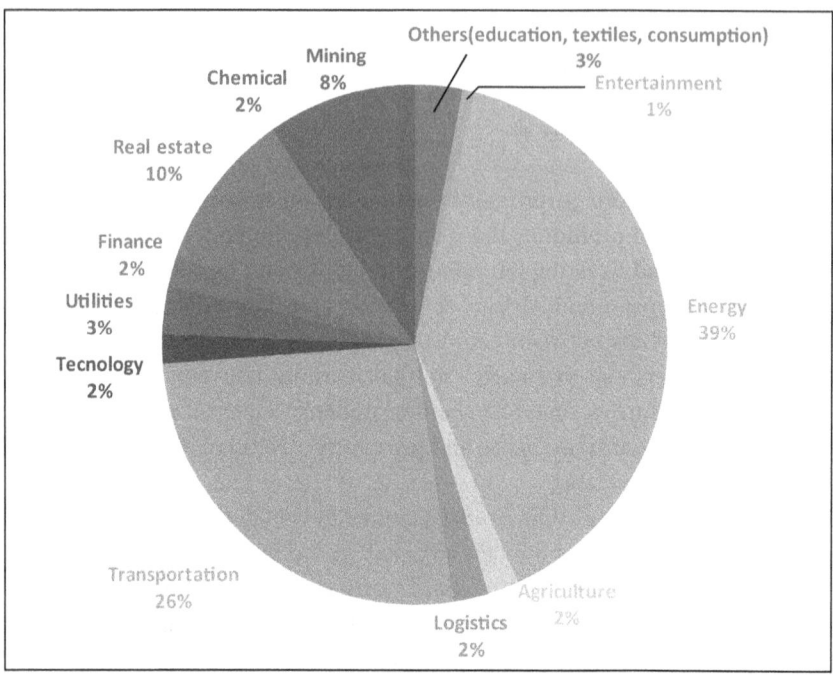

FIGURE 4.4 Belt and Road – Sector distribution of total investment (2013–2019)
SOURCE: AUTHOR'S OWN ELABORATION BASED ON DATA FROM THE CHINA GLOBAL INVESTMENT TRACKER (2020).

especially for the BRI, the Silk Road Fund, which has US$ 40 billion available for investments (OECD, 2018).

According to Zhexin (2018), although presenting itself as a grand strategy, the BRI can be considered somewhat vague, insofar as it represents yet another series of political objectives with poorly detailed proposals. According to the author, the BRI was created to respond both to economic challenges, such as the drop in growth and the increase in idle capacity in previous years, as well as geopolitical objectives, easing tensions with neighboring countries and dissolving hostilities.

According to Naughton (2020), it is important to understand the BRI not as a multilateral organization, that is, although countries "join" the BRI, this only means that they will negotiate bilateral agreements with China, through which these countries will be able to negotiate projects beneficial to themselves. This explains the expansion of the group of countries that have been adhering to the BRI, such as countries in Latin America, far from the region of the former Silk Road. According to the author, "the key objective of the BRI is thus to

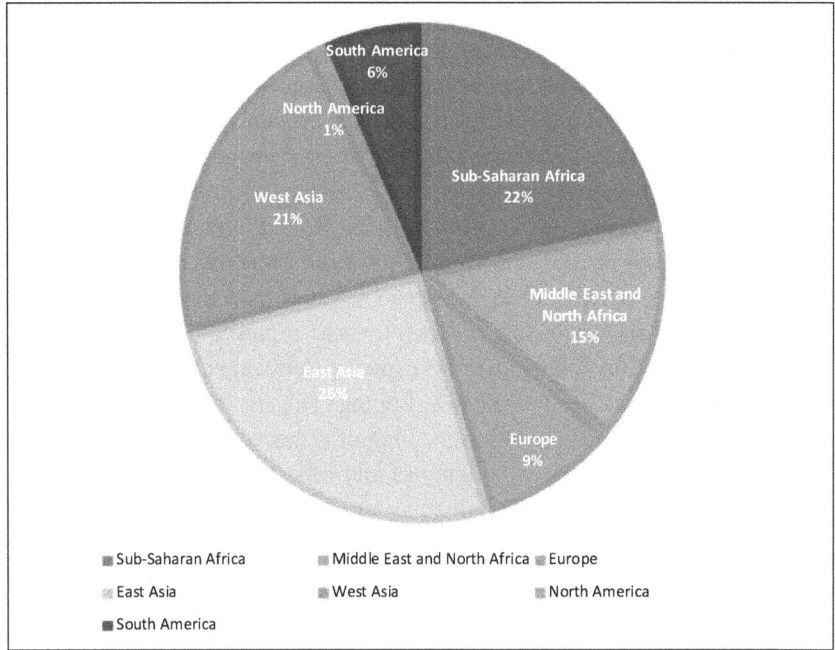

FIGURE 4.5 Belt and Road – Destination of investments by world region (2013–2019)
SOURCE: AUTHOR'S OWN ELABORATION BASED ON DATA FROM THE CHINA GLOBAL INVESTMENT TRACKER (2020)

strengthen political coordination between China and other nations, especially those on the periphery" (Naughton, 2020: 126). The BRI therefore represents a Chinese strategy to expand its global influence, paving the way for strategic objectives in the supply of energy resources, for example, and the expansion of its companies in the negotiation of investment and trade agreements.

According to Lee Jones and Jing Zeng (2019), it would be a mistake to see the BRI as a grand strategy coherently articulated from the central government. For the authors, the BRI is in fact much more incoherent and indeterminate, besides responding to competing domestic interests. According to the authors, Chinese foreign policy is shaped less by the action of a central state and more by the contestation and evolution of fragmented, decentralized and partially internationalized party apparatuses along with their social allies. The authors highlight how regulatory agencies, ministries, banks and state-owned companies have expanded their power base and their control of their own resources, adjusted central policies in their own way and shaped the direction of internationalization projects. Projects like the BRI are not meticulously planned by top leaders: instead, they are shaped by internal struggles for power and resources. This process is a reflection of changes in the Chinese Communist Party itself, which, despite exercising strong leadership, is increasingly having to deal with diverse interests springing from a complex government structure.

Unlike a grand strategy, the most prevalent influences in shaping the BRI were economic interests such as state-owned enterprises and provincial governments. After the 2007/2008 crisis, the Chinese government increased stimulus via loans to provincial governments, in order to finance infrastructure projects; this, however, did not actually solve the problems and several companies revealed problems of excess capacity, just as banks faced its own over-accumulation crisis. Given this context, the BRI represented an opportunity to internationalize its domestic excess capacity. Political-economic actors lobbied hard for the transformation of Xi Jinping's slogans into concrete policies in order to capture the gargantuan volume of resources. Dozens of domestic agencies, banks, state-owned companies and others have been forming new transnational coordination mechanisms with their partners abroad (Jones and Zeng, 2019).

According to the authors, so far, the winners of all these disputes within the scope of the BRI between provincial governments, banks, agencies, are state-owned companies, particularly construction companies. From January 2014 to June 2018, Chinese construction activity in 117 BRI countries totaled US$ 256 billion.

Despite the strong presence of state-owned companies, projects carried out through the BRI in the construction area and in several other areas have paved the way for the internationalization of Chinese private companies. According to data from the China Global Investment Tracker, it is possible to identify the presence of private companies among the investments made. Table 4.3 shows some of these investments made by private companies throughout the existence of the BRI.

As one can see, these companies invest in several countries, mainly in Asia. According to Jin et al. (2019), in regard to Chinese FDI in ASEAN, it was possible to identify that after the BRI both state and private companies have been attracted by the large markets of the countries in the region and seek to relocate their labor-intensive and low-technology sectors there. Between 2010 and 2015, private companies invested around RMB 2.57 billion in ASEAN countries, while state-owned companies invested RMB 890 million (Jin et al., 2019).

Thus, the BRI can be seen as a strategic project, articulated within the scope of the Chinese central government and aimed at expanding China's international influence; at the same time and related to this objective, the BRI also reflects the current moment of capital accumulation in China, marked by the imperative of investment diversification and technological catch up, with

TABLE 4.3 Selected Chinese private companies with projects via BRI (2013–2019)

Enterprise	Amounts (millions of dollars)	Sector	Country
Alibaba	$ 2.000	Others	Singapore
HNA	$ 1.030	Logistics	Singapore
ZTE	$ 1.010	Technology	Italy
Alibaba	$ 1.000	Others	Singapore
Alibaba	$ 1.000	Others	Singapore
Roadbot Tyre	$ 610	Transportation	UAE
Tencent	$ 500	Entertainment	South Korea
Alibaba	$ 500	Others	Indonesia
Alibaba	$ 480	Technology	Russia
ZTE	$ 460	Energy	Pakistan
Alibaba	$ 360	Logistics	Singapore
Tencent, JD.Com	$ 340	Transportation	Indonesia
Alibaba	$ 320	Others	Thailand
Suning	$ 310	Entertainment	Italy
Huawei	$ 280	Technology	New Zealand
Country Garden	$ 280	Real estate	Malaysia
GoerTek	$ 260	Technology	Vietnam
Huawei	$ 240	Technology	Guinea
HNA	$ 230	Finance	Austria
JD.com	$ 230	Others	Thailand
Alibaba	$ 200	Others	South Korea
Huawei	$ 200	Technology	Papua New Guinea
Alibaba	$ 180	Finance	Pakistan
Huawei	$ 170	Technology	Serbia
ZTE, China Telecom	$ 170	Technology	Nepal
Huawei	$ 170	Technology	Kenya
ZTE	$ 150	Technology	Bangladesh
Huawei	$ 150	Technology	Israel
Tencent	$ 150	Transportation	Indonesia
Alibaba	$ 150	Others	Pakistan
Alibaba	$ 150	Logistics	Singapore
Huawei	$ 120	Energy	Cameroon
JD.com	$ 100	Transportation	Indonesia
ZTE	$ 100	Technology	Turkey

SOURCE: AUTHOR'S OWN ELABORATION BASED ON DATA FROM THE CHINA GLOBAL INVESTMENT TRACKER (2020)

maintenance of the presence of state-owned companies, but with the growing presence of private companies.

The complexity and scope of the BRI have raised several criticisms regarding the impacts that the project has been causing in the countries involved. Among them, the possibility of increasing debts contracted by companies from poor countries with Chinese financial institutions stands out, forming what is called "debt-trap-diplomacy". The case at the Hambantota port in Sri Lanka was seen as evidence of the risks of Chinese lending.[10]

Some authors highlight the concern that most projects (about 90%) are carried out by Chinese companies, which puts into question the idea of cooperation and mutual benefit. In addition to that, there is the lack of a more detailed analysis of projects, which makes the vast majority of the routes established for projects, such as Europe Railway Projects, economically useless and their operating profit unlikely (Hart-Landsberg, 2018).

Problems linked to environmental degradation in BRI projects have also been pointed out. Simpson (2019) points out that there are doubts about whether the BRI would work as a smokescreen for China to outsource its pollution and environmental degradation to poorer and more vulnerable countries. Despite assurances that the "new silk road" will be "green, healthy, smart and peaceful", the World Bank noted that many of the countries where these projects are already underway or still in the planning stages have poor track records in terms of respect for transparency and environmental safeguards. What is even more serious is the fact that many of the infrastructure projects directly overlap with protected areas and further fragment environments deemed essential for the survival of vulnerable and endangered species and can lead to the collapse of ecosystems (Simpson, 2019).

4 Conclusion

Over nearly four decades since the beginning of the economic opening process, China has grown substantially and changed its productive structure towards an industrialized economy. This transformation was linked to a pattern of growth

---

10   China has struck a deal with former President Mahinda Rajapaksa to build a series of infrastructure mega-projects in Hambantota. The projects were financed mainly by borrowing from China, and a few years later, Sri Lanka struggled to pay as it sank into a series of debts of its own making. China ended up seizing 70% of the Hambantota port for 99 years, for $1.12 billion. After that, some countries like Malaysia and Pakistan canceled some projects under the BRI. (Shepard, 2020).

based on broad state investments and the opening of space for the expansion of private capital, in addition to the extensive use of available labor.

In recent decades, growth was based mainly on the expansion of industry via heavy investment, increases in productivity and the incorporation of the workforce that migrated from the countryside to the city. This process supported growth at very high rates, the expansion of exports of manufactured products and the high import of natural resources.

This pattern has been undergoing important transformations, as structural changes have been imposing limits on the continuity of expansion at high rates. The country is currently facing challenges related to the need to move from a manufacturing economy based on the production of final goods to the production of articles with high technological content, which requires a recalibration of domestic investment: a dislocation from infrastructure and heavy industry towards an economy based on "soft innovation" and the expansion of consumption (Naughton, 2018).

Allied to these transformations, over the years the path of opening and privatization has opened space for private capital, which is increasingly becoming an important part of the country's economy, whether through investments or job creation. The expansion of private capital points to the existence of a capitalist class, whose interests in the expansion of capital accumulation are increasingly asserted in the midst of the development project articulated by the government.

All these internal dynamics influence the way China has been projecting itself externally. The country's centrality in terms of international trade is now combined with the expansion of foreign direct investment, with Chinese companies investing in traditional sectors (but also in new ones) via mergers and acquisitions in different parts of the world, in search of access to technology and consumer markets.

Investments have become more diversified. Investments in the areas of energy and construction are increasingly accompanied by the sectors of technology, finance, real estate and pharmaceuticals, directed not only to developing countries, but also to central economies. These voluminous investment flows are fundamental to meeting the internal objectives of the current stage of Chinese accumulation, the expansion of the country's technological capacity.

China's external projection, therefore, today is largely connected with the challenges of continuing the internal accumulation process, and it is essential for the economy to advance towards modernization and expansion of income levels.

In addition, the Chinese external projection presents itself as the expression of state strategic objectives, but these objectives are increasingly interrelated with the objectives of private interests on the part of an expanding capitalist class. This establishes a dialectical relationship, which manifests itself both internally and externally. As Souza (2018) suggests, dialectically, the Chinese State cannot renounce the strengthening of capital to build an advanced economy; at the same time, the strength of capital is gradually incorporated into the State and society.

The Chinese external projection thus appears as the result of a dialectic relationship between state strategic interests and private interests, resulting from the expansion of capital accumulation, whose objectives are linked to the expansion of profitability.

The movements of intervention and political control with regard to the liberalization process (via blockade of the internationalization movements of private companies, for example) prove the importance of the State in the accumulation process, but also the concrete reality of a movement of expansion of private capital whose accumulation logic now transcends the limits of national borders.

From the point of view of the broader sense of external projection, it is worth questioning and reflecting on the way in which China intends to build its global insertion. The analysis made here does not exhaust future investigations on the directions of Chinese internationalization, nor does it capture all the elements surrounding this process; it only seeks to demonstrate that, like other capitalist countries, Chinese internationalization follows imperatives linked to internal processes of accumulation.

Thus, as Chun (2018) pointed out, the projection of the Chinese model comes up against deep contradictions linked to the country's subordination to the logic of capitalism. Thus, what today presents itself as Chinese "globalism", in fact, represents a complete rupture with the revolutionary socialist and anti-imperialist internationalism that was present during the Maoist period.

As Lee points out when analyzing the presence of Chinese capital in Zambia,

> even if Chinese state capital, with its peculiar logic of accumulation, productive organization and managerial ethos, offers more room for bargaining, China does not show interest, intention, or ability to challenge or replace the existing institutional infrastructure of 21st century capitalism.
> LEE, 2017

As stated by Katz, the well-disposed portraits of China's presence in the world,

> omit that the consolidation of capitalism in China accentuates all the imbalances already generated by surplus goods and surplus capital. ...

> Ignorance of these contradictions prevents us from realizing how China's international defensive strategy is undermined by the competitive pressure imposed by capitalism. ... It postulates that the new eastern power develops respectful international behavior, so as not to humiliate its western opponents (Guigue, 2018).. But he forgets that this coexistence is not only eroded by Washington's harassment of Beijing. The prevailing in China of an economy increasingly oriented towards profit and exploitation amplifies this conflict.
>
> KATZ, 2020

Thus, from a peripheral perspective, it is urgent to deepen the critical debate on China's internationalization, seeking to weigh its contradictions in the face of the country's current context of capital accumulation on a global scale. The challenges posed by developing countries are enormous in the face of an international context historically marked by disputes between Western nations and the entry of China. It is essential to prioritize the maintenance of sovereignty and of the development of the poorest countries.

References

ACFIC – All-China Federation of Industry and Commerce. (2019). *China Top 500 Private Enterprises Summit 2019 held in Xi'ning*, September 1st. Accessed August 16, 2020. http://www.chinachamber.org.cn/News/201909/t20190920_141282.html.

Amin, S. (2013). China 2013. *Monthly Review*, March 1st. Accessed August 16, 2020. https://monthlyreview.org/2013/03/01/china-2013/.

Anderson, P. (2018). *Duas Revoluções: Rússia e China*. São Paulo: Editora Boitempo.

Badiou, A. (2020). *Petrogrado, Xangai*. São Paulo: Editora Ubu.

Bettelheim, C. (1979). *Revolução Cultural e Organização Industrial na China*. Rio de Janeiro: Editora Graal.

Bugiato, C. (2014). A Cadeia Imperialista das Relações Interestatais: a Teoria do Imperialismo de Nicos Poulantzas. *Revista Quaestio Iuris*, 7 (2): 453–466.

China Global Investment Tracker – CGIT. 2020. https://www.aei.org/china-global-investment-tracker/.

Chun, L. (2018). China's New Globalism. In: Panitch, L.; Albo, G. (Eds.) *Socialist Register 2019: A World turned upside down?*, 55 .

Colório, A. G. (2019) Huawei e a Disputa pelo Mercado Internacional das Telecomunicações. *Instituto Humanitas Unisinos*, March 11. Accessed August 16, 2020. http://www.ihu.unisinos.br/78-noticias/587316-huawei-e-a-disputa-pelo-mercado-internacional-das-telecomunicacoes.

Dougherty, S.; Herd, R. (2005). Fast-falling Barriers and Growing Concentration: the Emergence of a Private Economy in China. *OECD Economics Department Working Papers*, 58 (471), December 16.

Hart-Landsberg, M. (2018). A Critical Look at China's One Belt, One Road Initiative. *Monthly Review*, October 5. Accessed August 16, 2020. https://mronline.org/2018/10/05/a-critical-look-at-chinas-one-belt-one-road-initiative/.

Jessop, B. (2002). *The Future of the Capitalist State*. Cambridge, UK: Polity Press.

Jin, S.; Xiaohui, H.; Yunxiong, L; (2019). Does the Belt and Road Initiative Reshape China's Outward Foreign Direct Investment in ASEAN? Shifting Motives of State-owned and Private-owned Enterprises. *Singapore Economic Review*, August.

Jones, L.; Zeng, J. (2019). Understanding China's 'Belt and Road Initiative': beyond 'Grand Strategy' to a State Transformation Analysis. *Third World Quarterly*, 40 (8): 1415–1439.

Katz, C. (2020). *O Gigante Chinês: Tão Distante do Imperialismo como do Sul Global*. A terra é redonda, June. https://aterraeredonda.com.br/o-gigante-chines/.

Khanapurkar, U. (2019). *The Rising Tide of Technology Denial against China*. ICS Occassional Paper, n. 32. Institute of Chinese Studies, Delhi.

Lee, C. K. (2017). *The Specter of Global China: Politics, Labor, and Foreign Investment in Africa*. Chicago; London: The University of Chicago Press.

Li, C. (2014). China's Communist Party-State: The structure and dynamics of power. In: Joseph, W. A. (Ed.) *Politics in China: An Introduction*. New York: Oxford University Press.

Lima, W. B. (2017). *Leia Íntegra do Discurso de Xi Jinping na Abertura do 19º Congresso do Partido Comunista da China*. Site Ópera Mundi, October. https://operamundi.uol.com.br/politica-e-economia/48290/leia-integra-do-discurso-de-xi-jinping-na-abertura-do-19-congresso-do-partido-comunista-da-china.

Lo, D. (2020). Towards a Conception of the Systematic Impact of China on Late Development. SOAS. Version of the article accepted for publication in Third World Quarterly published by Routledge: https://doi.org/10.1080/01436597.2020.1723076.

Losurdo, D. (2004) *Fuga da História? A Revolução Russa e a Revolução Chinesa vistas de hoje*. Rio de Janeiro: Editora Revan.

Majerowicz, E. (2019). *A China e a Economia Política Internacional das Tecnologias da Informação e Comunicação*. Universidade Federal do Rio Grande do Norte. Departamento de Economia. Discussion Paper, 001.

Majerowicz, E.; Medeiros, C. A. (2018). Chinese industrial policy in the geopolitics of the information age: the case of semiconductors. *Revista de Economia Contemporânea*, 22 (1): 1–28.

Marti, M. E. (2007). *A China de Deng Xiaoping: o Homem que pôs a China na Cena do Século XXI*. Editora Nova Fronteira.

Medeiros, Carlos Aguiar de. (2011). A China e as matérias primas. In: Fazzio, A. et al (org). *Brasil e China no reordenamento das relações internacionais: oportunidades e desafios*. Brasília. FUNAG - Fundação Alexandre Gusmão.

Medeiros, C. A. (2013). Padrões de Investimento, Mudança Institucional e Transformação Estrutural na Economia Chinesa. In: Centro de Gestão e Estudos Estratégicos. *Padrões de Desenvolvimento Econômico (1950–2008): América Latina, Ásia e Rússia*. Brasília: Centro de Gestão e Estudos Estratégicos.

Milanovic, B. (2020). *Capitalismo sem Rivais. O futuro do sistema que domina o mundo*. São Paulo: Editora Todavia.

MOFCOM – Ministry of Commerce. *Statistical Bulletin of China's Outward Foreign Direct Investment* 2017.

Motta, L. E. (2013). Sobre a Transição Socialista: Avanços Teóricos e os Limites das Experiências do Chamado "Socialismo Real". *Revista Praia Vermelha*, 22 (3).

National Bureau Statistics of China (2016). https://www.stats.gov.cn/english/.

National Development and Reform Commission; Ministry of Foreign Affairs; Ministry of Commerce. Action Plan on the Belt and Road Initiative. http://english.www.gov.cn/archive/publications/2015/03/30/content_281475080249035.htm.

Naughton, B. J. (2016). Economic Growth from High-speed to High-quality. In: Shambaugh, D. *The China Reader: Rising Power*. New York: Oxford University Press.

Naughton, B. J. (2018). *The Chinese Economy: Adaptation and Growth* (2nd Ed.). Cambridge, MA; London: MIT Press.

Nogueira, I. (2018). Estado e Capital em uma China com Classes. *Revista de Economia Contemporânea*, 22 (1).

OECD. (2018). China's Belt and Road Initiative in the Global Trade, Investment and Finance Landscape. *OECD Business and Financial Outlook 2018*.

Power, M.; Mohan, G.; Tan-mullins, M. (2012). *China's Resource Diplomacy in Africa Powering Development?*. London: Palgrave Macmillan.

Ribeiro, V. L. (2013). *A Expansão Chinesa e seus Impactos na África na Primeira Década do Século XXI*. Thesis (PhD in International Political Economy) – Universidade Federal do Rio de Janeiro, Rio de Janeiro.

Rithmire, M. (2019). Varieties of Outward Chinese Capital: Domestic Politics Status and Globalization of Chinese Firms. *Working Paper* 20-009. Boston: Harvard Business School.

Santos, G. A. G. (2020). *China: Desenvolvimento Nacional, Socialismo de Mercado e sua Internacionalização*. Master Thesis (Master in World Political Economy) – Universidade Federal do ABC, Santo André.

Shambaugh, D. (2013). *China Goes Global: The Partial Power*. New York: Oxford University Press.

Shambaugh, D. (2016). *The China Reader: Rising Power*. New York: Oxford University Press.

Shepard, W. (2020). How China's Belt and Road Became a 'Global Trail of Trouble'. *Forbes*, January 29. Accessed August 16, 2020. https://www.forbes.com/sites/wadeshepard/2020/01/29/how-chinas-belt-and-road-became-a-global-trail-of-trouble/#41aca93f443d.

Simpson, K. (2019). Just How Green is the Belt and Road? *The Interpreter*, January 23. Accessed August 16, 2020. https://www.lowyinstitute.org/the-interpreter/just-how-green-belt-road

Souza, R. (2018). *Estado e Capital na China*. [online]. Salvador: Edufba.

UNCTAD. *UNCTAD Statistics*. Accessed 2020.

Van Apeldoorn, B. (2017). Estratégia Geopolítica e Hegemonia de Classe: para uma Análise Materialista-histórica de Política Externa. [trad. de Caio Bugiato]. *Revista Plural*, 24 (2): 135–160.

World Bank. (2018). *China – Systematic Country Diagnostic: towards a more inclusive and sustainable development*. Washington, D.C.: World Bank Group.

World Bank. (2020). *World Bank DataBase*. https://databank.worldbank.org/source/world-development-indicators.

World Bank. (2021). *World Bank DataBase*. https://databank.worldbank.org/source/world-development-indicators.

Xinhua. (2019). Huawei Heads List of China's top 500 Private Firms. *Xinhua Net*, August 22. Accessed August 16, 2020. http://www.xinhuanet.com/english/2019-08/22/c_138329314.htm.

Zhexin, Z. (2018). The Belt and Road Initiative – China's New Geopolitical Strategy?. *China Quarterly of International Strategic Studies*, 4 (3): 327–343. Accessed August 16, 2020. https://www.worldscientific.com/toc/cqiss/04/03.

CHAPTER 5

The Sino-American Dispute in Information and Communication Technologies

Esther Majerowicz

1 Introduction

The digitalization of social life and the economy, along with a series of major developments, such as the rise of platforms and automation based on artificial intelligence (AI), have contributed to important transformations in the dynamics and competitive strategies of technology corporations and the great powers. Information and communication technologies (ICT) became the core of national projects and industrial policies aimed at restructuring manufacturing, while technological rivalry between the great powers has intensified. The deepening of digitalization in a context of increased competition between China and the U.S. has led several analysts to predict the emergence of a "digital divide", with two compartmentalized ICT systems, headed by each of these great powers, often referring to a new Cold War (Kaplan, 2019; Rachman, 2020; Smith, 2020; Yao, 2021).

Nonetheless, the postulation of this supposed new Cold War underpinned by the idea of a digital divide not only undervalues or denies the fact that there are no two "contending modes of production and opposed models of society" in dispute (Dyer-Witheford and Matviyenko, 2019: 21),[1] but also disregards the implications posed by the eminently global technical and productive aspects of the ICT system. To highlight the limitations of this interpretation, based on an analytical reformulation of a past configuration of the international system, it is necessary to take a step back and seek to understand the productive

---

1 "As several critics have observed, applying the Cold War metaphor to these tensions is deceptive (Ciuta and Klinke 2010; Sakwa 2013; Budraitskis 2014). At stake in the old Cold War were contending modes of production and opposed models of society, organized respectively around markets and planning – a compelling binary whose hold over both popular and elite imaginations was scarcely diminished by the actual corruption or occasional collusion of the antagonists. In the New Cold War, no such epic binaries are in play; all protagonists are participants in the world market, differentiated at best along a spectrum that runs from free-market neoliberalism to variants of state capitalism" (Dyer-Witheford and Matviyenko, 2019: 21).

structure and technological dynamics under which the said competitive processes between capitals and states are based. That is, the apprehension of the strategies and competitive dynamics of large technology companies and technological great powers presupposes the specification of the general characteristics of the key technologies that make up this technological system, their interrelations, and their differentiated dynamics of diffusion, considering that "technology discloses man's mode of dealing with Nature, the process of production by which he sustains his life, and thereby also lays bare the mode of formation of his social relations, and of the mental conceptions that flow from them " (Marx, 1887: n.p.).

By clarifying these key factors, the material elements that provide the limits of possibilities for the unfolding of the real, although we cannot predict the exact paths of the world economy and the interstate system, which are the fruit of multiple determinations and surrounded by contingencies, we can stress the limitations of this thesis. In addition, such expedient enables us to establish some central axes and general trends underpinning the technological dispute between China and the U.S. and their technology companies.

Thus, this chapter aims to provide an analysis of the Sino-American dispute based on a reading of ICT in its own technological and productive terms. Section 2 starts by examining the main characteristics of the three key technologies composing the ICT system – semiconductors, mobile telecommunications infrastructure, particularly 5G, and AI – in the context of two distinct ICT-based modernization waves. These three technologies are considered in an integrated manner, highlighting their development as a technological system historically constituted from a stacking of technologies submitted to coevolution, which were ultimately incorporated into a global machinery system. Besides considering the technological system as a whole, the section identifies the main nexuses of technological development in this system, namely, the fundamental nexus and the downstream nexus, and emphasizes the role of diffusion for technological progress. Based on this characterization, section 3 emphasizes two general competitive vectors that emerge from the technological development and historical evolution of this system, that is, the coexistence of processes of centralization and pulverization of machinery and productive capacity. In sections 4, 5, and 6, we examine the competitive imperatives involved in the Sino-American dispute arising from the global technical and productive aspect of the ICT system, and the competitive dynamics in the fundamental nexus and the downstream nexus of this system. Given the role of diffusion for technological development and the dynamics of pulverization of machinery and productive capacity in this system, we also consider the competitive dimensions associated with the waves of modernization in sections 7 and 8. While section 7 focuses on the state's role for the current wave of modernization, section 8 discusses the strategies and policies of China and the U.S. in the race for the implementation of these technologies. The last section is dedicated to the conclusions.

2 The Three Key Technologies and the Modernization Waves

ICT diffusion in recent decades had both as presupposition and consequence the rapid technical progress in its production base, particularly in the branches producing capital goods and high-tech inputs, in which are located semiconductors and semiconductor manufacturing equipment (Majerowicz and Medeiros, 2018; Majerowicz, 2020). Based on drastic reductions in production costs, along with the increased number of transistors in and the miniaturization of its fundamental inputs, this accelerated diffusion had its first wave in the escalation of consumption of mixed-use electronic devices (unproductive and productive consumption), especially computers and smartphones, and the expansion of Internet access, accompanied by successive renovations of telecommunication infrastructure, particularly mobile.[2]

In the 1970s and 1980s, the diffusion of digitalization was more or less restricted to the use of computers and dedicated networks in military applications, research institutions, the public sector, international agencies, and companies – both in the financial and productive sectors, enabling, for example, the creation of the SWIFT in 1973 (Scott and Zachariadis, 2013), the restructuring of white-collar occupations (Huws, 2014), and the emergence of global value chains in manufacturing. It was only in the 1990s and 2000s that digitalization and Internet access gained traction among consumers in general, manifested in the first wave of modernization based on computers and smartphones. In the 2010s, these processes led to several substantial developments – namely, the process of plataformization of the economy and sociability; the rise of Big Data and deep neural networks; the starting-up of the digitalization and networking of objects in general, especially surveillance cameras and the widespread implementation of urban and home sensors; and the deepening of diffusion in manufacturing production processes. These developments have put in motion a second wave of ICT-based modernization.

---

2 Since 2G, the mobile telecommunication networks are digital (Ssemboga and Restrepo, 2018). Mobile telecommunication networks are enabled by and are consumers of semiconductors (for instance, in switches and routers).

Thus, in recent years, the process of digitalization and networking has been rapidly extrapolating its initial scope – focused on devices whose primary functions were eminently computing and communication –, taking the form of embedded diffusion, that is, whose characteristic is to provide communication and computing capabilities to objects in general, from machines and equipment to traditional consumer goods and infrastructures, which have other primary functions. This built-in diffusion is a matter of incorporating the building blocks of ICT capabilities, semiconductors, in objects and structures. Therefore, the digitalization of the physical world consists in the implementation of semiconductors, both sensors and integrated circuits (chips). Although this process is not genuinely new – as it is enough to recognize the relatively long existence of computerized industrial control systems and machinery with electronic modules used in manufacturing production processes (Gutierrez & Leal, 2004) –; what is postulated is, in a certain way, a universalization of this process, with its rapid intensification, extending even to the most trivial goods. This ubiquitous computing project is well translated by industrial jargons such as the Internet of Things (itu, 2012; McKinsey Global Institute, 2015; Ogonda, 2017) and the Internet of Everything (Cisco *apud* Miraz et al., 2015; Qualcomm *apud* Miraz et al., 2015).

The maturation of the first wave of ICT diffusion was responsible for generating gigantic masses of data (Big Data) with a high degree of granularity, particularly for online activities and the geographical position of individuals through the Global Positioning System accessed by smartphones – and, therefore, as Greenwald (2014) stresses, also for recomposing their trajectories. The emergence of Big Data for financial transactions, consumption, mobility, political preferences, and personal contact networks, among other activities and attributes, enabled the implementation of statistical techniques based on the identification and synthesis of patterns and correlations present in large masses of data through the intensive use of computational capacity (Jason, 2017; Katz, 2017; Pasquinelli and Joler, 2020). Such statistical techniques, sometimes labeled as Big Data Analytics, sometimes labeled as machine learning, deep learning or AI – "whose common denominator is the use of expensive computing power to analyze massive centralized data" (Katz, 2017: 2) – have experienced important development and diffusion with deep neural networks, and depend on the intensive use of integrated circuits, AI training chips. What is meant by AI is, therefore, the application of these techniques to the large masses of data, enabling a certain type of partial or complete automation of various labor processes and human activities.

The commercial pursuit for such data production and centralization, both by search engines and the emergence of platform business models, engendered the concentration of computational capacity in large Data Centers to make possible the storing and processing of data (with cutting-edge chips), eventually giving way for the emergence of cloud computing strategies and business services (Srnicek, 2021). It is in this marriage between data and computational capacity centralization (Katz, 2017; Srnicek, 2016, 2021) that deep neural networks became viable and proliferated as information compression techniques (Pasquinelli and Joler, 2020) able to provide some kind of intelligibility to the astronomical amount of data and, from the patterns recognized, act back on the ICT system, automating it.

Coetaneous to the second wave of modernization, AI was initially applied to the voluminous masses of data derived from the first wave – considering that for each type of activity to be "intelligentized" it is generally necessary to have Big Data of the same nature –, while the scope of its application has been expanding as the second wave acquires momentum in different productive sectors, infrastructures, and activities, even though these processes are markedly uneven. This second wave, or the generic project of "digital intermediation of everything" (Morozov, 2018), finds in the new round of renewal of the global telecommunications infrastructure, 5G, an adequate material base. Developed and designed to sustain and enable the spread of such a wave, 5G is the first mobile telecommunication system intentionally designed to support massive amounts of devices, industrial systems, and mission-critical applications (Triolo and Allison, 2018). To deal with the different needs of the distinct types of users that will be connected to the network, 5G was conceived as a flexible infrastructure, in which network resources are allocated by software according to the specificities of the user – hence, departing from the principle of network neutrality (Lee and Chau, 2017). The complexity in defining these functions and allocating resources are managed by AI (Triolo and Allison, 2018).[3]

2.1   ICT *as a Technology and Machinery System*

Thus, it can be said that semiconductors, mobile telecommunication systems, particularly 5G, and AI are the three central technologies that currently make up the ICT technological system, constituted through two differentiated waves of diffusion.

---

3   In this sense, AI also becomes part of contemporary digital infrastructure – being explicitly recognized as such, for instance, by the Chinese government (Liu *et al.*, 2020. Xinhuanet, 2020) – due to both its direct implementation in the telecommunication system and its incorporation into productive, logistics, urban, and governmental structures, in the second wave of ICT-based modernization.

As parts of a technological system and as digital infrastructures, these three key technologies must be understood, on the one hand, as a stack of technologies – which historically superpose one another and maintain necessary technical relationships. Each layer of the stack has as technological presupposition and feasibility the development and implementation of the previous layers. On the other hand, once developed, the latest technological layers retroact on the technological development of the previous layers, engendering a process of coevolution and codetermination. Such coevolution, however, does not deny or suppress the technical preconditions of existence of the technologies at the top of the stack in relation to those at the base, whose technical progress and its rhythm delimit the conditions of possibility and evolution of the upper layers and can propagate and impact the entire system. Moreover, the emergence of the technologies of the top layers and their coevolution, in general, depend on a certain advanced, if not massive, degree of diffusion of the previous technologies. In this sense, digitalization is a prerequisite for networking, while these are requirements for AI.

Figure 5.1 synthetizes these relationships of stacking and coevolution of the key technologies in the ICT system. From data to the cloud, the entire ICT system rests on its foundation in the industrial base, that is, in semiconductors and semiconductor manufacturing equipment. As semiconductors are the building blocks of computing and communication capabilities, the rest of the technological system consists of semiconductor users.

According to Majerowicz and Medeiros (2018), semiconductor users in manufacturing (e.g., electronics industry), together with the semiconductor and semiconductor manufacturing equipment industries, constitute the modern industrial system. The development of ICT and its dissemination were strongly based on technical progress in the production of semiconductor manufacturing equipment, especially in lithography machines. These machines make possible to manufacture integrated circuits with more and more transistors in the same space by reducing the size of its elements, resulting in increasingly smaller and more powerful chips, while defining both the parameters for the manufacturing process and the design rules of integrated circuits (Atta and Slusarczuk, 2012; Platzer et al., 2020). The most critical interaction of this system, or its fundamental nexus, consists of the productive, technical, and commercial relationships – including preferential access (Atta and Slusarczuk, 2012) and technical support/cooperation – between semiconductor manufacturing equipment firms and those in semiconductor manufacturing.

The interactions between semiconductor users and the semiconductor industry occur primarily through the demand for characteristics and specifications posed by users, which are incorporated into chips by the design segment

THE SINO-AMERICAN DISPUTE IN ICT 149

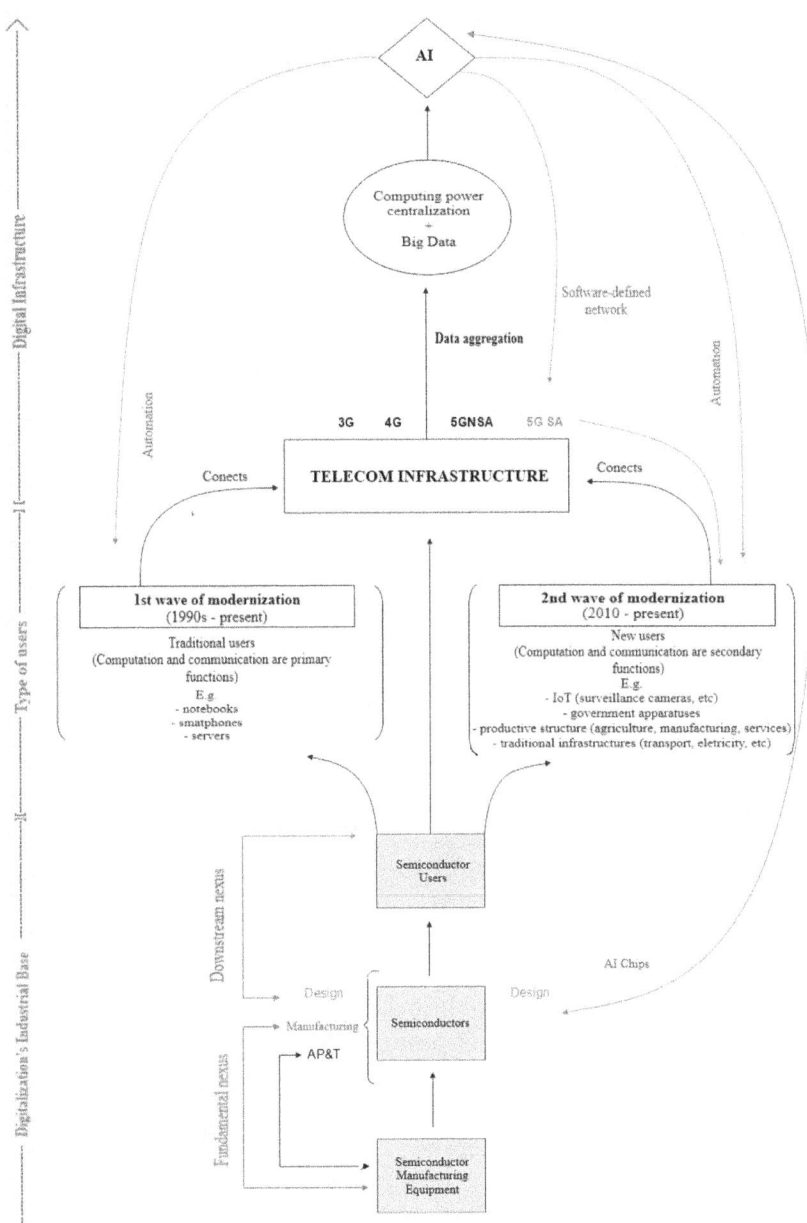

FIGURE 5.1   The stacking and coevolution of the key technologies in the ICT system
Note: "5GNSA" stands for 5G non-stand alone, a hybrid form of 4G (LTE) and 5G, which enables increased speed. "5GSA" stands for 5G stand alone, which also enables massive connection between machines and ultra-reliable and low latency connection. "AP&T" stands for assembly, packaging, and testing of semiconductors.
SOURCE: AUTHOR'S OWN ELABORATION

of industry, the downstream nexus of the industrial base. As semiconductor-based applications increase in character and spread, as well as new demands for their use arise, semiconductor design adapts to these needs, engendering the proliferation and diversification of semiconductor types. Thus, the development and proliferation of semiconductor users engender transformations, through the downstream nexus of the industrial base, on the production of semiconductors.

The integrated analysis of this key technological system of contemporary capitalism exposes to the naked eye the physical and productive aspects of data, the cloud, and AI. If we extrapolate the frontier of the firm as an analytical unit, we can understand it as a vast machinery system with a surprising degree of socialization, whose historical development has made it eminently global. This contemporary machinery system is composed by the industrial base of digitalization, the digital infrastructure, and electronic devices and objects with electronic modules connected to the digital infrastructure.

The global machinery system that incorporates the ICT technological system, on the one hand, negates the factory, by displacing it as the *locus par excellence* of its operation, due to both its character of infrastructure and the incorporation of mobile electronic devices in the subsistence wage, given their central role in the mediation and production of everyday life in modern societies. On the other hand, such a global machinery system reaffirms the factory and the factory system. From the stricter or more traditional point of view in designating the machinery system, as in Marx (1887) – what we have so far called the "industrial base of digitalization" –, it can be said that the "silicon machinery system", that is, the machines that produce semiconductors for the production of other machines, is what gives genesis, sustains, and conditions the pace of technical progress and development of the ICT machinery system *lato sensu*, this "global electronic monster". Hence, as will be argued, the strategic character of the rivalry among the industrial and technological great powers for the mastery of this manufacturing system and the recent movement, which acquires the character of a competitive compulsion, of descent from the cloud to the industrial base by several US and Chinese Big Tech. The supposed post-industrial world has never depended so much on the shop floor.

3   Competitive Vectors: Concentration and Pulverization

The comprehension of these technologies as a key technological system underpinning distinct waves of modernization, which is constituted by the stacking of technologies that coevolve and engenders a historical process of formation of a global machinery system, is essential for the apprehension of the competitive dynamics among the technological great powers – as well as their strategies – and their main technological companies. In Figure 5.1, it is possible to highlight two types of general dynamics in the technological development and historical evolution of this system, namely, the coexistence of processes of centralization and pulverization of machinery and productive capacity, that is, its centralization at the base and at the top and pulverization in the middle of the stack. While its base and top are extremely concentrated, due to both economic and political factors, its development presupposes and depends on diffusion and pulverization, in what we understand as waves of modernization.

Concentration is especially marked in semiconductor manufacturing equipment and the manufacturing of the most advanced semiconductors – whose productive and technological interactions constitute the fundamental nexus of the system. Such concentration derives from both economic factors – such as the large scale of capital requirement and R&D expenditures, the long maturation time of investments, the increasing returns to scale, and the very high degree of technical complexity involved in productive processes (Majerowicz, 2015; Platzer et al., 2020) – and political factors, such as technological transfer by and relations with the U.S. defense sector and the fierce protection of industrial and technical secrets (Atta and Slusarczuk, 2012; Goodwin, 1998; Sandia, 2001; Williams, 2019). Illustratively, for the productive processes in the manufacturing of the most sophisticated chips today, only one company in the world – the Dutch ASML, which has historical technological ties with the US defense sector (Atta and Slusarczuk, 2012; Majerowicz and Medeiros, 2018) – produces the Extreme Ultraviolet lithography (EUV)[4] capable of carrying out these processes. Only a few semiconductor companies from the US, Taiwan, and South Korea (TSMC, Intel, Samsung, SK Hynix, and Micron) are able to access these tools and employ or plan to use them in chip manufacturing (Lin, 2022).[5]

Just like the base, the top of the system is also marked by a strong concentration of machinery and productive capacity. It is the centralization of cutting-edge computing capacity – the productive consumption of semiconductors – that acts as material support for Big Data private production and the statistical models resulting from machine learning. The storage and processing of these data requires large scales of capital for acquiring the machinery

---

4 Lithography machines largely dictate the pace of technical progress in semiconductors to date, and access to new machines is a key factor in determining superprofits in the semiconductor and electronics industry (Atta and Slusarczuk, 2012).
5 China's SMIC was denied access to such equipment due to U.S. pressures (Alper et al., 2020).

in Data Centers, as well as sustaining their substantial energy consumption and maintenance. Here, technical barriers co-constituted by technological exclusivist policies are significantly less relevant. Thus, even though the number of companies operating in the business is small, it is much higher than in the base, with companies such as Google, Amazon, Microsoft, IBM, Apple, Huawei, Alibaba, Tencent, and Baidu.

In contrast, the concentration at the top is predicated and depends on the diffusion and pulverization of semiconductors and electronic devices in the economy, civil society, government, and traditional infrastructure. The more widespread the pulverized consumption of semiconductors, the greater the imperative for the concentration of machinery at the top and the greater the scope for the development of AI-based partial and full automation, expanding the branches and activities susceptible to AI's application.[6]

4 Competition in the ICT System as a Whole: No Cold War

In this context, some central elements for competition between China and the U.S. and their large technology companies come to light. First, it becomes evident that, from the coevolution and the wide diffusion of these technologies to different areas, a system of high complexity emerges, with an enormous and

---

6 The dynamics of concentration and pulverization of semiconductor consumption are manifested in the very structuring of the AI industry, whose production has two phases, training and inference. Training the algorithm with Big Data – to obtain the statistical model that embodies extracted patterns – occurs with AI training chips, which are highly sophisticated and consumed centrally in dedicated facilities. Once the model is obtained, a simple software, it is then embedded in electronic devices and objects through AI inference chips, which are low cost and low power chips, whose function is to face unknown data and classify them using the embedded statistical model. Thus, the pulverization of semiconductor consumption is both a premise and a result of AI, in as much as inference chips become the manifestation of the centralized power of data over the scattered parts of the global machinery system. This particular arrangement of computational power and its centralization-pulverization dynamics support and reflect the understanding postulated by Durand (2020) regarding Big Data: "The symbolic productions that emanate from individuals but that, when multiplied and aggregated, assume a form that becomes unrecognizable to them, this is what Big Data is: a 'sea of data' where algorithms will extract a surplus that emanates from individual actions but which, in the aggregation process, comes to transcend them and returns to them metamorphosed.

Between the social and Big Data, there is more than one analogy. Big Data is certainly not all the social but belong to the social. They come from a dialectical movement: first, the symbolic crystallization of collective power captured in statistical regularities; then feedback from this power on individuals and their behaviors".

growing degree of differentiation in its inputs, final goods, and applications. Therefore, it is highly unlikely if not impossible to internalize this system in its completeness inside the borders of a single country, no matter how large the country is, without sacrificing its complexity.

Although the ICT system has its genesis in the U.S. academic-military-industrial complex, which keeps being fundamental to ICT technical progress[7] (Medeiros, 2003; Noble, 2011; Morris, 1990; Mazzucato, 2013; Platzer et al., 2020), the process of converting these military technologies to the civil sector – which occurred especially from the 1970s onwards – and their diffusion in the first wave of modernization are simultaneous to neoliberalism, so that the very constitution of the global ICT machinery system was predicated in the globalization of production. The formation of the ICT technological system was, therefore, based not only on the global diffusion of the consumption of electronic devices and digital infrastructure, but also on the international productive fragmentation of its industrial base (e.g., electronics industry, semiconductors). The developments and coevolution of this system are also expressed in the increase in the breadth and depth of global value chains (GVC), as the GVC of personal computers was followed by the mobile communications GVC, and further succeeded by the emergence of the AI GVC, "involving a greater diversity of stakeholders on multiple GVC layers" (Ernst, 2020: 13).

Illustratively, analyzing just one of the most recent components of this system, AI chips, Ernst (2020: 14) states: "That chip can only function if it is integrated into a multilayered ecosystem and if developers are willing to develop AI applications around this specific chip". As a result, the author concludes: "No country, not even the United States or China, can bring together all the different layers of that ecosystem. Hence, access is needed to highly specialized GVCs that transcend national borders" (Ernst, 2020: 14).

If for only a specific high-tech input of this system it is already difficult to envision the viability of a complete nationalization of the supply chain, the ambitions to internalize the entire industry and, further, the whole system, seem even more detached from the limits of possibilities imposed by the materiality of the contemporary machinery system as historically constituted. Therefore, the idea that the current Sino-American dispute acquires the contours of a new Cold War is not only unreasonable from the point of view that

---

7 "Modernizing our military requires successful research, technology maturation, prototyping, systems integration, and test capability to turn innovative and disruptive technology into fielded and sustainable military systems. The Fiscal Year 2022 President's [of the Department of Defense] Budget requests $2.3 billion for various microelectronics efforts crucial to long-term national security". (Dod, 2021: 3–2).

there are no two "contending modes of production and opposed models of society" in dispute (Dyer-Witheford and Matviyenko, 2019: 21), but also for postulating a digital division into two compartmentalized blocs, disregarding the implications posed by the eminently global technical and productive aspects of this system.

Although the machinery system is global, the most sophisticated productive and technological part of this system's industrial base, its fundamental nexus, is controlled by a handful of developed economies that are military allies, namely the U.S., South Korea, Taiwan, Europe, and Japan. China is not only technologically lagging in this fundamental nexus, but also has very low productive capacity vis-à-vis its consumption[8] (ICinsights, 2021, 2022 *apud* Evertiq, 2022), and it does not even have certain productive subsectors – in this respect, like all other countries. Thus, the most plausible hypothesis is that, instead of "two antagonistic blocs", if the U.S. and allies decide to tighten the pressure on China, it would constitute only a greater or lesser degree of exclusion of the country from the global machinery system than the formation of two rival blocs.

Moreover, even if it were possible for a country to internalize this entire system, replicating it in its entirety on a national scale – as it has been expressed in Chinese ambitions and rhetoric of technological self-sufficiency in general and in semiconductors in particular (State Council, 2014, 2015; Buck and Chenne, 2021; Sutter, 2021) –, such an undertaking would reduce not only the degree of complexity of the system – compromising, for example, the variety of semiconductors dedicated to the most diverse applications – but also would impact the degree and speed of diffusion of semiconductor consumption, which would be limited by domestic productive capacity. This limitation would impose technological obstacles, since the degree of diffusion of these technologies and the expansion of the contemporary machinery system are important for the very

---

8 According to ICinsights (2022 *apud* Evertiq, 2022) data, in 2021, the IC market in China amounted to $186,5 billion dollars, or 36,5% of the world IC market. China IC production represented 16.7% of its consumption/market, of which only 6.6 percentage points, or $12.3 billion dollars were produced by enterprises headquartered in China. Despite the rise in the rate of consumption over production in China from 10.2% in 2010 (Icinsights, 2021), this number falls short from Made in China 2025 (State Council, 2015) target of 40% for 2020 and is still very far from the projected target of 70% for 2025. Regarding semiconductor manufacturing equipment, China's rate of consumption over production is even lower: "The localization rate of semiconductor equipment in Mainland China is merely 11.5%, and the China-made semiconductor equipment makes up roughly 2% of the global market". (Research and Markets, 2019).

unfolding of the system and its technological development, especially with regards to data production and the possibility of automation.

5   The Fundamental Nexus: US Structural Power in the ICT System

Despite ICT productive globalization, globalization occurred in a controlled manner (Majerowicz and Medeiros, 2018), considering that the all-encompassing character of the contemporary machinery system – therefore, the myriad of uses to which it lends itself and the new mediations it engenders with its expansion – makes economic, political, and national security issues inseparable. Therefore, the globalized constitution of this system, and, in particular, of its industrial base, took place in a heterogeneous way, under the control of the U.S., maintaining the following general characteristics:

i)   the unskilled labor-intensive productive stages were offshored to any and all parts of the globe where there were cost advantages;

ii) the manufacturing of semiconductors had a much timider degree of globalization[9] and tended to be subjected to regulations[10] – which sought to keep these manufacturing processes in the domestic economy, particularly those at the technological frontier –, as well as the production and export of semiconductor manufacturing equipment[11] GAO, 2002; Khan, 2020);

---

9   According to the Semiconductor Industry Association (SIA, 2021), the U.S. semiconductor industry maintains the largest share of its manufacturing base (43%) in the US compared to any other single country. The inclusion of other economies, particularly in East Asia, as relevant players in the manufacturing of semiconductors depended less on transnational corporations offshoring plants and more on national development strategies, industrial policies, and technological transfer for the emergence of domestic companies (Yeung, 2022). China may constitute an exception among the major players in manufacturing, for most of the production of integrated circuits in the country is the result of the operation of foreign companies, even though industrial policy and its national strategy are fundamental for the rise of domestic firms.

10 For example, in 2016, the Taiwanese government required TSMC, the largest foundry of the world, to initiate more sophisticated new productive processes in Taiwan before creating productive capacity with the current technological process in mainland China, which should be limited to a maximum of three plants (Clarke, 2016). Government limitations on the transfer of Taiwanese companies' cutting-edge productive capacity in semiconductor manufacturing have been in place for a significant period (Chu, 2013).

11 In addition to domestic regulations, semiconductor manufacturing equipment are also under the scope of the Wassenaar Arrangement, a voluntary international agreement on export controls of conventional weapons and dual-use (civil-military) goods and technologies.

iii) only a few military allied countries – due to particular geopolitical circumstances – received technical assistance and technological transfer from the U.S. to extrapolate 'i' and develop 'ii' (Majerowicz and Medeiros, 2018);

iv) even with the development of some of the allies in the fundamental nexus, the U.S. has shown a great capacity to handle them over the decades, both by the political restriction of their industries (Japan) and the help provided in creating other economic competitors among the military allies (South Korea and Taiwan) to prevent losing its dominance over the fundamental nexus (Majerowicz and Medeiros, 2018; Morris, 1990).

This control over the fundamental nexus – that is, the semiconductor manufacturing equipment industry and semiconductor manufacturing, as well as the interactions between these segments of the industrial base – is what gives the U.S. structural power in the ICT system. This power is revealed in its direct and indirect dominance, together with its military allies, of the semiconductor manufacturing equipment industry[12] and the semiconductor industry.[13] In semiconductors, historically, the U.S. has been able to recover market share from its economic competitors in the world market stemming from changes in the signal of U.S. domestic policy (Morris, 1990; Majerowicz and Medeiros, 2018). Moreover, considering that the interactions expressed in this nexus are central to the technological development of the entire system, they become the focus of technological exclusivist practices.[14]

---

12 The world's leading semiconductor machinery companies are from the U.S., Japan, and the Netherlands.

13 According to SIA (2022), the global semiconductor market by enterprise headquarters, excluding foundries, was divided as follows in 2021: US (46%), South Korea (21%), Japan (9%), Europe (9%), Taiwan (8%), and China (7%). ICinsights (2022 *apud* Sheen, 2022) offers statistics in which American dominance is even greater: US (54%), South Korea (22%), Taiwan (9%), Europe (6%), Japan (6%), and China (4%). According to SIA data, China would have gained 2 percentage points since 2021, while ICinsights (2021, 2022 *apud* Sheen, 2022) estimates a loss of 1 percentage points because of the US sanctions on HiSilicon.

14 The tacit or uncoded knowledge, in the terms of academic literature on innovation, or industrial secrets, long discussed by classical political economists, are evident in this sensitive industry, given the sophistication of the equipment and production processes in question (Majerowicz, 2019): "part of this is due to the fact that both foundries and equipment vendors work together to fine tune how to extract maximum yield out of the production lines. This co-developed knowledge is often locked under NDA [non-disclosure agreements]" (Williams, 2019).

In this context, facing the unviability of a country to replicate the complete system in its diversity, the second-best strategy is to control the key elements of technological development and the key subsectors. Considering that this system is formed by a stack, it follows that no matter how developed the country or company is in the upper layers, without the production and/or access to the goods of the lower layers, this development is halted.[15] This is one of the main aspects that gives the U.S. structural power in the ICT system stemming from the control of the fundamental nexus. It is not, however, just a matter of controlling supplies essential to digitalization, because the structural power also emanates from the fact that the set of technological possibilities in the upper layers are given by the industrial base – so that the pace of technical progress on that base propagates throughout the system.[16]

It is precisely through the leverage of this structural power derived from the control over the industrial base of digitalization – whether it is established directly over US producers, or indirectly over the economies and producers of military allied countries, particularly through the extraterritoriality conferred by the foreign direct product rule in US sanctions[17] – that the U.S. has been seeking to contain China's ICT ambitions and the effective Chinese success in the upper layers of this system (Majerowicz, 2019; NSCAI, 2021). If, initially, the sanctions were focused on specific companies that were being added to the US Entity List, such as Huawei, the US has significantly increased the use of its structural power by amplifying the scope of the sanctions in October 2022. With the latter, the US has been attempting to block the Chinese development

---

15   This diagnosis is also reflected in the Final Report of the U.S. National Security Commission on Artificial Intelligence (NSCAI, 2021), in which semiconductor manufacturing equipment are identified as a critical bottleneck for Chinese development in AI. Thus, the report recommends: "Utilize targeted export controls on key semiconductor manufacturing equipment (SME). Where possible, the United States should use export controls to prevent competitors from obtaining AI capabilities that would grant them strategic or military advantages. The primary U.S. export control target to constrain competitors' AI capabilities should be sophisticated SME necessary to manufacture high-end chips" (NSCAI, 2021: 230).

16   The U.S. Department of Defense (2021) is explicit about the impacts of advances in semiconductors on technological development at the top of the stack when requesting a budget for research and investments in microchips. According to the DoD (2021: 3–2), "Advanced capability microelectronics technology development directly influences success in fielding disruptive technologies, including the following Advanced Capability Enablers", namely, hypersonic, AI, and 5G.

17   This rule establishes that foreign firms using controlled US technology or software are in the scope of US export restrictions. If these foreign firms fail to comply, they might lose access to US technology and software themselves.

in AI and supercomputers, while seeking to degrade the actual technological capacity of China's leading semiconductor manufacturing enterprises, such as SMIC and YMTC (Allen, 2022). Hence, the US has forbidden the supplies of AI high-end chips used in data centers and supercomputing facilities to China, as well as blocked Chinese AI and supercomputing chip designs from being manufactured in any facility outside China either because these designs were made using US electronic design automation (EDA) tools (whose purchase have presumption of denial) and/or because the manufacturing facilities employ US semiconductor manufacturing equipment (SME) – which encompass virtually all facilities.[18] In line with the recommendation advanced in the 2021 final report by the US National Security Commission on Artificial Intelligence, chaired by Google's former-CEO Eric Schmidt, the US has also cut Chinese access to advanced SME (NASCAI, 2021), and blocked the supply of American components necessary for manufacturing SME to prevent the building of Chinese SME alternatives (Allen, 2022). Moreover, US nationals and residents have been prohibited to work in and support the production of advanced chips in in China (Sheehan, 2022).[19] The US was also successful in convincing the other two major players of the SME industry, the Netherlands and Japan, to impose export controls to China – virtually locking the market for advanced SME to the country (Toh and Ogura, 2023).

However, the leverage of the US structural power does not unfold without contradictions. By denying access to some of the most sophisticated fundamental inputs and the advanced machines – and their parts – at the base of the ICT system, China is put back and forced to broaden even more its strategy of import substitution and dedicate more efforts and resources to developing its own industrial and technological capabilities. This is one reason why several analysts in the US have been against the US sanctions, claiming that ultimately they would benefit more China than the US (Kumar, 2022; Castellano, 2023). For instance, in November 2022, Huawei has filed a patent for key elements of the EUV lithography machine, an important step in a long road toward the commercial development of such machine and the mastering of its productive

---

18 "With the new rules, no Chinese chip design company will be allowed to outsource manufacturing abroad for advanced AI and supercomputing chips. For those Chinese organizations on the BIS Entity List, they will be blocked from outsourcing the manufacturing of any types of chips at all" (Allen, 2022: 5).

19 Biden's strategy also seeks to rearticulate U.S. relations with allied countries to provide a coordinated response to China. If more difficulty has been found in Biden's initiative in forging the chip 4 alliance with Japan, Taiwan, and South Korea, reportedly he has been able to achieve an agreement with Japan and the Netherlands to increase restrictions on SME and associated technologies to China (Pan, 2023).

use (Shilov, 2022). Meanwhile, as a response to the US sanctions, China has been reportedly planning to further intensify its efforts to develop the semiconductor industry, with a five-year plan encompassing US$143 billion (Gooding, 2022). In the long run, some of the technologies, inputs and even machines, may find domestic substitutes, affecting the own US structural power in the ICT system – that is, if this was not a race with moving targets, and hence, did not depend on what is happening in the technological frontier and how players are moving along it. However, the success of China's import substitution strategy, be it self-determined and/or imposed by circumstances, is still contingent in China being part of global value chains. Illustratively, the same EUV machine discussed above has more than 100,000 parts, which are sourced by specialized producers across the globe, some of these, being supplied by just one firm (Lin, 2022).

Another contradiction of the leverage of the US structural power emerges from China's economic importance to the US tech sector. China joined the world market during the neoliberal period and began to play a central role in the global constitution of the ICT system, both from the point of view of final consumption – since it has become the fastest expanding market in recent decades and the main market for a myriad of electronic goods in units sold – and the point of view of internationally fragmented production – becoming the world's leading electronic producing center and, therefore, the main consumer of semiconductors on the planet since 2005 (ICinsights, 2020). This important role imposes domestic resistances to the U.S. full leverage of its structural power in the ICT system, given the various circuits of capital accumulation of US technology companies that have in China their main market for realization. The US tech sector is not fully on board with US sanctions. The US semiconductor industry, for instance, defends industrial policy support as a competitive mechanism instead of sanctions in order to continue with business as usual (Hamblen, 2022). Hence, in the decisions of whether and how to leverage the U.S. structural power, there are tensions between those defending the politically motivated goals of national security – which are also growingly supported by capitalists facing competition with Chinese businesses (see, for instance, Google's former-CEO recommendation to NASCAI supporting export controls) – and those whose businesses are strongly tied to the Chinese economy, such as the overall U.S. semiconductor industry.

While the leverage of the U.S. structural power can place serious obstacles to Chinese development in ICT, at least in the short to mid-term, the U.S. cannot use this strategy very effectively without hampering itself, given the economic losses entailed in its intertwining with China. Meanwhile, beyond the war of short-term positions based on prohibitions to halt China's productive capacity and generate technological obsolescence, competition tends to intensify in the quest to move forward the technological frontier with a long-term horizon – as signaled at the end of the Obama administration (PCAST, 2017), and affirmed in the Biden administration, especially with the CHIPS and Science Act, whose budget of $280 billion for the next ten years provides $200 billion for scientific R&D and commercialization, and $52,7 billion for semiconductors (manufacturing, R&D, and workforce qualification) (Badlam et al., 2022). In this sense, if the U.S. can move faster on the technological frontier, China's technological obsolescence is also a corollary and occurs without the need to short-circuit capital accumulation in many of the country's large and important technology companies. On the long-term horizon, if there is no technological disruption that supplants the "silicon machinery system", the U.S. also gets ahead in the race due to its structural power stemming from the control over the fundamental nexus, with all the implications this has to the pace of technical progress.

Meanwhile, in the medium term, the U.S. seeks to strengthen its dominance over this nexus of the industrial base of digitalization, pursuing the implementation of policies that increase domestic manufacturing capacity for "supply chains for critical sectors and subsectors of the information and communications technology (ICT) industrial base" (The White House, 2021b). This concern stems mainly from the facts that much of the global semiconductor manufacturing capacity is no longer in the U.S. – whose share felt from 37% in 1990 to 12% in 2020 (Varas et al., 2020; The White House, 2021a) – and that all manufacturing capacity of high-end chips (below 10nm) is now concentrated on the territory of its Asian military allies, with Taiwan detaining a share of 92% and South Korea, 8% (Varas et al., 2021, The White House, 2021a). The US establishment is worried due to the geographical proximity of such industrial base to China (Moore, 2021), particularly in the event of Taiwan being absorbed by the mainland. Besides strengthening the US domestic capacity, the US is also supporting "allyshoring" or "friendshoring", or "an approach ... to diversify away from countries that present geopolitical and security risks to our supply chain" (Yellen *apud* Aggarwal, 2022). In the case of semiconductor manufacturing, the aim is not only to reduce China's share, but also to deconcentrate productive capacity out of Taiwan.

6 The Race for the Downstream Nexus: Big Tech, from Consumption to Semiconductor Production

Unlike the fundamental nexus, marked by U.S. dominance, the downstream nexus is where the fierce competition between Chinese and U.S. companies becomes visible. This intensification of competition has driven the Big Tech of both countries to assume a greater productive character at the expense of merely engaging in activities for the redistribution/predation of surplus value. In this section, we will turn to this dimension of intercapitalist competition.

It is undeniable that there is, contemporary, a sharp competition among the Big Tech for the collection and capture of data (Durand, 2020; Zuboff, 2019). However, in several academic analyses, this competitive dynamic tends to be separated from the analysis of the ICT technological and machinery systems as a whole, focusing only in the most visible surface of the stack, with more direct implications in everyday life. In Figure 5.1, this dynamic can be seen simply as the dispute for data aggregation, that is, the centralization at the top of the technological and machinery system.

An important contribution to the analysis of intercapitalist competitive dynamics is offered by Srnicek (2016), who examines the different models of digital platforms. Beyond postulating the tendency towards monopolization engendered by network effects and highlighting the digital "enclosures" of platforms, Srnicek (2016) advances two competitive dynamics that consider the broader ICT system. Predicated as extensions of the imperative of collecting more data, these dynamics are: i) the imperative of platforms to develop the full stack, that is, "a tendency to increasingly take on all the features of the stack,[20] from hardware to software" (Srnicek, 2016); ii) and, considering the stack, the tendency of large platforms to pursue key and strategic positions, in a rhizomatic integration, in which "the strategic importance of a position has much more to do with controlling data from businesses and customers than with just being lower in the stack" (Srnicek, 2016). In relation to the first trend, he highlights both the centrality of "the extension of sensors" – particularly stressing the electronic consumer devices of the Internet of Things, in which sensors are embedded in homes and the most trivial consumer goods – and "the means of analysis", emphasizing the role of advances in computer servers and hardware and investments in AI.

If it is a fact that the production of raw data and its subsequent transformation into Big Data and AI-derived statistical models require both the embedded diffusion of semiconductors and their technological development – since more powerful servers come from more powerful chips –, the relationships of individual capitals with these machines are distinct and bear consequences for competition. The diffusion of semiconductors, in general, and the Internet

---

20 Srnicek's (2016) stack is not exactly the same, as here we have included the entire industrial base of digitization.

of Things, in particular, takes place extra-frontier of the technology firm. That is, the ownership of these machines does not tend to accrue to the companies, which sell them – i.e., they are not their fixed assets –, even if the permanent integration of these machines in the contemporary machinery system engenders the creation of constant channels for applying AI and absorbing the data produced by the use and/or automatic operation of such devices.

This dissemination, in general, takes place in the form of tie-in sales – electronic devices and embedded software –, therefore constituting differentiated sources of profit for the company(s) involved, or in the sale of electronic devices with free embedded software, whose counterpart may be access to data, as Srnicek (2016) stresses. This process of embedded diffusion of semiconductors, therefore, does not occur, in general, as a mere counterpart to data and, for total capital, as discussed in the next section, it is much more conditioned to national strategies than those of individual capitals. That is, the ICT machinery system as ubiquitous machinery, which denies the factory as a *locus par excellence* of the machinery system, finds central determinations in state policies that drive technical progress in semiconductors and the development and implementation of digital infrastructure, national industrial strategies, and capital accumulation patterns.

In contrast, the machinery held by Big Tech in the form of concentrated and centralized computing power, "the means of analysis", is in fact fixed capital of these companies. Here, the productive consumption of semiconductors is key to the quality and the expansion of Big Tech services and to competition between individual capitals in this sphere of accumulation. Moreover, it has been widely recognized in the academia and the industry that both the emergence of large masses of data and technical progress in semiconductors (computing capacity) were the enabling elements for the emergence of the AI industry, and that both continue to be central to competition in this industry (Ding, 2018; Ernst, 2020; Lee, 2018).[21] There is also, therefore, a race for computing capacity that is not limited to data access.

It is this centrality of technical progress in semiconductors for the technological development of the upper layers of stack that explains Big Tech's recent movement of descent from the mere consumption to semiconductor production, albeit in general only at the semiconductor design stage.[22] Thus,

---

21 According to Ding (2018: 4), technological development in AI has four central parameters, namely "(1) hardware in the form of chips for training and executing AI algorithms, (2) data as an input for AI algorithms, (3) research and algorithm development, and (4) the commercial AI ecosystem".
22 In addition to the demand for higher performance, Fitch (2020) also highlights the search for minor costs implied in this movement: "Amazon, Google and Microsoft each are

large U.S. and Chinese technology companies began to seek to develop their own designs of AI and/or cloud computing chips. This is the case of Google, Apple, Amazon, Microsoft, Baidu, Alibaba, Tencent, ByteDance – the owner of TikTok – and possibly even Facebook (Fitch, 2020; Global Times, 2021). And this move towards the industrial base of digitalization is strategic for competition between large technology companies, but not because it is 'rhizomatic' and associated with the control of third-party data. It is about the competitiveness gains associated with the internalization of one of the key nexuses of technological development in the ICT system, namely, the downstream nexus in Figure 5.1, in which interactions occur between semiconductor consumers and semiconductor producers through customer's specifications of the parameters that should drive chip design. By internalizing this relationship, this interaction occurs in a much more refined way, resulting in chip designs much more suitable for the computing needs of each firm and their applications. The October 2022 sanctions, however, may create a further disadvantage for the Chinese tech giants since they attempt not only to deny access to advanced AI chips but also to close the space for the pursuit of the internalization of such relationship in AI, either by denying access to EDA software for developing chip designs or blocking the access to manufacturing facilities.

Such as for countries, it is impossible for companies to internalize the entire ICT machinery system. This impossibility makes them seek to build strategic partnerships with firms in the adjacent layer – as in the case of the special relationships established between certain semiconductor manufacturing companies and the producers of lithography machines, in the fundamental nexus, to obtain priority of access to the newest machines (Atta and Slusarczuk, 2012) – or, when feasible, to internalize the very nexus of key technological interactions – expressed in this movement of internalization of semiconductor design by the large technology firms that consume them. The latter movement applies not only to the case of cloud companies, but also to the case of producers of electronic devices, such as Huawei, whose chip design subsidiary, HiSilicon, was credited by much of the success of Huawei's products (Triggs, 2018) before being added to the US Entity List.

Thus, the aspect of the ICT machinery system that affirms the factory is also felt in intercapitalist competition even for those companies that have been associated only with business models of value predation and not production

estimated to operate millions of servers in globe spanning networks of data centers for their own use and to rent out to their millions of cloud-computing customers. Even small improvements in performance and minute reductions in the cost of powering and cooling chips become worth the effort when spread across those vast technology empires".

by parcel of the academic literature[23] – such as cloud companies and even advertising-focused companies such as Facebook. As a machinery system that extrapolates the factory, the ICT system, in order to develop technologically, must always return and refer to the shop floor.

7 The Waves of Modernization and the Acceleration of Diffusion: the Role of the State

Technical progress in semiconductors and semiconductor manufacturing equipment not only enabled the computing capacity needed for the development of AI or Big Data Analytics, but also the very emergence of Big Data. It was the cheapening, the increase of performance, and the miniaturization of semiconductors that enabled the mass diffusion of semiconductors in both the goods whose computing and communication capacities are primary functions and those in which they are secondary functions, referring here, respectively, to the first and second waves of modernization based on ICT.

Despite this same determination to both waves of modernization – and, consequently, the role of the state in them can be already perceived, particularly that of the U.S., for the advancement of the technological frontier in these crucial sectors of the "silicon machinery system" –, it can be said that the propagation dynamics of these modernization waves keep important determinations that differentiate them. This is particularly valid when considering the role of the state and interstate competition, since the project of "digital intermediation of everything", or the ubiquity of the modern global machinery system, entails state action and coordination that go far beyond corporate strategies and workers' decisions regarding consumption.

It is true that the state was also fundamental to the first wave – just think of its role in the emergence of the Internet and the implementation/regulation of telecommunications infrastructure, as well as in the computerization of public companies and services or the encouragement for the adoption of computers and computerized industrial control systems by private companies. But the first wave really gained momentum due to the explosion of personal consumption of these goods. If initially the first wave, on the one hand, moved due to the cheapening of personal computers and smartphones, on the other hand, it found limitations in the income level of working families. However, as smartphones became indispensable for the insertion in the labor

---

23 See, for instance, Durand (2020).

market, including the informal sector, and to access public services (Morozov, 2018), they were incorporated into workers' subsistence wage, even in much of the capitalist periphery. This process did not occur with the other mixed-use goods of the first wave, such as personal computers and tablets. In this sense, the hypothesis presented here is that a significant portion of the global demand that sustained the boom of the first wave of modernization largely decoupled from the income level of workers, possibly shifting the level of consumption of other subsistence goods, which would provide support to personal demand for smartphones even in the face of stagnation or decline in workers' incomes.

In contrast, it is not to be expected or there is nothing to ensure that the advertised personal consumer goods of the second wave – e.g., smart surveillance cameras, smart appliances, voice assistants, smartwatches – will have such a strong demand, with an explosive trajectory, such as the one experienced by smartphones. In a historical period of fierce global competition between workers and the informalization of domestic labor markets – made possible by ICT themselves –, with a vast industrial reserve army (Foster et al., 2011; Huws, 2019; Fontes, 2017), the pressure of these factors on workers' wages does not seem to make wages a promising source of demand for the support of the second wave of modernization. And, as far as we know, Big Tech is not providing this entire range of products – for "the extension of their sensors" (Srnicek, 2016) – free of charge in exchange for data, as data is far from the only relevant source of profitability associated with the modern global machinery system. Thus, in addition to the determinants that involve state action for the formation and propagation of the first wave, the second wave seems to require an even more prominent role of the state, especially when we consider that the state should assume the role of a central demander for the products of this wave, since personal demand tends to be much more restricted compared to the previous wave.

Moreover, the project of "digital intermediation of everything" has only one of its relevant components in the goods used for personal consumption. Three other components associated with this project are worth highlighting. First, the transformation of traditional and urban infrastructure (e.g., smart grids, smart cities), in addition to the very renewal of the mobile telecommunication system with 5G, which introduce new intermediations in the most distinct areas of social life. Secondly, the transformations in the productive structure stemming from the diffusion of the most recent developments of the ICT technological system. These refer not only to the manufacturing industry – a component of "the digital intermediation of everything" translated into the projects of "Industry 4.0" –, but also to services and, especially, agriculture, which has remained, so far, the sector relatively less touched by the diffusion of semiconductors in productive processes. Finally, the transformations in the state apparatus itself, including public services, with emphasis on two processes, namely: i) the technological upgrade and the development of state repressive apparatuses, including ubiquitous surveillance, which is also implemented through the first component, with smart cities and intelligent transport systems (Graham, 2010); and ii) the reconfiguration of the state itself in relation to capital, with privatization within the public machine, which will depend on Big Tech to be operational, both for providing public services as education and its day-to-day activities (Morozov, 2018).

Thus, the state is a direct executor (e.g., smart cities, transport infrastructure), activator and coordinator, through industrial policies, and the object of the second wave of modernization based on ICT. These instances of state action highlight what Medeiros (2018) provides due centrality, namely, the role of government procurement for technological development and dissemination. Analyzing China's economic development, Medeiros (2013, 2018) diagnoses that infrastructure investments were one of the engines of the country's growth, while government procurement and demand for innovation have propelled its technological development. As previously discussed, the technological development of the ICT system has in the degree of diffusion one of its important determinants, thus establishing another sphere in which the state appears as fundamental to contemporary technological development.

Therefore, it is mainly around the states of the great technological powers that the second wave of modernization has gained momentum and not around the corporate strategies of Big Tech, even though these are the major suppliers and beneficiaries of the projects of "digital intermediation of everything" headed by these states. Diffusion affects technological development and enables the emergence of new branches of accumulation and the reconfiguration of different markets stemming from the new mediations made possible by ICT. This makes room not only for Big Tech to enter established sectors challenging incumbents, but also to privatize public services, urban spaces, and part of the state's operational structure. As a result, a race is established for the implementation and dissemination among the technological great powers in close alliance with their technology companies, tending to provoke the acceleration of the second wave. This is particularly true for the cases of China and the U.S.

8 The Sino-American Dispute and the Race for Implementation

The Chinese Communist Party (CCP) has been implementing a plan for the manufacturing industry in general, Made in China 2025 (State Council, 2015), along with sectoral industrial policies aimed at the ICT sector – including the 2014 National Guidelines for the Promotion and Development of the Integrated Circuit Industry (State Council, 2014), the 2017 New Generation Artificial Intelligence Development Plan (State Council, 2017), and the 2020 Policies for Promoting the High-Quality Development of the Integrated Circuit Industry and the Software Industry (State Council, 2020; Zhang, 2020). In addition, the CCP has launched several policies aimed at the dissemination of ICT on the different aspects of the economy, society, and national security. After initially controlling what could have become a serious health crisis, in March 2020, China saw as a way out for its economy a package of public-private investments, with a large participation of domestic Big Tech, in what it has been calling the "new infrastructures", namely: 5G infrastructure, AI, Big Data, Data Centers, Industrial Internet, ultra-high voltage power transmission lines, batteries for charging electric vehicles, and high-speed long-distance transportation (Liu et al., 2020).[24] From the point of view of ICT, this perspective reveals a strategy for disseminating these technologies as a package, a set whose implementation should go *pari passu* and in which the implementation of each technology tends to strengthen and propel the dissemination of the others.

It should be noted, however, that the role of government procurement in the development of the ICT system in China goes far beyond such an investment package. The case of the development of the AI industry in the country is emblematic. In 2019, the AI software and application market in China totaled US$ 2.89 billion,[25] approximately 51% of which was related to computer vision technology (IDC, 2020; Shiyue, 2020). The main vector of demand in computer vision was government spending on public security and smart cities (IDC, 2020; Shiyue, 2020). The highlight in this technology is facial recognition

---

24 This investment package seeks to achieve short- and long-term objectives, acting macroeconomically to maintain the growth rate and ensuring the infrastructures considered as a precondition for the deepening of digitalization, "networkization", and "intelligentization". The centrality of the CCP's leitmotiv "digitalize, networkize, and intelligentize" (Xinhuanet, 2018; People's Daily, 2019; Xu, 2019) is such that it gained expression in the methodology of GDP measurement, with the National Bureau of Statistics producing metrics on the "new economy" and the "three new" sectors, accounting for digitalized and internet-connected activities in agriculture, manufacturing, and services as portions of GDP (NBS, 2020b).

25 Including hardware, this market reached $6 billion (IDC, 2020).

– one of the applications in which China leads worldwide, followed by the U.S. (Ding, 2018; Financial Times, 2021) –, whose demand in China was basically destined to public security (72% in 2015), followed by far by finance (20% in 2015) (Chyxx, 2020). Thus, in addition to the start-up unicorns in AI (Megvii, Yutu, Sensetime, Cloudwalk), the big companies in the security industry are rapidly gaining market shares of the computer vision market in China, particularly the state-owned Hikvision and the mixed capital company Dahua (IDC, 2020).

Here, it becomes clear how the Chinese advantage in the technological diffusion of AI, stemming from government procurement, contributed to the conversion of the country to the position of primacy in facial recognition. According to official statistics, in the 2010s, government public security spending in China exceeded spending for national defense, so that, in 2019, it was 22% higher (NBS, 2020a). In this sense, in addition to the importance of China's military modernization strategy for its technological development and the civil-military nature of ICT (Majerowicz and Medeiros, 2018; Trebat and Medeiros, 2014), social control is consolidated as one of the main objectives of the state's action in pursuing the project of "digital intermediation of everything".

The U.S. stance in the technology dispute during the Trump administration had a short-term logic, with the series of restrictions on Chinese companies (e.g., Huawei, Hikvision, Dahua, Megvii, Yutu, Sensetime) and the interference and pressure on the relations of U.S. allies and their companies with Chinese companies (Alper et al., 2020; BIS, 2019a, 2019b;). Trump mobilized the escalation of tension in the technological dispute with China for electoral purposes, but his policies reverberated deep concerns of the US establishment.

At the end of the Obama administration, several documents were published stressing the need for government resource targeting and support, with industrial policy, to the ICT sector, particularly in the call for strengthening the semiconductor industry and the outline of a national plan for AI (NSTC, 2016; pcast, 2017; The White House, 2016;). In addition to emphasizing the need to ensure U.S. supremacy in semiconductors, the President's Council of Advisers on Science and Technology (PCAST, 2017) warned about Chinese industrial policies. These had been achieving great results in ICT, in a context in which the ambitions and determination of the party-state showed no signs of cooling down if left by themselves.

The Trump administration represented a solution of continuity to this response that had been outlined by Obama. The Republican's long-term response to this competition was piecemeal, delayed, and disjointed. Several analysts also highlight that China's 2017 national plan for AI would have been, in practice, the implementation of the Obama plan (Allen and Kania, 2017; Metz, 2018). It was late in 2019 when Trump served the industry's calls and presented a national plan for AI (The White House, 2019). However, the piecemeal and disjointed nature of this initiative should be emphasized. Still in the final days of the administration, Trump implemented a new round of restrictions on Chinese companies and applications (e.g., Xiaomi, Alipay, WeChat Pay, QQ wallet) (The White House, 2021c).

These short-term responses bequeathed to the Biden administration were welcomed, even if some of the restrictions were initially revoked. Indeed, in the short-term, tensions have risen, and the US sanctions have been significantly widened. However, Biden's responses are not restrained to short-term measures; they are multi-temporal. A key component of Biden's response is systematic, long-term, and structural, deepening the technological race. With the abbreviated name "Made in America" (Biden, 2020), referring directly to the Chinese industrial policy, Biden's administration plan foresaw a comprehensive industrial and innovation policy based on infrastructure investments, government procurement based on local content criteria – signaling for a shift in posture in trade negotiations – and vast R&D investments, especially in disruptive technologies. In terms of industries, the focus was placed not only on telecommunications (5G) and AI, but also on clean energy and clean vehicles and the relocation of critical production chains (e.g., semiconductors, pharmaceuticals) (Biden, 2020; The White House, 2021a, 2021b). By 2022, these general directives were manifested in what the Biden administration has called the modern American industrial strategy (Deese, 2022; The White House, 2022b), which had materialized in the Infrastructure and Jobs Act, the CHIPS and Science Act and the Inflation Reduction Act.[26]

There is, therefore, a growing convergence between Chinese and US domestic policies and practices: China mimics the U.S. civil-military national system of innovation, adapted to its specificities (Trebat and Medeiros, 2014), and the US explicitly affirms in its strategy many of the key instruments that have underpinned the Chinese development in recent decades, such as infrastructure investments and government procurement. This tendency to convergence of Chinese and U.S. state action – both from the point of view of the innovation system and the domestic instruments of economic action – is another central element that differentiates the current Sino-American competition from that existing during the Cold War.

---

26   The U.S. national security strategy also mentions the National Biotechnology and Biomanufacturing Initiative as being part of the modern American industrial strategy (The White House, 2022).

In general terms, it can be said that the Cold War was marked by two fundamental encapsulations that dictated both the paths of the dispute between the U.S. and the USSR. and its ultimate result, namely: the economic encapsulation of the USSR in relation to the global capitalist economy, and the encapsulation of the Soviet innovation system in the military sector relative to the civilian sector. The latter encapsulation implied the absence or the very low degree of propagation of technical progress developed in the military sector to the upgrading of civilian productive capacity, as opposed to the American innovation system. In contrast, the contemporary Sino-American dispute is marked by economic intertwining and the convergence of the national innovation systems, in particular, and state action, in more general terms, reflecting characteristics of contemporary intercapitalist competition and imposing distinct dynamics on the technological and economic race vis-à-vis the Cold War.

Thus, the ongoing transformations point to the deepening of the technological competition between the U.S. and China, with the significant repositioning of the U.S., which has not only significantly increased the use of its structural power, but also has settled the understanding that the inevitable path to maintain its technological supremacy is the leap forward, pushing the technological frontier. This exit forward, however, is also a race for militarization (Medeiros, 2003; Majerowicz and Medeiros, 2018) – including the domestic spheres, in what Graham (2010) called a new urban militarism – and the deepening of public-private digital surveillance (Greenwald, 2014; Majerowicz, 2020). Moreover, it is a fierce dispute over the markets and infrastructures of other countries, especially those peripherals, whose insertion is in the condition of technological consumers – which in general tends to increase their technological distances from the center and to provide global propulsion to the second wave of ICT-based modernization.

Before the pandemic, large U.S. and Chinese companies were already exporting technological packages and competing in third markets, in a process largely driven and made possible by their states. In January 2020, on the eve of the pandemic's arrival in the U.S., the U.S.-China Economic and Security Review Commission of the U.S. Congress addressed a report on China's development in smart cities to instruct closing measures of the U.S. market and competition in third markets (Atha et al., 2020). Under the brand of smart cities, these large technological and digital infrastructure packages, which include sensors, surveillance cameras, telecommunications, software systems, chips, and AI have become an important expansion vector for Big Tech and unicorn startups, as well as the security industry, where automation and digitalization are at full steam. The ramifications and consequences of this process in deepening the dependency of the countries receiving these packages, highly integrated with critical government and civilian infrastructure, when not military, are still incalculable.

Additionally, the pandemic has acted as a catalyst for the second wave of ICT-based modernization, paving the way for the explosive growth of online activities, through the migration and digitalization of various services and the production of digital content, accelerating the development of algorithmic automation and the subsumption of intellectual labor to capital. It has also concurred for the sudden opening of several and vast national markets, including public health and education services. In this context, the digital sphere and all the infrastructure that sustains and automates it tend to have their role strengthened. Meanwhile, major markets are opening to intercapitalist competition between the U.S. and China mediated by the development of ICT, resulting in the accumulation of factors that tend to intensify the technological competition.

9 Conclusions

The present chapter sought to consider how ICT, read in their own productive and technological terrain and in their historical developmental process, impose material constraints on the dispute between China and the U.S. and their large capitals in the technology sector. Marked by the coexistence of processes of centralization and pulverization of machinery and productive capacity, these competitive dynamics were considered from four dimensions extracted from the conceptual discussion, namely, from the global technical-productive character of ICT as a machinery system, the fundamental nexus, the downstream nexus, and the technological diffusion embodied in the second wave of modernization.

The global technical-productive character of ICT as a machinery system emerges not only from the global diffusion of electronic devices' consumption and digital infrastructure, but also from the international productive fragmentation of its industrial base, simultaneous to neoliberalism, even though this process has been heterogeneous. The result of this historical development is the constitution of a system of high complexity and with a huge and growing degree of differentiation in its inputs, final goods, and applications. Consequently, efforts to internalize or achieve self-sufficiency in this system are highly unlikely to be successful, when not impossible without sacrificing its complexity and delaying diffusion speed and technological development.

The postulation, therefore, of a digital division into two compartmentalized blocs, disregards, on the one hand, the implications posed by the global technical-productive aspect of this system. On the other hand, the idea of a new Cold War ignores that the most sophisticated productive and technological part of the industrial base of this system, its fundamental nexus, is controlled by the U.S. and military allies, so that, instead of "two antagonistic blocs", if the US and allies decide to tighten the pressure on China, it would constitute only a greater or lesser exclusion of the country from the global machinery system than properly the formation of two rival blocs.

In face of the unviability for a country to replicate the complete system in its diversity, the second-best strategy is to control the key elements of technological development and key subsectors. Considering the stack, we concluded that no matter how developed the country or company is in the upper layers, without the production of and/or access to the goods from the lower layers, this development is derailed. This is one of the main aspects that give the U.S. structural power in the ICT system from the direct and indirect control of the fundamental nexus. The structural power also emanates from the fact that the set of technological possibilities in the upper layers are given by the industrial base.

It is precisely through the leverage of this structural power stemming from the control over the industrial base of digitalization that the U.S. has been seeking to contain China's ICT ambitions and the effective Chinese success in the upper layers. However, the leverage of the US structural power does not unfold without contradictions. On the one hand, China is put back and forced to broaden even more its strategy of import substitution and dedicate more efforts and resources to developing its own industrial and technological capabilities. In the long run, some of the technologies, inputs and even machines, may find domestic substitutes, which can affect the own U.S. structural power in the ICT system, depending on how the players are moving in the technological frontier. On the other hand, the fact that China joined the world market during the neoliberal period and assumed a central role in the global constitution of the ICT system imposes domestic resistances to the full leverage of the US structural power, given the various U.S. technology companies whose circuits of capital accumulation have China as their main market. While the leverage of this structural power can put serious obstacles to China, the U.S. cannot use this strategy very effectively without hampering itself. Hence, beyond the short-term measures, competition tends to increase in the search for moving forward the technological frontier, with a long-term horizon, while the U.S. seeks to strengthen its dominance over the fundamental nexus, implementing policies that increase domestic manufacturing capacity.

In contrast, in the downstream nexus, competition between Chinese and U.S. companies is much tighter. Here there is also the centralization of machinery and productive capacity – necessary for transforming pulverized raw data into private production of Big Data and AI-generated statistical models. As productive consumers of semiconductors and owners of machinery in the form of concentrated computing power, U.S. and Chinese Big Tech compete not only for access/monopoly of data sources, but also for computing capacity, which is expressed in the recent movement of Big Tech from the mere consumption to production of semiconductors, even if in the design stage. Such a movement is strategic because of the competitiveness gains associated with the internalization of one of the key nexuses of technological development in the ICT system. Thus, the aspect of the ICT machinery system that affirms the factory is also felt in intercapitalist competition, even for those companies that have been associated only with models of value predation and not production. As a machinery system that extrapolates the factory, the ICT system, to develop technologically, must always return and refer to the shop floor. Nonetheless, for Chinese companies, this movement has also been affected in AI chips by US sanctions.

Finally, we considered the race for technological diffusion embodied in the second wave of modernization, given the role of machinery pulverization in the middle of the stack for the technological development of the system. In this dimension of the ICT system as a machinery system that goes beyond the factory, the role of the state and interstate competition is central, since the project of "digital intermediation of everything" entails a state action and coordination that go far beyond companies' strategies and workers' consumption decisions. Unlike the first wave, which had in the subsistence wage a central component of demand, the support for the second wave does not seem to find in wages a promising source of demand. In addition to the determinants that involve state action for the formation of the first wave, the second seems to require an even more prominent role of the state. The state must assert itself as a central buyer, direct executor, activator and coordinator, through industrial policies, and the object of the second wave – which implies the reconfiguration of the state in relation to capital and the strengthening of state repressive apparatuses, including ubiquitous surveillance. Therefore, it is mainly around the states of the great technological powers that the second wave has been gaining momentum.

In this context, the analysis of the Sino-American race for diffusion revealed a tendency towards the convergence of Chinese and U.S. state action, both from the point of view of the national innovation system and the domestic instruments of economic action. This trend, added to the Sino-American economic intertwining, presents itself as another central element that differentiates the Sino-American competition from that existing during the Cold War, which was based on two encapsulations vis-à-vis the USSR. This differentiation reflects characteristics of contemporary intercapitalist competition and imposes distinct dynamics on the technological and economic race in relation to the Cold War.

Thus, the ongoing transformations point to the deepening of technological competition between the U.S. and China, with the U.S. repositioning. This, however, is also a race for militarization – including the domestic spheres –, the deepening of public-private digital surveillance, and the conquest of foreign markets and infrastructures, especially in the periphery, with serious implications for the autonomy and sovereignty of countries receiving these technological packages.

References

Aggarwal, R. (2022). To Globalize or Not: Everything You Need to Know about Friendshoring. *Business Standard*, November 14.

Allen, G. (2022). *Choking off China's Access to the Future of AI*. Center for Strategic and International Studies, October 11.

Allen, G.; Kania, E. B. (2017). China is Using America's Own Plan to Dominate the Future of Artificial Intelligence. *Foreign Policy*, September 8.

Alper, A.; Sterling, T.; Nellis, S. (2020). Trump Administration Pressed Dutch Hard to Cancel China Chip-equipment Sales. *Reuters*, January 6.

Atha, K.; Callahan, J.; Chen, J.; Drun, J.; Green, K.; Lafferty, B.; Mulvenon, J.; Rosen, B.; Walz, E. (2020). *China's Smart Cities Development*. Research Report Prepared on Behalf of the U.S.-China Economic and Security Review Commission, January.

Atta, R.V.; Slusarczuk, M.M.G. (2012). The Tunnel at the End of the Light: The Future of the U.S. Semiconductor Industry. *Issues in Science and Technology* 28 (3).

Badlam, J. et al. (2022) The CHIPS and Science Act: Here's what's in it. *McKinsey*, October 4.

Biden, J. (2020). *Made in America*. Accessed June 25, 2021. https://joebiden.com/made-in-america/.

BIS – Bureau of Industry and Security of the US Department of Commerce. (2019a). Addition of Certain Entities to the Entity List. *The Federal Register* 84 (196): 54002–54009.

BIS – Bureau of Industry and Security of the US Department of Commerce. (2019b). Addition of Entities to the Entity List. *The Federal Register* 84 (98): 22961–22968.

Buck, G.; Chenne, J. D. (2021). China Aims for Self-sufficiency. Deutsche Bank AG, March 26.

Castellano, R. (2023). U.S. Sanction are a Catalyst for China's New Semiconductor Fab Expansion. *Seeking Alpha*, January 3.

Chu, M. M. *The East Asian Computer Chip War*. London and New York: Routledge, 2013.

Chyxx. (2020). 2015–2020年中国人工智能市场规模统计及增长情况预测[图]. *Chyxx*, 28 February.

Clarke, P. (2016) TSMC's 300mm Chinese Wafer Fab Wins Approval. *EENews Europe*, February 3.

Deese, B. (2022). Remarks on a Modern American Industrial Strategy by NEC Director Brian Deese. Washington D.C.: The White House. Accessed August 29, 2023. https://www.whitehouse.gov/briefing-room/speeches-remarks/2022/04/20/remarks-on-a-modern-american-industrial-strategy-by-nec-director-brian-deese/.

Ding. J. (2018). Deciphering China's AI dream: The Context, Components, Capabilities, and Consequences of China's Strategy to Lead the World in AI. Report, University of Oxford, UK, March.

DOD – United States Department of Defense. (2021). *Defense Budget Overview*. Office of the Under Secretary of Defense (Comptroller)/Chief Financial Officer, May 19.

Durand, C. (2020). *Technoféodalisme: Critique de l'Économie Numérique*. Paris: Zones.

Dyer-Witheford, N.; Matviyenko, S. (2019). *Cyberwar and Revolution: Digital Subterfuge in Global Capitalism*. Minneapolis and London: University of Minnesota Press.

Ernst, D. (2020). Competing in Artificial Intelligence Chips: China's Challenge amid Technology War. Report, Centre for International Governance Innovation, Canada, March.

Evertiq. (2022). China-based IC Production to Represent 21.2% of China IC Market in 2026. *Evertiq*, May 19.

Financial Times. (2021). In Charts: Facial Recognition Technology – and How Much Do We Trust It? *The Financial Times*, May 17.

Fitch, A. (2020). Chip Giants Intel and Nvidia Face New Threats from Amazon to Google to Apple. *The Wall Street Journal*, 20 December.

Fontes, V. (2017). Capitalismo em Tempos de Uberização: do Emprego ao Trabalho. *Revista de Estudos Galegos*, n. 2.

Foster, J. B.; McChesney, R. W.; Jonna, R. J. (2011). The Global Reserve Army of Labor and the New Imperialism. *Monthly Review* 63 (6).

GAO – US Government Accountability Office. *Export Controls: Rapid Advances in China's Semiconductor Industry Underscore Need for Fundamental U.S. Policy Review*. Washington: US Congress, 2002.

Global Times. (2021) TikTok Owner ByteDance Makes Foray into AI Chipset amid In-house R&D Wave. *Global Times*, March 16.

Gooding, M. (2022). China has a $143bn Semiconductor Plan to Beat US Chip Sanctions. *TechMonitor*, December 13.

Goodwin, I. (1998). Washington Dispatches. *Physics Today* 51(7): 48.

Graham, S. (2010). *Cities Under Sieges: The New Military Urbanism*. London: Verso.
Greenwald, G. (2014). *No Place to Hide: Edward Snowden, the NSA, and the U.S. Surveillance State*. New York: Metropolitan Books.
Gutierrez, R. M. V.; Leal, C. F. C. (2004). Estratégias para uma Indústria de Circuitos Integrados no Brasil. *BNDES setorial*, n. 19: 3–22.
Hamblem, M. (2022). How Chip Executives React to US Trade Sanctions on China. *Fierce Electronics*, December 16, 2022.
Huws, U. (2014). *Labor in the Global Digital Economy: The Cybertariat Comes of Age*. New York: Monthly Review Press.
Huws, U. (2019). *Labour in Contemporary Capitalism: What Next?* London: Palgrave Macmillan.
ICinsights. (2020). China to Fall Short of its "Made-in-China 2025" Goal for IC Devices. Research Bulletin, May 21.
ICinsights. (2021). China Forecast to Fall Far Short of its "Made in China 2025" Goals for ICs. *Research Bulletin*, January 6.
IDC. (2020). IDC 2019 年中国AI软件及应用市场份额报告发布：数据智能卷土重来，市场竞争方兴未艾. *IDC*, June 22.
ITU – International Telecommunication Union. (2012). Overview of the Internet of Things. *Recommendation ITU-T Y.2060*, June.
JASON Program Office, The MITRE Corporation. (2017). *Perspectives on Research in Artificial Intelligence and Artificial General Intelligence Relevant to DoD*.
Kaplan, R. D. (2019). A New Cold War Has Begun. *Foreign Policy*, January 7.
Katz, Y. (2017). *Manufacturing an Artificial Intelligence Revolution*. http://dx.doi.org/10.2139/ssrn.3078224.
Khan, S.M. (2020). U.S. Semiconductor Exports to China: Current Policies and Trends. *CSET Issue Brief*, University of Georgetown, US, October.
Kumar, R. (2022). Chip Bans on Countries like China Will Hurt the U.S. More Than They'll Help. They Won't Even Work. *Fortune*, September 28.
Lee, E.; Chau, T. (2017). *Telecom Services: The Geopolitics of 5G and IoT*. Jefferies Franchise Note, September 14.
Lee, K-F. (2018). *AI superpowers: China, Silicon Valley, and the New World Order*. Boston, Mass: Houghton Mifflin.
Lin, J. (2022). Huawei Confirms Breakthrough in EUV Lithography Process Optimization. *Digitimes*, December 22. https://www.digitimes.com/news/a20221226VL203/euv-huawei.html.
Liu, C.; Li, L.; Ting-Fang, C.; Kawase, K. (2020). China Bets on $2tn High-tech Infrastructure Plan to Spark Economy. *Nikkei Asia*, June 1.
Majerowicz, E. (2020). A China e a Economia Política Internacional das Tecnologias da Informação e Comunicação. *Geosul*, 35 (77).

Majerowicz, E. (2019). China and the International Political Economy of Information and Communication Technologies. *Texto para Discussão*, DEPEC-UFRN, n. 002.

Majerowicz, E. (2015). Relações Econômicas entre China e Malásia: Comércio, Cadeias Globais de Produção e a Indústria de Semicondutores. In: Cintra, M. A. M.; Filho, E. B. S.; Pinto, E. C. (Eds.). *China em Transformação: Dimensões Econômicas e Geopolíticas do Desenvolvimento*. Brasília: IPEA.

Majerowicz, E.; Medeiros, C. A. (2018). Chinese Industrial Policy in the Geopolitics of the Information Age: The Case of Semiconductors. *Revista de Economia Contemporânea*, 22 (1): 1–28.

Marx, K. (1887). *Capital: A Critique of Political Economy*, vol. I. Moscow: Progress Publishers. https://www.marxists.org/archive/marx/works/1867-c1/index.htm.

Mazzucato, M. (2013). *The Entrepreneurial State: Debunking Public vs. Private Sector Myths*. London: Anthem Press.

McKinsey Global Institute. (2015). *The Internet of Things: Mapping the Value Beyond the Hype*, June.

Medeiros, C. A. (2003). The Post-War American Technological Development as a Military Enterprise. *Contributions to Political Economy*, 22: 41–62.

Medeiros, C. A. (2013). Padrões de Investimento, Mudança Institucional e Transformação Estrutural na Economia Chinesa. In: Bielschowsky, R. (Org.). *Padrões de Desenvolvimento Econômico (1950–2008)*. Brasília: CGEE, 435–491.

Medeiros, C. A. (2018). *Progresso Técnico como um Empreendimento de Estado*. Aula Magna ANPEC.

Metz, C. (2018). As China Marches Forward on A.I., the White House Is Silent. *The New York Times*, February 12.

Miraz, M. H.; Ali, M.; Excell, P. S.; Picking, R. A Review on Internet of Things (IoT), Internet of Everything (IoE) and Internet of Nano Things (IoNT). (2015). *2015 Internet Technologies and Applications (ITA)*, 219–224.

Moore, S. K. (2021). U.S. Takes Strategic Step to Onshore Electronics Manufacturing. *IEEE Spectrum*, January 6.

Morozov, E. (2018). *Big Tech: A Ascensão dos Dados e a Morte da Política*. São Paulo: Ubu.

Morris, P. R. (1990). *A History of the World Semiconductor Industry*. London: P. Peregrinus.

NBS – National Bureau of Statistics of China. (2020a). *2019 China Statistical Yearbook*. Beijing: China Statistics Press.

NBS – National Bureau of Statistics of China. (2020b). China's "Three New" Economic Added Value Was Equivalent to 16.3 Percent of GDP in 2019. *NBS*, July 8.

Noble, D. F. (2011). *Forces of Production: A Social History of Industrial Automation*. New Brunswick and London: Transaction Publishers.

NSCAI – National Security Commission on Artificial Intelligence. (2021). *Final report*. NSCAI.

NSTC – National Science and Technology Council. (2016). *The National Artificial Intelligence Research and Development Strategic Plan*. The White House, October.

Ogonda, T. (2017). *Internet of Things: Cisco's Vision & Approach*. ITU.

Pan, C. (2023). How US-Japan-Netherlands Agreement on Chip Export Restrictions May Play Out in China. *South China Morning Post*, February 1.

Pasquinelli, M.; Joler, V. (2021). The Nooscope Manifested: AI as Instrument of Knowledge Extractivism. *AI & Society*, 36: 1263–1280.

PCAST – The President's Council of Advisors on Science and Technology. (2017). *Ensuring Long-term U.S. Leadership in Semiconductors*. PCAST.

People's Daily. (2019). 数字化、网络化、智能化深入发展 助力智能制造热卖. Central Cyberspace Affairs Commission, April 30.

Platzer, M. D.; Sargent, J. F.; Sutter, K. M. (2020). Semiconductors: U.S. Industry, Global Competition, and Federal Policy. *Congressional Research Service Report*, R46581, October 26.

Rachman, G. (2020). A New Cold War: Trump, Xi and the Escalating US-China Confrontation. *The Financial Times*, October 5.

Research and Markets. (2019). *Global and China Semiconductor Equipment Industry Report, 2019–2025*. Research and Markets.

Sandia National Laboratories. (2001). *Partner Unveil First Extreme Ultraviolet Chipmaking Machine: Milestone in Making Computer Chips*. Sandia National Laboratories, April 11.

Scott, S. V.; Zachariadis, M. (2013). *The Society for Worldwide Interbank Financial Telecommunication (SWIFT): Cooperative Governance for Network Innovation, Standards, and Community*. London: Routledge.

Sheehan, M. (2022). Biden's Unprecedented Semiconductor Bet. *Carnegie Endowment for International Peace*, October 27.

Sheen, J. (2022). US companies capture 54% of global IC market in 2021, says IC Insights. *Digitimes*, April 11.

Shilov, A. (2022). Huawei EUV Scanner Patent Suggests Sub-7nm Chips for China. *Tom's Hardware*, December 23.

Shiyue, Z. (2020). China's AI Software and Application Market Hit $2.89b in 2019. *China Daily*, June 22.

SIA – Semiconductor Industry Association. (2021). *2021 State of the U.S. Semiconductor Industry*. SIA, 2021.

SIA – Semiconductor Industry Association. (2022). *2022 State of the U.S. Semiconductor Industry*. SIA, November 2022.

Smith, C. (2021). Overcoming US/China Digital Cold War. *Digital Divide Institute*.

Srnicek, N. (2016). *Platform Capitalism*. Cambridge: Polity Press.

Srnicek, N. (2021). Construir Plataformas Pós-capitalistas. In: Grohmann, R. (Ed.). *Os Laboratórios do Trabalho Digital*. São Paulo: Boitempo.

Ssemboga, A. R.; Restrepo, J. (2018). The Economic Impact of 5G: Ensure Regulation and Keep Pace of Innovation. *ITU Regional Economic Dialogue for Africa*, Burkina Faso.

State Council. (2014). *Guideline for the Promotion of the Development of the National Integrated Circuits Industry*. Beijing: State Council.

State Council. (2015). *Made in China 2025*. Beijing: State Council, July 7.

State Council. (2017). *A New Generation of Artificial Intelligence Plan*. [Trans. Sapio, F.; Chen, W.; Lo, A.]. The Foundation for Law and International Affairs.

State Council. (2020). *Policies of Promoting High-quality Development of Integrated Circuit Industry and Software Industry*. Beijing: State Council.

Sutter, K. M. China's New Semiconductor Policies: Issues for Congress. *Congressional Research Service Report*, R46767, April 20, 2021.

The White House. (2016). *Preparing for the Future of Artificial Intelligence*. The White House, October.

The White House. (2019). Maintaining American Leadership in Artificial Intelligence. *The Federal Register*, 84 (31): 3967–3972, Feb. 14. www.govinfo.gov/content/pkg/FR-2019-02-14/pdf/2019-02544.pdf.

The White House. (2021a). *Building Resilient Supply Chains, Revitalizing American Manufacturing, and Fostering Broad-Based Growth*. The White House, June. https://www.whitehouse.gov/wp-content/uploads/2021/06/100-day-supply-chain-review-report.pdf.

The White House. (2021b). *Executive Order on America's Supply Chains*. The White House, February 24. https://www.whitehouse.gov/briefing-room/presidential-actions/2021/02/24/executive-order-on-americas-supply-chains/.

The White House. (2021c). *Executive Order Addressing the Threat Posed By Applications and Other Software Developed or Controlled By Chinese Companies*. The White House, January 5. https://trumpwhitehouse.archives.gov/presidential-actions/executive-order-addressing-threat-posed-applications-software-developed-controlled-chinese-companies/.

The White House. (2022). *National Security Strategy*. Washington D.C.: The White House.

Toh, M.; Ogura, J. (2023). Japan Joins the US and Europe in Chipmaking Curbs on China. *CNN*, March 31. https://edition.cnn.com/2023/03/31/tech/japan-china-chip-export-curbs-intl-hnk/index.html.

Trebat, N.; Medeiros, C. A. (2014). Military Modernization in Chinese Technical Progress and Industrial Innovation. *Review of Political Economy*, 26 (2).

Triggs, R. (2018). HiSilicon: What you Need to Know About Huawei's Chip Design Unit. *AndroidAutorithy.com*, April 12.

Triolo, P.; Allison, K. (2018). The Geopolitcs of 5G. *Eurasia Group White Paper*, November.

Varas, A.; Varadarajan, R.; Goodrich, J.; Yinug, F. (2020). *Government Incentives and U.S. Competitiveness in Semiconductor Manufacturing*. Boston Consulting Group and Semiconductor Industry Association, September. https://www.semiconductors.org/wp-content/uploads/2020/09/Government-Incentives-and-US-Competitiveness-in-Semiconductor-Manufacturing-Sep-2020.pdf.

Varas, A.; Varadarajan, R.; Goodrich, J.; Yinug, F. (2021). *Strengthening the Global Semiconductor Supply Chain in an Uncertain Era.* Boston Consulting Group and Semiconductor Industry Association, April.

Williams, S. (2019). China Is Still Multiple Generations Behind in Chip Manufacturing. *Wccftech*, June 13.

Xinhuanet. (2018). 徐静：用数字化、网络化、智能化培育新动能. *XinhuaNet*, June 11.

Xinhuanet. (2020). 新基建，是什么？ *XinhuaNet*, April 26. http://www.xinhuanet.com/politics/2020-04/26/c_1125908061.

Xu, Z. (2019). 数字化网络化智能化 把握新一代信息技术的聚焦点. *People's Daily*, March 1.

Yao, Y. (2021). The New Cold War: America's New Approach to Sino-American Relations. *China International Strategy Review*.

Yeung, H. W. C. (2022). *Interconnected Worlds: Global Electronics and Production Networks in East Asia.* Stanford, CA: Stanford University Press.

Zhang, Z. (2020). China's Incentives for Integrated Circuit, Software Enterprises. *China Briefing*, August 6.

Zuboff, S. (2019). *The Age of Surveillance Capitalism: The Fight for a Human Future at the New Frontier of Power.* London: Profile Books.

Conclusion

Esther Majerowicz and Edemilson Paraná

The first two decades of the 21st century have indisputably proven the significance of China and its ability to reshape global geopolitics.[1] Several crucial questions then arise: How can we understand the complex socioeconomic structure that is responsible for orchestrating the phenomena such as China's impressive and sustained economic growth? Is this remarkable growth a result of China's departure from its socialist roots or, alternatively, its firm commitment to the renewal of socialism from within? What role does the Communist Party, which still governs the country, play in this context? In our book, we address these and other critical questions with an eye toward the ongoing evolution of the global capital accumulation process, examining China's role in contemporary capitalism.

China's economic development and ascension in the international system have been interpreted differently by diverse states, political forces, and social movements around the globe. While many have been characterizing these processes as a challenge or a threat, others have been envisioning an opportunity for development and a more inclusive world order. So far, the US interpretation of China as a threat has resulted in an increased geopolitical polarization between both countries in the international order, strongly asserted through geoeconomics, with the active promotion of an anti-China rhetoric by the US. This growing polarization has been molding the debate about China, tending to impress at least two tendencies in current discussions. First, there has been an overwhelming focus on the geopolitical aspect of the Chinese ascension and what it may represent for the historical development of contemporary capitalism. Often, such a strand of scholarship neglects social class interests in shaping state policies and the role of class struggle in history, or worse, mistakes interstate rivalry for class struggle as in some theses currently in vogue in certain sectors of the left. These theses postulate reading reality as primarily and fundamentally framed by the polarity between an imperialist and a supposedly anti-imperialist bloc – the latter including Russia and China. Second, the proliferation of derogatory and celebratory outbursts; in some cases substituting the analysis based on concrete reality, theoretical rigor, and critical thinking, as stressed previously. In this scenario, the present volume sought to

---

1 We thank Carlos Aguiar de Medeiros for the constructive comments to a version of this text.

frame the debate about China through a critical political economy perspective, undertaking a double movement required to approach the two connotations *China in Contemporary Capitalism* may convey, that is, China's contemporary development *of* capitalism and China's contemporary insertion *in* global capitalism. As these dimensions are intrinsically intertwined, what differentiated the two parts that structured the book – i) *The fundamentals of the Chinese economic transition,* and ii) *China's global expansion and the technological dispute* – was the emphasis placed on each of these dimensions.

1 China's Contemporary Development of Capitalism

Part 1 delved into China's contemporary development of capitalism. Opening the volume, "Developmentalism with Chinese Characteristics" established a debate with different positions on the nature of the current economic system in China. As Medeiros and Majerowicz argue, "actually existing capitalism" is always a hybrid system. The metaphor they recover from Polanyi (2001) of the oscillation between social regulation and regulation by the market is instrumental not only in understanding China's socioeconomic reality since the 1990s, but also the greater or lesser strength of certain ideas in the interpretation of China's economic system and regime over the last decades. The characterization of China as a version of neoliberalism, or "neoliberalism with Chinese characteristics" (Harvey, 2005), had a greater influence when the pendulum moved towards the market and when the subsequent change of direction was not as strongly established. Since mid-2000s, the pendulum began to shift toward the social regulation of the market, a movement that was accentuated under Xi Jinping. When this movement became clearer, the official CCP ideology of China as a "socialist market economy", representing "socialism with Chinese characteristics", started to increasingly gain ground. Moreover, the greater the economic success and the unsubordinated insertion of China in the international system, the greater the influence of the official ideology and its academic versions (Gabriele, 2020; Jabbour and Gabriele, 2021).[2]

---

2 Given this current conjuncture, assessing whether the claim of the party-state corresponds to reality is relevant in at least two manners. On the one hand, from a leftist standpoint, this discourse that associates China with socialism – even if in its socialist market economy form – covers with a veil of (potentially) emancipatory legitimacy China's current economic system – particularly its relations of production, which are based on wage labor exploitation, and the associate distributive outcomes – and its authoritarian political regime. On the other hand, as socialism has a universal appeal, in as much as the working class is global, China can occupy a role model of what concretely represents socialism for workers' organizations

CONCLUSION

Fundamental to establishing capitalism in China was the process of commodification of labor power.[3] Medeiros and Majerowicz argue that the alteration of the social relations of production through the constitution of a vast labor market and the privatization of the economy, which included the privatization of small and medium SOEs and the increased opening for foreign private enterprises, asserted capitalism in China in the second cycle of structural reforms put in motion by Deng's Southern Tour in 1992. The establishment of capitalism, hence, was politically induced by the CCP as a national development strategy. It was there that developmentalism with Chinese characteristics, as a growth regime, was inaugurated. Underpinned by economic nationalism, its objectives have changed since then, as political and class conflicts emerged, shifting from accelerating capital accumulation to, in the mid-2000s, achieving harmonious development and accelerating technological development, which were further reinforced under Xi Jinping, who placed greater emphasis on social cohesion and in the overall reform goal of modernizing the armed forces.

Since the beginning of reforms, fundamental characteristics of the Chinese economic and political structure were maintained, namely, comprehensive planning, large SOEs forming the commanding heights of the economy, and the CCP's monopoly of political power and strong penetration over economic interests. However, the permanence of these characteristics, which is claimed to be the cornerstone of China's socialist market economy, was accompanied by fundamental changes. Medeiros and Majerowicz highlight the alteration in the nature of planning, which ceased to be mandatory and became indicative – the characteristic type of planning in capitalist economies when planning is present. The large presence of SOEs in the economy, comparable to the Taiwanese experience in the 1950s in terms of industrial production, as the authors stress, affirm a form, but not a content. The latter was increasingly provided by the process of corporatization through SOEs reform, which subordinated SOEs to capitalist rationality oriented to increasing productivity through profitability-focused business practices. The CCP's monopoly on political power and strong penetration over economic interests, although maintained, has changed the

---

around the globe, or at least for developing countries, since the formulation of "socialist market economy" would apply for countries with lesser development of the productive forces. However, a very different working-class politics inside and outside China is entailed if instead of China being any sort of socialism, initial stage of socialism, or "trapped" transitional stage to it (Roberts, 2022), it is a capitalist economy, even if governed by a developmental state.

3 For a discussion on the process of proletarianization in China and the formation of its industrial reserve army, see Majerowicz (2022).

party's own nature, which transited from a class to a national party. The strong penetration over economic interests has also represented a penetration of economic interests over the party, as capitalists were admitted in the CCP and, hence, started participating in political power, in a tension that has not evolved linearly.

Ultimately, the social composition, the materiality, of the party-state, adapted to and found correspondence in its strategy inaugurated by Deng, that is, a party-state-led strategy of economic nationalism that, in Chinese political history, is not intellectually tributary to Mao's project, but to Sun Yat-sen's project – or, in the European political history, to List's (1904) "prosperity, civilization, and power". Within the framework of such strategy and amidst all the highlighted "changes in continuity", emerged developmentalism with Chinese characteristics, in which planning has been effectively driving Chinese industrial development based on five-year plans. Hence, developmentalism with Chinese characteristics has been reproducing, in a particular manner – especially considering the role of SOEs in the commanding heights of the economy and the structure of China's political power – the successful trajectory of postwar Japan and Southeast Asia.

Even though the chapter focused on the internal dimensions of developmentalism with Chinese characteristics, it stresses to the reader that China's essential difference from these other developmental experiences is its autonomous military power relative to the US, as well as the fact that the country was a great protagonist in the Cold War. Moreover, the constitution of developmentalism with Chinese characteristics is a process with a different historical temporality than that experienced by the rest of the world, which converged into the direction of neoliberalism. Neoliberalism represented not only the crisis of the Keynesian welfare state in industrialized countries, but also the crisis of developmental states across the world (Medeiros, 2013).

This external dimension and its imbrication with China's developmentalism are at the very core of "The Trajectory of Chinese Developmentalist Action and Its Contemporary Challenges". In this chapter, Paraná and Ribeiro also consider nationalism as structuring Chinese developmentalist action. The authors stress that Chinese nationalism unequivocally tied together the promotion of economic development to strategies and national defense policies with the ultimate goal of recovering a superior position in the hierarchy of the international system. They defend that this is the common thread in China's trajectory since 1949. Surely, as Paraná and Ribeiro highlight, the Revolution also had a communist content, while, since Reform and Opening, the CCP seeks to, in Deng's terms, give primacy to the development of the productive forces over class struggle, a formulation that has "a conceptual blueprint of

Marxist extraction", but whose categories are mobilized as rhetorical elements, providing political legitimation to the CCP among the people.

Focusing on how China's articulation with the world economy and its international insertion were operationalized by the CCP (*virtù*) to serve the country's economic development, in a favorable international conjuncture (*fortuna*), Paraná and Ribeiro characterize that a symbiotic relationship was established with globalization. If China was able to make high use of it for its economic development and international projection, it was also fundamental to propelling financialization, international productive fragmentation, commercial liberalization, and, consequently, depressing global production costs, all of which were fundamental responses of capitals in central countries, particular in the US, to the 1970s crisis. As a result, the main structural transformation entailed in this two-sided movement was the shift in the dynamic center of gravity of the world economy. Capital accumulation in the 21st century has been led by the Sino-American axis, predicated on multiple dimensions of economic complementarity between the two economies, in a relationship characterized as a "collaborative or amiable competition", until the Great Financial Crisis, which represented its moment of crisis. Hence, at least up to that moment, there may not have been a "neoliberalism with Chinese characteristics", but China was definitely a central piece in materially sustaining the neoliberal globalized form of capitalism.

The fact that the CCP has been able, so far, to operationalize China's insertion in the global economy to achieve its developmentalist goals, as well as manage the mounting domestic contradictions – such as those related to the deceleration of China's economic growth and the tensions that arise from the acute social inequalities – has neither suppressed their existence nor guaranteed that the party-state will be able to indefinitely administer them to its satisfaction in a greater or lesser degree, as Paraná and Ribeiro argue. China's successful trajectory of development over the last decades might give the impression and reinforce some open or presupposed myth of infallibility associated with the CCP and its leaders, as well as the idea, perhaps in some versions and to some degree linked to the former, that China is in an inescapable path towards the apex of world power, as, for example, conveyed in the hegemonic transition hypothesis. The undeniable fact is that *virtù* will be summoned in an even greater degree to sustain China' development trajectory now that *fortuna* has turned its back on China, as the international context is becoming increasingly unfavorable to the country with "the geopolitical and geoeconomic repositioning of the US against China, which was chosen by both the Pentagon and the Department of Commerce as the US main contender" (Medeiros and Majerowicz, 2023: 4), a subject that we will return to later on. Moreover, it must be remembered, as the authors do, that history is not over, as "China's place in the history of our time remains open". Hence, if one is to think of the possible historical paths that may open for China, one must not forget the role of class struggle and the subaltern classes, which repeatedly demonstrated in the history of China how to forge new paths, either through different peasant uprisings that put an end to dynastic cycles in the imperial period, or through the Popular Revolution of 1949.

The Chinese state and class struggle come together in "The State and Domestic Capitalists in China's Economic Transition" by Nogueira and Qi, as the state must be put into terms dynamically with the socioeconomic processes it sets into motion when unleashing the capitalist reforms, and this is, in the first instance, a matter of class formation and arising class antagonisms. On the one hand, the state has concurred to the formation and the evolving configuration of the domestic capitalist class., On the other hand, the state has also started to be shaped by this new class, which in many circumstances emerges from the bureaucratic ranks, but also enters the ranks of the party-state from outside. This mutual influence exerted between the state and domestic capitalists is traversed by the fundamental conflict of the capitalist society, namely between wage labor and capital, and by the contradictions of the regimes of capital accumulation.

Nogueira and Qi, hence, embed the state in society and historicize it in an way whose result is to dethrone the Chinese state as a supraclassist, autonomous, "disinterested" one that establishes the long-term goal of economic development or "a particular version of socialism", and is capable of instrumentalizing at will the domestic capitalist class under its control. It is noteworthy that, when it comes to an approach to the theory of the state, Nogueira and Qi find more commonality than divergence in the thesis of the Chinese developmental state and the official CCP ideology of socialism with Chinese characteristics, despite their different characterizations of the Chinese economic system. They argue that the theory of the developmental state presupposes the autonomy of the state by exerting control over capitalists, which finds correspondence in the ideology of the CCP regarding the matter. Although this is not the direct subject of the chapter, by stressing what is not the nature of the Chinese state – neither socialist, nor developmentalist – it begs the question, what is actually the nature of the Chinese state? Is it bourgeoisie? In scrutinizing the concrete relations between the domestic capitalist class differentiated along factions and the state historically, the authors provide important clues to construct an alternative approach to the subject. In doing so, they also assert that one may not fall into the opposite temptation of treating the state as a mere servant of the capitalist class.

The relationship between the state and the domestic capitalist class has evolved, since Deng's Southern Tour, which marks the beginning of the period in which emerged a domestic capitalist class proper, from what Nogueira and Qi denominate a "great compromise" to a "strained alliance", the 2008 Great Financial Crisis marking its watershed moment. In the earlier reform period, price reforms produced a new elite that accumulated wealth but did not control production. A domestic capitalist class proper would emerge, based on the "great compromise" between the new elites and the state, in the 1990s with the privatization of small and medium SOEs and collective enterprises and, subsequently, the expropriation of rural land, while the state would retain the control of large and strategic SOEs. This process gave rise to the low-road faction, depending on low costs, particularly of labor and land, for its manufacturing export insertion and real estate boom, which corresponded to the export-led and investment-led regime of accumulation, counting also with large infrastructure and SOEs investments. This regime would be put in check by social unrests, rising labor costs, an unfavorable insertion in global value chains due to technological disadvantages, and the corresponding decline in profitability of domestic capitalists.

As a response, by the mid-2000s, the state decided to re-adjust its relationship with capitalists, insomuch as it gave primacy to domestic technological development and to mitigate the social costs provoked by capitalist development. Selective support to capitalists was provided, among a series of policies to promote indigenous innovation, giving rise to the innovation faction, while the financial faction that had grown after the Great Financial Crisis was repressed, characterizing a "strained alliance". According to the authors, an important aspect of the new strategy based on indigenous innovation – which entailed a re-adjustment in the state relationship with the domestic capitalist class – is that it was not confined to achieving a superior position in the hierarchy of the international system by catching up technologically. It also sought to address the domestic labor question by lessening the dependence on cheap labor.

Here is a thread that indirectly links class struggle with geopolitical shifts, but not as mechanically as proposed by the current interpretations that conveniently and apologetically displace the locus of class struggle in China from the national sphere to that of interstate rivalry and equate them,[4] seeking to

---

4 Class struggle would equate to the geopolitical confrontation of the imperialist bloc and the supposed anti-imperialist bloc. Any criticism to and any struggle against the Chinese regime would imply reinforcing the imperialist bloc, while any enemy of the US should be deemed antiimperialist and be supported.

invalidate and mutate the struggles and criticisms against exploitation and oppression in China, and thereby shielding the regime.

2   China's Contemporary Insertion in Global Capitalism

The new strategy discussed by Nogueira and Qi implied not only a re-adjustment of the state's relationship with the domestic capitalist class, but also with foreign capitalists, particularly those with operations headquartered in the US, with eventual repercussions in state-to-state relations. Cheap labor was paramount for the profitability of foreign capitalists operating in China. China's incorporation into the global capitalist economy appeared as a central piece in capital's decades-long overall offensive over labor in advanced countries, as the profitability crisis that hit central countries in the late 1960s and 1970s, particularly the US, responded in a great extent to increased labor bargaining power and active social movements. Enabled by the diplomatic rapprochement between the US and China, the exploitation of Chinese wage labor, an "opportunity" made available by the CCP and seized by transnational corporations, helped bounce up the profitability of central countries' capital. This occurred both by directly exploiting low wage Chinese labor power and by exerting downward pressures on manufacturing wages in central countries, particularly the US, thereby contributed to tilting the balance of power towards capital and eroding labor bargaining power in the latter (Majerowicz, forthcoming). Hence, not only a "great compromise" was achieved domestically, but also an alliance was affirmed between the state and foreign capitalists investing in China. And just like the "great compromise", this alliance was also eventually put in check along with the regime of accumulation to which it corresponded by social unrest and other concurrent factors, as argued by Nogueira and Qi regarding the domestic relations. Therefore, the CCP's response also included readjusting its relations with foreign capitalists for the establishment of its new strategy.

As argued by Majerowicz and Carvalho (2024), based on Medeiros' contributions, "since the Great Financial Crisis, in 2008, China's greater technological convergence with advanced countries, especially in dual-use technologies (civil-military) such as digital technologies," even though still relying upon technology import, "has increasingly shifted its relation of complementarity to a relation of competition with several large US enterprises". As a result, this increased competition was expressed politically in a change of position of large US entrepreneurial sectors, whose interests started to oppose China, aligning with the national security interests represented by the hawkish forces that always existed in the US, and altering the configuration of US domestic forces in the making of the China policy (Hung, 2020, 2022). Hence, the geopolitical and geoeconomic repositioning of the US against China: China ceased to be an "amiable competitor" and became the US main contender.

It is in this context that Part 2 of this volume dealt with China's contemporary insertion in global capitalism, particularly with China's global expansion and the technological dispute. China's increased competition with US-headquartered capitals, and with advanced countries' capitals in general, refers not only to the already decades-long and much-complained impact of Chinese exports – which include products from transnational corporations of advanced countries operating in China and exporting back to advanced countries –but also to the ascension of highly competitive Chinese global brands in the world market, particularly in technological areas, as well as to the dispute for spheres of capital valorization and strategic assets in the globe, including technological assets, as Chinese-headquartered capitals internationalize.

The latter process of internationalization of domestic capitals, in the form of foreign direct investments (FDI), is the subject of "Recent Chinese Expansion: State, Capital and Accumulation on a Global Scale". China's search for new spaces of capital accumulation and exploitation is examined by Ribeiro considering the relations between the state and capital and the domestic patterns of capital accumulation. In the official rhetoric, China's growing external projection, which has been especially prominent since the second decade of the 21st century, would entail a new era of "socialism with Chinese characteristics", expressing the export of its model to the globe, particularly an opportunity for development with sovereignty when presented to developing countries. However, as Ribeiro stresses, China's "globalism" represents a rupture with the building of socialism inasmuch as it increasingly integrates China in global capitalism. Incorporating much of Chun's (2018) critique, Ribeiro highlights that this "globalism" also breaks with the long-gone class nature of China's third-world foreign policy and with anti-imperialism, given China's alliance with the US[5] starting in the early 1970s. According to Ribeiro, ultimately, China's "globalism" expresses a strategy to amplify the projection of its domestic capitals internationally, including through privatizations around the globe.

Ribeiro highlights that China's external projection at the beginning of the 21st century, marked by its "going out" or "going global" strategy, was mainly

---

5   Note that the current US-China rivalry emerges from the US repositioning against China, not China's anti-imperialist principles. The Chinese rupture with an anti-imperialist policy can also be seen in its position in face of Russian imperialism, which, although a minor imperialism comparatively to the US, it is still imperialism in nature.

dominated by big SOEs investments in oil, mining, and construction in resource-rich regions, such as Latin America and Africa. This responded to the imperative of accessing primary goods (raw materials and energy) stemming from the domestic pattern of accumulation since 2001, which was based on investments in infrastructure and heavy industry, closely associated to the urbanization process. However, this pattern of accumulation has undergone transformations, which were also felt in China's external projection.

According to Ribeiro, the slowdown of China's economic growth, associated with a series of structural changes, implied if not a new pattern of growth, at least the exhaustion of the previous one, with growing wages undermining its low-cost manufacturing competitiveness. China sought, hence, to increase the reliance of its growth on innovation and consumption, especially through the search to produce articles with high technological content. The latter strategy implied a shift from a high growth to a high-quality model (Naughton, 2018), which would require a correspondent adjustment on investments. In addition to the traditional need to access primary goods, new imperatives became responsible for projecting Chinese capitals in the world, including the saturation of many domestic markets and the need to access technology. Ribeiro's analysis of Chinese FDI demonstrates this adjustment at the external level. Chinese FDI has become increasingly diversified with respect to its destination – penetrating also advanced countries – sectors and activities – including financial, technological, trade-related services, and manufacturing, with the growing presence of non-state-owned enterprises, including mixed-owned enterprises – so that their stock of FDI in the period analyzed by Ribeiro was slightly higher than the stock of SOEs – and the expressive presence of mergers and acquisition, particularly as a form to acquire technology. Even in the Belt and Road Initiative, in which infrastructure projects – both traditional and digital – are core, and hence, SOEs predominate, there is a trend towards the increased presence of private capital and sectorial diversification, as SOEs presence paved the way for the entrance of private capital.

Based on Rithmire (2019), the author stresses that different types of enterprises entail distinct aims orienting their external projection. While all types of enterprises would seek to enhance profitability in internationalization, state capital would also search for greater prestige and political power, while competitive (private) capital would seek markets and competitive advantage areas, entailing, for instance, low costs, and the acquisition of technology and knowhow. Finally, there would be a third type of capital, "crony capital", which would also seek to increase its domestic political influence, associating with the state in order to internationalize. Regarding the Belt and Road Initiative, Ribeiro argues that, from the economic standpoint, it would have the objectives of conquering markets – helping deal with excess capacity, transferring activities abroad, solving debt problems, and helping China move up in global value chains, as demand for its technology and know-how is created.

Ribeiro stresses that, although the state retains a high capacity to shape this process of internationalization, for instance by blocking FDI, China's expansion occurs like that of other capitalist economies, in search of spaces of valorization, responding to the profitability imperative, the conquest of new markets, natural resources, and the acquisition of technology.

China's expansion through FDI, however, has been met with responses from advanced countries. The most prominent case derives from a central characteristic identified by Ribeiro associated with the transformations in the patterns of domestic accumulation; that is the growing penetration in advanced countries in search for mergers and acquisitions with the objective of acquiring technology. This trait became the most contentious dimension of the Chinese FDI, leading ultimately to the closure of this road for the acquisition of technology, at least in critical sectors. There was both the conformation/creation of, where it did not exist, and the strengthening of FDI screening mechanisms, such as in the EU and the US respectively, enabling the blockade of this type FDI and the protection of technological strategic assets. These measures against China are inscribed in a broader context of the technological dispute between the US and China that started under the Trump administration and continues under the Biden administration, which was the subject of the volume's last chapter.

In "The Sino-American Dispute in Information and Communication Technologies", Majerowicz debated with the twin theses that a digital divide was under way, engendering a new Cold War between the US and China. The author argued that the analogy of a new Cold War was misleading not only from the standpoint of the working class, since no alternative economic system is currently in this dispute as in the Cold War, but also due to the fact that the Cold War was marked by two encapsulations, an economic one, which separated the USSR from the global capitalist economy, and a technological one, which constrained the Soviet innovation system to the military sector. In contrast, contemporary China is deeply integrated into the global capitalist economy, and its national innovation system, mimicking its American counterpart, is highly integrated into the civilian sector. Moreover, the author also stressed that the interpretation of a new Cold War based on a "digital divide" in two blocs is proposed in a context in which the productive structure and the technological system incorporated in it, which underpin the current competitive dynamics, conform a global technological and machinery system of high complexity that is not likely to be nationalized without losing complexity and slowing the pace of technological development. Furthermore, while the global players of this system are the US, its military allies, and China, one cannot properly speak of two blocs in this system. If the US and its allies increase the measures against China, what will tend to occur is China's greater or lesser exclusion from the global machinery system and not the formation of another bloc.

Once nationalizing the productive and technological system was not a competitive strategy for the technological dispute, Majerowicz stressed that the second-best strategy was to control the key nexuses of technological development and key subsectors. Although the author identifies two key nexuses in the global productive and technological ICT system, namely, the downstream and the fundamental nexuses, which encompass interactions between semiconductor design and its consumers and semiconductor manufacturing and semiconductor manufacturing equipment, respectively, it is the latter that has a special character. Majerowicz highlights that the globalization of the ICT machinery system occurred without compromising the US direct and indirect control, along with its military allies, of the fundamental nexus, that is, the control over the semiconductor manufacturing equipment and thus the semiconductor industries by dominating production and technological development, which is a condition *sine qua non* for the development of the technologies in the upper layers of the stack such as 5G and AI, in which China either dominates or is the US major rival.

Hence, the author postulates that this control confers the US a structural power in the ICT ecosystem, which has been leveraged by denying access, for instance, to key semiconductors and machinery to contain China's development in the upper layers of this system. This strategy, however, does not unfold without contradictions, particularly as China is pushed to increase efforts to develop its own productive and technological capabilities through import substitution – which can eventually affect back the US structural power itself, given the Chinese semiconductor market is the main semiconductor market in the world, short-circuiting many US companies circuits of capital accumulation. According to the author, however, competition between the US and China has acquired a multidimensional temporality since the Biden administration, as sanctions (i.e. export controls, denial of access to global manufacturing plants), whose impacts are felt immediately, have been also accompanied by strategies of manufacturing relocation – onshoring and friendshoring – and long-term strategies that aim to move the technological frontier, such as those in the CHIPS and Science Act, and sustain the bases of the US structural power.

Majerowicz argues that the technological dispute between the US and China also appears as a race for diffusion of these technologies, in the second wave of modernization, based on the project of "digital intermediation of everything"

(Morozov, 2018). Different from the first wave of modernization based on ICT, which mostly involved personal computers and smartphones, the second wave has other important components beyond personal consumption as their drivers, such as smart cities, smart grids, industry 4.0, and the transformation of states apparatuses, particularly repressive apparatuses and public services, reconfiguring public-private relations. The state has, hence, a prominent role as a direct executor, an activator and a coordinator, and an object of this wave of modernization. The author stresses that it is mainly around the states of the great technological powers, particularly China and the US, that the second wave of modernization has been gaining momentum, establishing a race for implementation between these states in close alliance with their technology companies. In analyzing the Sino-American race for diffusion, Majerowicz argues that there is a tendency for convergence of Chinese and US state action, as not only China mimics the US national innovation system adapted to its reality, but also the US has started to explicitly affirm the main instruments that sustained China's development in recent decades, such as investments in infrastructure, industrial policy, and public procurement.

This race for implementation between the US and China has also acquired global contours, becoming a dispute for the markets and infrastructures of other countries, particularly peripheral countries, in the form of export of technological packages. Here, the functions attributed to the states, in a certain way, are differentiated, as China and the US hyper-develop the functions of direct executor, activator and coordinator, while states in other countries appear, especially peripheral ones, mostly as objects of this wave of modernization. As these packages become highly integrated with critical governmental and civilian infrastructure, they tend to increase dependency and bear consequences for the autonomy and sovereignty of the receivers.

As Ribeiro argues, it is of utmost importance for developing countries to deepen a critical approach to China's internationalization, given the numerous contradictions imposed by capital accumulation and the disputes engendered with Western countries as China seeks to expand its spaces of valorization. From a resource-constrained peripheral standpoint, the overflow of Chinese FDI, especially in digital infrastructure and digital applications, has been received with the enthusiasm of many, several times in the name of development, even though, at least in the history of Latin America, distinct waves of FDI from great powers and advanced countries were observed while the region remains underdeveloped. Inasmuch as China's expansion occurs like other capitalist economies – which also count on the state and in close state-capital relations for internationalization – the reproduction of China's domestic capitals at a global scale is amenable to the same tendencies of capital accumulation at the world level, with significant consequences for developing countries, particularly considering the tendency toward the polarization of wealth. Here, the same base mechanisms that generate the peripheral condition or dependency are reproduced by China's expansion. For much of the primary resource-rich periphery, such as Latin America, Chinese investments in primary activities and the infrastructure necessary to integrate this production into China's economy, to a certain extent resembling the pattern of FDI during the British hegemony, reinforce their traditional pattern of international insertion – the export of primary goods (to China) and the import of manufactured goods (from China).

China's exports of technological packages, goods, and services for digital infrastructure and the digital applications they enable involve many enterprises and Big Tech that not only have been growingly controlling ample swaths of global computing power through the vast expansion of their fixed capital at transnational scale, but also whose models, as a trend of contemporary capitalism, count with the monopolization of knowledge (Rikap, 2021). This monopolization entails the transfer of value and knowledge from the periphery to the center in the form of technological/knowledge rents and data extraction, creating new forms of reproduction of the peripheral condition or dependency. As Chinese and US digital platforms are closely intertwined with their states, Rolf and Schindler (2023) argue that the incorporation of users and nations in their state-platform nexuses is a form of projecting extraterritorial economic and political power. Here, China's digital infrastructural projection, just like that of the US and in fierce competition with it, resembles an imperialist expansion due to the extraterritorial dimension of power it entails.

China's ascension, hence, carries a central contradiction, while China breaks away from the peripheral condition or dependency, it reproduces the central-peripheral junction, since it also reproduces the mechanisms that sustain this junction. Nonetheless, the geopolitical dimension of China's ascension, the current dispute with the US, may enable peripheral countries, especially Latin America, which has for a long time been the US backyard, to engage in negotiations with both sides to extract some concessions and better terms in international deals and cooperation – for instance, attracting FDI to strategic sectors such as semiconductor manufacturing or obtaining technological transfer. These greater or lesser economic and technological gains, however, come with a price tag, for their condition of possibility, the intensification of great power competition and, hence, of militarization, increases the systemic risks of war.

Inasmuch as advanced countries are concerned, the challenge posed by China's ascension is the major driver, along with the environmental question

– which is intertwined with the former, because China is the dominant "green manufacturer" – for the contemporary return of planning in major OECD economies, especially in the US and the EU, since the Global Financial Crisis (Medeiros and Majerowicz, 2023). As argued by Medeiros and Majerowicz (2023: 11), "the Chinese challenge is posed both from the point of view of industrial production, with its impacts on manufacturing employment resulting from the displacement of investments, particularly in the case of the USA, and of new technologies, whether dual-use or green, with repercussions for national and energy security". Consequently, "China's industrial and technological rise in digital technologies – for example, emerging as the great rival of the USA in AI (Lee, 2018) and leading 5G with Huawei – and in the green industries, being the main producer across the board, required American responses in different areas" (Medeiros and Majerowicz, 2023: 5). Such responses were manifested not only in the negative dimension (e.g., sanctions) but also in the positive dimension, with the formulation of active industrial and technological policies. Hence, the current scenario of heightened inter-capitalist and interstate competition provoked by China's ascension appears to be reversing the disjunction of temporalities posed by the constitution of developmentalism with Chinese characteristics, as, if not the world – because austerity keeps reigning in many peripheries – at least advanced countries[6] appear to be converging to non-neoliberal practices in the direction of the instruments that have been affirmed in China's experience over the last decades – especially with the return of planning and the embrace of explicit, centrally coordinated, and comprehensive industrial policies as weapons in competition.

Meanwhile, the developmentalist bloc inside China is reinforced as the current situation is diametrically opposed to the one which engendered the crisis of the developmental state in the 1970's, which occurred to a great extent because large enterprises undermined national development strategies as they bypassed the state for their strategies of internationalization (Medeiros, 2013). In order to internationalize and compete in the world market, particularly in the context of an aggressive technological dispute with the US, Chinese enterprises need the state not only to expand but also, in many cases, to keep surviving.

---

6 While the convergence of US and China state action was delt in the context of the technological dispute, it is noteworthy that in the case of the EU, China's FDI seeking for technological assets was the trigger for the return of the industrial policy at the bloc's level, since the acquisition of the German robotics company Kuka by Midea in 2016 was a decisive element to change Germany's position in favor of industrial policy, conforming a coalition with France that established a political base for an EU industrial policy (Di Carlo and Schmitz, 2023).

Overall, this again places the economic significance of the political actions of the state as well as the politically strategic importance of economic endeavors at the center stage. In that sense, China's situation is special not only because it entangles politics and economics in its own new and innovative manner, but also by making these entanglements somehow "transparent" in the international order – for itself and as much as for other countries in the current conjuncture. China's international projection forces Western major powers to openly declare – by words or actions – their aggressively reactive intentions when it comes to fiercely holding on their hegemonic control of large shares of the world. The time for "soft power" seems to have ended for all parties involved. That these have also been years of crisis, austerity, and poor world economic growth is no coincidence. US-China tensions are very much immersed in the winds of change within global contemporary capitalism in the last decades.

In sum, we hope to have demonstrated that – from part to part – all these moves are not coming out of some masterminds playing a game of global geopolitics chess. Nor out of a mere change of moods within "state reason". In this book, we delivered an explanation that connects and somehow derives these processes from capitalism's dynamic reconfigurations, first, within China and, related to that, in the global system encompassing China. It turns out that if it is not possible to properly explain contemporary capitalism without directing our gaze to China, we hope to have convinced you, that it is also not possible to understand what happens in and to China without asking ourselves about the relevant transformations in capital accumulation on a global scale. This can sound circular, or tautological, only to the ones not used to the works of the dialectic materialistic thinking. This is the complex China challenge of which we hope to have contributed to advancing our understanding, following the two intrinsically intertwined parts that structured the book, and the differentiated emphasis placed on each of these dimensions in the five chapters. Considering the much-needed critical understanding of the two interlaced strategic aspects of these structural changes, we paid special attention to the 'fundamentals of the Chinese economic transition' and to the current 'China's global expansion and the technological dispute'.

How China will cope with the limits we have indicated in these pages – rising debt and financialization, labor and social unrest, inequality, mounting tensions with economic elites, geopolitical tightening, and environmental change – is yet to be seen. The same can be said about China's role in the world to come. Until now, its economic and technological feats have been impressive. Its internal politics is going strong in maintaining social control, and its international positioning is cautious but growingly active in defense of its spaces of influence and decision *vis à vis* its growing economic and military importance. What will be of these trends from now on? And how to deal with them? We hope this volume has helped to better equip the readers with new perspectives and analytical tools to apprehend the logic behind these processes.

References

Chun, L. (2018). China's New Globalism. In: Panitch, L.; Albo, G. (Eds.) *Socialist Register 2019: A World turned upside down?*, 55.

Di Carlo, D.; Schmitz, L. (2023). Europe first? The Rise of EU Industrial Policy Promoting and Protecting the Single Market. *Journal of European Public Policy* 30 (10): 2063–2096.

Gabriele, A. (2020). *Enterprises, Industry and Innovation in the People's Republic of China*. Singapore: Springer Nature Singapore.

Harvey, D. (2005). *A Brief History of Neoliberalism*. Oxford: Oxford University Press.

Hung, H-F. (2020). The US-China Rivalry Is About Capitalist Competition. *Jacobin Magazine*, July. Available at: https://jacobin.com/2020/07/us-china-competition-capitalism-rivalry.

Hung, H-F. (2022). *Clash of Empires: From "Chimerica" to the "New Cold War"*. Cambridge: Cambridge University Press.

Jabbour, E; Gabriele, A. (2021). *China: O Socialismo do Século XXI*. São Paulo: Boitempo.

List, F. [1841] (1904). *The National System of Political Economy*. Reprint, London: Longmans Green.

Majerowicz, E. (2022). The Industrial Reserve Army and Wage Setting in China. *Bulletin of Political Economy* 16 (1): 21–56.

Majerowicz, E. (forthcoming). *The Globalization of China's Industrial Reserve Army: its Formation and Impacts on Wages in Advanced Countries*. London: Palgrave Macmillan.

Majerowicz, E.; Carvalho, M. H. (2024). China's Expansion into Brazilian Digital Surveillance Markets. *The Information Society*, DOI: 10.1080/01972243.2024.2315880.

Medeiros, C. A. (2013). The Political Economy of the Rise and Decline of Developmental States. In: Levrero, E. S.; Palumbo, A.; Stirati, A. *Sraffa and the Reconstruction of Economic Theory: Volume Two*. London: Palgrave Macmillan.

Medeiros, C. A.; Majerowicz, E. (2023). Contemporary Industrial Policy and Challenges to South America. Proceedings of the 35th European Association for Evolutionary Political Economy, 13–15 September, Leeds.

Morozov, E. (2018). *Big Tech: A Ascensão dos Dados e a Morte da Política*. São Paulo: Ubu.

Naughton, B. J. (2018). *The Chinese Economy: Adaptation and Growth* (2nd Ed.). Cambridge, MA; London: MIT Press.

Polanyi, K. [1944] (2001). *The Great Transformation: The Political and Economic Origins of Our Time*. Reprint, Boston: Beacon Press.

Rikap, C. (2021). *Capitalism, Power and Innovation: Intellectual Monopoly Capitalism Uncovered*. Abingdon and New York: Routledge.

Rithmire, M. (2019). Varieties of Outward Chinese Capital: Domestic Politics Status and Globalization of Chinese Firms. Working Paper 20–009. Boston: Harvard Business School.

Roberts, M. (2022). China as a transitional economy to socialism? *Journal of Global Faultlines* 9 (2): 180–197.

Rolf, S.; Schindler, S. (2023). The US–China rivalry and the emergence of state platform capitalism. *Environment and Planning A: Economy and Space* 55(5): 1255–1280.

Index

1989 social movement   86
5G. *Consulte* telecommunications infrastructure

advanced countries. *See* developed countries
Africa   114, 190
agrarian reform   16
Alibaba   126, 163
Amazon   163
Amer International   125
Anbang Insurance   128
anti-corruption movement   86
anti-cyclical program   24, 95
anti-imperialism   110, 111, 120, 189
anti-imperialist bloc   181
Apple   163
arable land   61, 89
artificial intelligence   144, 146, 147, 152, 158, 161, 162, 163, 167
    national plan   168
Asia   55–56, 121, 134
ASML   151
authoritarianism   vii, 16
automation   146
autonomy   51, 53

Baidu   163
Belt and Road Initiative   5, 25, 120, 130–136, 190
    criticisms   136
    economic corridors   131
    economic interests   134
    infrastructure   130
    objectives   131, 132–133, 134–136, 190
    private enterprise   134
Biden   160, 169, 192
Big Data   146, 152n6, 161
Big Tech   96, 150, 161, 162, 165, 166, 173, 194
bourgeoisie. *See* capitalist class
Braudel   48
BRICS   viii
British hegemony   194
ByteDance   163

cadre-capitalist class   79

campaign against corruption   10, 24, 36, 96, 128
capital
    Chinese   129
    controls   95, 129
    crony   124, 128, 190
    domestic   124
    expansion   129
    fixed   162, 194
    private   29, 109, 124, 137, 190
    state   16, 124, 190
    structure   29
    trans-nationalization   48
    valorization   4
capital accumulation   12, 30, 32, 78, 117, 194, 196
    contradictions   86
    export-led   92
    global   181
    pattern   59, 116, 190
    regime   78, 83, 86, 92, 94, 96, 186, 188
        investment-led and export-led   90, 187
    social structure of. *See* social structure of accumulation
    stage of   4, 111
    structure of   28
capitalism   vii, 2, 10, 11, 12, 183, 196
    actually existing   13, 182
    global   107, 111, 182, 196
    international   105, 109
    neoliberal   185
    political   11
    regulated   14
    state   2, 11, 30, 108
    variety of   14, 16
capitalist class   2, 3–4, 77, 78, 96, 109, 137, 186, 187
    faction   x, 4, 78, 84t.3.1, 96
    finance faction   79, 83, 84, 94, 96
    financial faction   187
    foreign   188
    formation   82, 88
    innovation faction   79, 83, 84, 93, 94, 187
    low-road faction   79, 83–84, 87, 89, 187

capitalist economy   2, 13, 33
  actually existing   2
  global   3, 56, 58, 170, 191
    China's insertion   116, 120, 185, 189
capitalist rationality   31, 183
capital-labor conflicts   78, 84
capital-labor relations   33
Carlos Aguiar de Medeiros   5
Catholic Church   vii
central planning economy   10
central-peripheral junction   194
century of humiliation   50
cheap labor   83, 93, 187, 188
cheap land   83
China plus one strategy   65
China's "globalism"   189
China's ascension   vii, viii, 1, 54, 110, 111, 194, 195
  advanced countries' responses   191
  threat or opportunity   181
China's global expansion   4, 133, 191
China's market   159
Chinese "globalism"   110, 111, 120, 138
Chinese civilization   46, 50
Chinese Communist Party   vii, 36, 37, 49, 105, 107, 129, 134, 185
  legitimacy   71, 93, 98, 185
  monopoly of political power   35, 39, 183
  nature of   183
  official rethoric   26, 53, 54, 78, 182, 186, 189
Chinese economic miracle   57, 115
  end of   115–116
Chinese external projection   110, 113, 114, 116, 120, 137–139, 189, 190, 193, 196
  private interests   129, 137–138
  state strategic interests   129, 137–138
Chinese foreign direct investment   121, 127–129, 130, 189, 193
  ASEAN   134
  blockades   128–129, 191
  crony capital   128
  destination   121
  diversification   137, 190
  largest private enterprises   125
  mergers and acquisitions   122
  ownership   122
  screening   127, 191

  sector composition   122
  technology sector   x, 123f4.2, 127, 191
  volume   121
Chinese global strategy   110
Chinese world power strategy   35
CHIPS and Science Act   160
class
  formation   186
  interests   120, 181
  structure   112
class antagonisms   186
class conflicts   90
class struggle   33, 55, 98, 181, 184, 186, 187
cloud computing   147
Cloudwalk   168
Cold War   5, 36, 169, 170, 173, 184, 191
  new   5, 143, 153, 172, 191
collaborative competition   57, 185
commanding heights   16, 29, 40, 184
commercial surpluses   57
competition
  intercapitalist   161, 162, 163, 170, 172, 188, 189, 195
  interstate   164, 166, 195
competitive advantage   55
  loss of   116
computational capacity   161, 162, 173, 194
  concentration   147, 151, 173
computer vision technology   167
corporate structure   9
corporatization   31, 38, 183
corruption   86
Country Garden   125
crackdown   10, 96
crisis
  Asian financial   23
  Chinese stock market   vii, 24, 38
  global financial   59, 95, 117
  of the 1970s   185, 188
crucial reform   15, 39

Dahua   168
Dalian Wanda Group   128
data   146, 151, 161, 162, 173
  collection   161
Data Centers   147, 152
Datang   94
debt   115

debt-trap-diplomacy   136
deep learning. *See* artificial intelligence
deep neural networks. *See* artificial intelligence
defensive capability   52
defensive nationalism   21
demography   115
Deng Xiaoping   18, 87, 106, 107
Deng's Southern Tour   21, 87, 183, 187
dependency   170, 193
   mechanisms of reproduction   194
developed countries   1, 14, 55, 56, 121, 188, 189, 190, 191, 194, 195
developing countries   viii, 1, 16, 39, 121, 194
development   40, 48, 52, 53, 58, 78, 108, 181, 185, 193
   capitalist   108, 182
   contradictions   70–71
   model   vii, 69, 70–71
   national project   108
   strategy   3, 36, 53, 55, 183
      innovation-driven   35
development bank   131
developmental state   2, 3, 11, 16, 17, 27, 77, 78, 80, 186
   decline of   17, 195
developmentalism   39, 184
developmentalism with Chinese characteristics   2–3, 11, 25–26, 40, 183, 184, 195
developmentalist action   3, 47, 53, 58, 184
developmentalist bloc   195
digital divide   5, 143, 154, 171, 191
digital infrastructure   148, 150
digital platforms   161, 194
digitalization   143, 145–146
   of the physical world   146
domestic value added   64
dual price system   85–86

East Asia   11, 16, 27–28
economic growth   x, 59, 60f2.1, 63, 87, 89, 105, 109, 118, 181
   cycle   113–114, 115
   model   10
   pattern   59, 61, 63, 190
   per capita rate   113
   rate   113, 115

   regime   23, 25, 183
   slowdown   34, 70–71, 83, 95, 115
economic interdependence   170, 173
economic nationalism   14, 19, 20, 22, 24, 25, 26, 183, 184
economic performance   9
economic power   36
economic rebalancing   59, 61
economic system
   demand constrained   12
   interpretations of China   182
   nature of   182
   supply-constrained   18
electronic design automation tools   158
electronic devices   150, 152, 162
elites   82, 85, 86, 87, 187
employment composition   32–33
energy matrix   61
energy resources   113
environmental degradation   136
environmental question   195
Europe   127, 154
Evergrande   vii, 125
exchange rate policy   57
experimentalism   53
exports   63, 64, 115, 116, 194
   controls   158, 159
   model   116
   sector   92
external constraints   90
extraterritoriality   157, 194

Facebook   164
facial recognition   168
factory of the world   48, 90
factory system   150
fictitious goods   13, 16
financial expansion   64, 96
financial liberalization   68
financial market   37, 39, 67, 84, 94
financial system   38, 55, 67
financialization   84, 95
foreign direct investment   5, 23, 66, 110, 114, 116, 193
   Chinese. *See* Chinese foreign direct investment
foreign policy   110, 112, 120, 133, 189
foreign technology   35, 92, 117

foreign trade 63, 116
   bilateral agreements 132
forms of ownership 22
fortuna 46, 47, 47n3, 58, 70, 185
Fosun Group 128
Four Modernizations 20, 52, 106
friendshoring 160, 192

geopolitical ascension 51, 53, 184, 187
geopolitical polarization 181
geopolitics 19, 51, 181, 187, 194, 196
Gerschenkron 14
global demand 165
global economy 185
global imbalances 58
global machinery system 144, 150, 162, 171, 191
Global South viii
global surpluses 56
global value chains 64, 66, 90, 153, 159
globalization 3, 49, 55, 57, 67, 69, 185
   controlled 155
   financial 48, 52, 67
   productive 153, 155
going global 23, 114, 189
going out. *See* going global
Golden Age 15
Gome Holdings 126
Google 163
Gorbatchov 37
government
   local 88
      budgetary constraints 89
   neutrality 80
   procurement 94, 166, 167, 168
   spending 64, 167, 168
great compromise 4, 78, 79, 82, 85, 87, 98, 107, 187
great power 1, 166, 193, 194
great power rivalry 143, 150
gross domestic product
   components x, 62, 62t.2.1
      sector composition 113, 115
gross fixed capital formation 63
guandao 86–87

Hainan Airlines 128
Han Feizi 49

harmonious society 27
hegemonic transition hypothesis 185
Hengli Group 125
Hikvision 168
HiSilicon 163
historical bloc 80
HNA Group 125, 126, 128
Hong Kong 121
household consumption 62–63, 117, 118
Huawei 94, 125, 126, 157, 158, 163, 168
hybrid economy 2
hybrid system 13

ICT technological system x, 144, 147, 149/5.1, 150, 192
   downstream nexus 150, 160, 163, 172
   fundamental nexus 148, 154, 156, 157, 172, 192
   internalization 153, 154, 163, 171, 192
ICT-based modernization waves 144, 164
   first wave 145, 146, 164
   role of the state 164, 165–166, 173, 193
   second wave 145, 147, 165, 171, 173, 192
   sources of demand 164–166, 173, 193
imperialist bloc 181
imperialist expansion 194
import substitution strategy 158, 172, 192
imports 63
indigenous innovation 84, 93–94, 187
industrial bottleneck 35
industrial policy 159, 167, 168, 169, 195
industrial revolution 34
Industrial State 11, 15, 30, 40
industrial system 15
industrialization 11, 16, 19, 105
   late 14
industrialized economies 39
industry 63, 195
   value added 118
inequality 33, 119
information and communication technologies 5, 35, 143
   embedded diffusion 146, 161, 162
   industrial base 148, 150, 157, 160, 172
   key technologies x, 144, 145, 149/5.1
infrastructure 89, 165, 190
   new 167
infrastructure diplomacy 66

INDEX 203

innovation   117
institutional convergence   17
institutionalism   11, 12
institutions   17, 54
integrated circuits   146, 148
international division of labor   56
international monetary system   67
internationalism   111
internationalist nationalist project   111, 120
internationalization of Chinese
    enterprises   37, 38, 134, 189
internationalization strategy   129, 195
Internet access   145
Internet of Things   146, 161
interstate rivalry   187
investment   63, 90, 95, 113, 115, 117, 118
    infrastructure   64
    opportunities   118
    package   167
    recalibration of   116, 137, 190

Japan   15–16, 30, 154, 156, 158, 184
JD.com   125
joint ventures   92

labor bargaining power   188
labor market   64
labor relations   24
labor shortage   92
labor unrest   83
land
    expropriation   87, 88, 187
    transfers   90
Latin America   1, 114, 190, 193, 194
leapfrog   34
leftist tendencies   106
Legend Holdings   126
Lenovo   94
List   14, 26, 184
lithography machines   148, 163
    Extreme Ultraviolet lithography   151, 158
living standards   64

Machiavelli   46–47, 49, 58
machine learning. *See* artificial intelligence
Made in America   169
Made in China   24, 34, 63, 127, 167
Mao Zedong   107, 108, 184

Maoist period   110
market   12, 13, 18, 32
    incentives   86
    liberalization   55
    practices   36
    social regulation of   24, 33
market economy   30, 53, 82
market socialism   2, 10, 18, 22, 26, 27, 28, 30,
    31, 54, 182, 183
Marx   12
Marxism   12, 13, 78
Material Supply Bureau   85
Megvii   168
Microsoft   163
middle-income countries   viii
middle-income trap   117
militarization   170, 194
military
    modernization   21, 26
    modernization strategy   168
    power   184
    sector   170
    strategy   34
military-civil fusion   34
modern American industrial strategy   169
modern industrial system   148
monetary expansion   64
monopolization of knowledge   194

national brands   94
national defense   51, 184
National Development and Reform
    Commission   27
national innovation system   169, 191
national interests   112
national security   127, 159
national sovereignty   54, 108, 110, 193
national strategy   162
nationalism   107, 110, 120, 184
neoliberalism   3, 16–17, 153, 184
neoliberalism with Chinese
    characteristics   10, 182
Netherlands   158
networking   146
New Economic Policy   18, 55
new normal   59–60, 83
non-market relations   13
non-neoliberal practices   195

non-state enterprise   122, 123, 124

Obama   57, 168
oil   60
overcapacity   115, 134
ownership structure   88

pandemic   171
party-state   vii, 2, 3
peasant uprisings   186
peripheral countries   170, 174, 193, 194
periphery   193
personal consumption   164
planned commodity economy   22
planning   16, 26, 53, 69, 183, 184
   central   18
   developmental   28
   hybrid   20
   indicative   24, 183
   of investment   15
   return of   195
   system   85
Polanyi   23, 182
polarization of wealth   194
political apparatus   59
political interests   112
political power   36, 37, 40, 78, 87, 125
   expropriation of   18
   structure of   3, 26, 35, 87, 184
political realism   47
political system   10
political-diplomatic isolation   55
power   51
   relations   81
prices
   market   85
   planning   85
primary distribution   x, 81, 82f3.1
primary resources   61, 113, 190
primitive accumulation   79, 82, 87, 88
private enterprise   28, 32, 36, 118, 123
   political connections   128
private sector   118
privatization   17n5, 22, 23, 28, 32, 85, 87, 89, 106, 114, 187
production engineers   15
productive expansion   64
productive forces   53, 106, 109, 184

productive restructuring   52, 55
productive structure   165
productivity   64
profitability   31, 84, 90, 125, 128, 188, 190
profits   83, 125
   real estate   90
public security   167, 168
public services   91

real estate developers   89
red capitalists   79
reform and opening   9, 52, 58, 105, 107, 109, 184
reformist leadership   26
reforms   40, 53, 81, 85, 87, 183, 186
   liberalizing   20, 21, 38, 86
regulation   37, 84, 96, 129, 155
relations of production   13, 21, 39, 53, 106, 183
relationship between political and economic power   40–41
relationship between the state and capitalists   x, 3, 4, 77–79, 80, 89, 97t.3.2, 109, 111, 113, 129, 186, 187
   foreign capitalists   188
   re-adjustment   93–94, 187, 188
renminbi internationalization   67–69
rents   86, 88
repression   84, 94, 98
research and development   63
reserve army of labor   92
reserves   57, 66–67, 96
revolution
   Chinese   10, 19, 35, 50, 105, 184, 186
   Cultural   106
   in military affairs   34
Rule of Law   54

SASAC   23, 28, 29, 31n21, 36
savings   116
   excess   116
Schumpeterian   12
security industry   168
semiconductor manufacturing equipment   145, 148, 155, 156, 158, 192
   concentration   151
semiconductor users   148

semiconductors   144, 145, 146, 147, 148, 159, 161, 162, 164, 168, 192
   artificial intelligence chips   152n6, 153, 158
   design   150, 162, 163, 173
   diffusion   152
   global manufacturing capacity   160
   manufacturing   151, 155, 156, 158
   United States industry   159
Sensetime   168
sensors   161
services   63
shadow banking   95
shareholder remuneration   31
silicon machinery system   150, 160
Silk Road Economic Belt   66
Sino-American axis   56, 185
Sino-American dispute. *See* US-China rivalry
Sino-Asian manufacturing cluster   56
Sino-capitalism   30n18
Sino-Soviet split   52
smart cities   167, 170
SMIC   158
social cohesion   26, 34
social control   168
social egalitarianism   9
social protection   106
social structure of accumulation   11, 14, 40
social unrest   90–92, 188
socialism   10, 17, 105, 107, 108, 110, 181, 186
   actually existing   18
   construction   105, 106, 107, 108
   essence of   20
   international attractiveness of   19
socialism with Chinese characteristics   2, 10, 18, 26, 54, 78, 182, 186, 189
socialist market economy. *See* market socialism
soft landing   70–71
soft power   196
software   162
South Korea   15–16, 30, 151, 154, 156, 160
Southeast Asia   56, 184
special economic zone   21, 22, 32
speculation   83, 84, 86, 95
stability   54, 87
state   2, 4, 13, 51, 77, 78, 108, 109, 112, 119, 128, 133, 186, 193, 195

   agents   112
   apparatus   166
      repressive apparatus   166
   autonomy   80, 98, 186
   fiscal capacity   86
   nature of   186
   policies   162
   property   53
   sector   90
   theory of the   186
state bank   29
state-capital reconfiguration   166
state-owned enterprise   24, 28, 87, 94, 114, 118, 122, 124, 183, 184, 187, 190
   reform   114
   restructuring   24
statistical techniques   146
stock market bubble   95
strained alliance   4, 78, 79, 83, 90, 93, 98, 187
strategic partnerships   163
strategy of openness   21
structural change   64, 115, 116–117, 118, 137
structural transformation   9, 185
structural turning point   115
subaltern classes   186
Sun Yat-sen   19, 26, 184
Suning   125
supercomputers   158
superpower   54
surveillance   170

Taiwan   19, 28, 35, 151, 154, 156, 160
TD-SCDMA   94
technical progress   12, 117, 145, 148, 153, 157, 162
   control of   127
technical standards   94
technological dispute. *See* US-China rivalry
technology   195
   catch-up   23, 63, 93
   coevolution   x, 148, 149f5.1
   convergence   188
   development   148, 156, 161, 163, 166
   diffusion   148, 154, 166, 167, 170
      race for   166, 173, 192, 193
   enterprise   162, 170
   frontier   159, 160, 170, 172, 192
   modernization   20

technology (*cont.*)
  obsolescence   160
  package   167, 170, 193
  race   169, 170
  revolution   34
  sector   37
    China's importance   159, 172, 192
    United States   159
  self-sufficiency   154
  stack   x, 148, 149f5.1, 161, 172
  supremacy   170
  transfer   22, 92–93, 156
telecommunications   94
  infrastructure   144
    5G   144, 147
  systems   147
Tencent   126, 163
The Prince   46
third world   110, 111, 120
Trade Market for Technology   92
trade opening   106
trade policy   22
trade unions   33
transition   2, 19, 25, 36, 40, 77, 106
  Soviet   41
transnational corporations   188
Trump   168
twin American deficits   57

ubiquitous computing   146, 165, 166, 168, 173
unemployment   34
United States   1, 4, 15, 38, 39, 52, 55, 56–58, 96, 111, 127, 143, 151, 154, 155, 156, 168, 170, 172, 181, 188, 192, 193
  academic-military-industrial complex   153
  Committee on Foreign Investment in the United States   127
  defense sector   151
  dominance   156
  entrepreneurial sectors   188

  geopolitical repositioning against China   185, 189
  National Security Commission on Artificial Intelligence   158, 159
  sanctions   157, 158, 159, 163, 168, 169, 192
  structural power   156, 157, 158–159, 160, 170, 172, 192
  Treasury bonds   57, 66–67
urbanization   90
US-China
  convergence of state action   169, 173, 193
  rivalry   viii, 5, 153, 196
    technological dispute   5, 35, 144, 168–171, 191, 192, 195
  trade war   127
USSR   18, 19, 52, 170, 174, 191

Veblen   15
virtù   46, 47, 47n3, 58, 70, 185

wages   x, 33, 64, 65, 65f2.2, 83, 116, 165, 188, 190
  in developed countries   188
  subsistence   165
welfare
  policies   24, 27
  state   14, 25, 33, 40
  system   33
West   vii
  learn with the   21
  major powers   196
  thought   47
  workers   33, 83, 88
  workforce   48, 116
  working class   39, 191

Xi Jinping   10, 26, 28, 37, 110

YMTC   158
Yutu   168

ZTE   94

www.ingramcontent.com/pod-product-compliance
Lightning Source LLC
Chambersburg PA
CBHW070621030426
42337CB00020B/3873